California Politics
The Fault Lines of Power, Wealth, and Diversity

Edgar Kaskla
California State University, Long Beach

CQ PRESS

A Division of Congressional Quarterly Inc.
Washington, D.C.

CQ Press
1255 22nd Street, NW, Suite 400
Washington, DC 20037

Phone: 202-729-1900; toll-free, 1-866-4CQ-PRESS (1-866-427-7737)

Web: www.cqpress.com

Cover design: Matthew Simmons, Myself Included Design
Cover photo: Corbis

Photos: 23, 90, 98, 102, AP Images; 43, San Diego Historical Society

♾ The paper used in this publication exceeds the requirements of the American National Standard for Information Sciences—Permanence of Paper for Printed Library Materials, ANSI
Z39.48-1992.

Printed and bound in the United States of America

11 10 09 08 07   1 2 3 4 5

Library of Congress Cataloging-in-Publication Data

Kaskla, Edgar.
  California politics : the fault lines of power, wealth, and diversity / Edgar Kaskla.
    p. cm.
  Includes bibliographical references and index.
  ISBN 978-0-87289-276-7 (alk. paper)
  1. California—Politics and government. 2. Power (Social sciences)—California—History.
I. Title.

  JK8716.K37 2007
  320.9794—dc22

                                                                      2007026000

California Politics

To my family:
Linda, Taavi, Priit, and Aivar

Contents

Tables, Figures, and Map

Preface

California is a state of immigrants. Among them my parents, who came to California as refugees after the Soviet Union occupied Estonia toward the end of World War II. My story, however, is somewhat different in that although I am Estonian by nationality and come from an immigrant family I was born in California and therefore also qualify as a native Californian. Writing this book comes from the experience of growing up in Southern California and trying to make sense of what has been happening to this state in the past thirty to forty years.

What has happened? Growth, growth, and more growth, pushed by a unified understanding on the part of virtually all economic and political leaders that "we" need growth and that the more development "we" get, the better off "we" will be. I grew up in Burbank and remember a time when there were still some farms in the San Fernando Valley, where Burbank is located. They were scruffy farms at that point, to be sure, but they still had orange and lemon trees; they grew corn; and it was not out of the ordinary to see chickens, goats, and horses. The last of those farms disappeared about the time that I was an undergraduate student at UCLA. By the time I moved thirty miles south to go to graduate school at the University of California, Irvine, I saw the last remnants of Orange County's agricultural past also get plowed under. The orange and avocado groves disappeared, then the bean fields started to go, and finally the last strawberry fields that were still wedged between subdivisions were bulldozed and turned into tightly packed homes, big-box stores, and mini-malls. Between 1980 and the turn of the millennium, California added about ten million people to its population. But growth, it is repeated, is good.

Seeing these changes—the unbearable traffic, the strains that all these people place on resources like water, the sheer difficulty of figuring out just where to put everybody—led me to start thinking critically about the logic of growth and to question who really benefits from this unforgiving march of progress. Who are the "we" who benefit from growth? The answer can be found in California's own rich history, a history that has been dominated by an economic, political, and cultural elite from its very earliest days. Property owners and business leaders have transformed California, but it is not a transformation that has benefited all of us. Quite the contrary. Economic power has used political and cultural power to create a power elite in California that has been remarkably proficient at generating profit and wealth for the few, while the rest of society is left to deal with the so-called externalities that growth inevitably produces. What's a few extra cars on the road, and who cares that after it rains the ocean water is so laced with bacteria that the surfers risk getting sick? These are small prices to pay to be able to live in paradise. So "we" hold onto that image, while the reality all around us continues to change and becomes more dystopian than utopian.

California politics is about the power elite. Unlike textbooks that insist that democracy matters and that the system might be flawed but ultimately can be fixed, this book takes the approach that the state's political structure has to be analyzed as a system by and for the rich. It is a plutocracy, supported by a political system that has been hopelessly—at least in its present configuration—bought off by the ruling economic class through the injection of enormous amounts of money into the campaign process, reinforced later by millions of dollars spent on lobbying by corporations and a select few organizations that want something for themselves, not for "us."

In this text students *do* learn about the state's political history and its institutions—how its parties work, how the legislature operates, what powers its governors have, how its budget is formulated—but this information *does not* obscure the many ways that those institutions and the people that run them hinder, rather than facilitate, basic democratic practices and goals. In a nutshell, this is not a book that seeks a so-called balanced approach to understanding California politics. There is no balance and fairness when the power elite decide what is to be done and the public, in turn, is left to react to decisions already made. Moreover, the power elite's hold on power is getting stronger, as evidenced by the growing gap between the rich and poor in this state. For immigrants coming today, California is not a place of hope. There are no hills full of gold; this is just another place for survival.

Structure of the Book

Elite politics and the limits placed on democracy are not just part of California politics but are rooted in all of American politics. That is the main argument presented in the Introduction and chapters 1 and 2. There is inherent contradiction between a capitalist economic system, where inequalities are an inevitable outcome of competition, and a democratic political system, where the concept of equality is stressed in terms of one's right to vote, the principle of representation, and the idea of people's equality before the law. The contradiction has been resolved through a power elite structure that gives the appearance of democratic representation while allowing the power elite to stay in charge. In the American West, land itself has been a valuable resource for the power elite, and the development of land has been facilitated through the operation of what are called growth machines, which are examined in detail in chapter 2. In chapter 3 California's history is analyzed through the lens of elite politics. California's development has been organized through elite interests that have used these growth machines to increase wealth—and cheap immigrant labor to keep costs down and profits up.

The actual institutional structures of California politics are the focus of chapters 4 through 8. We look at party organizations, campaigning, and the central role that money plays in the electoral process in chapter 4. Then, in chapter 5, we look at the legislature, how bills become law, and how interest groups are able to steer the legislative process using money. Chapter 6 deals with the role of the governor in California. Although the governor has substantial formal powers, the governor's role as a symbolic leader is even more significant. Governor Arnold Schwarzenegger has been able to capitalize on his heroic film image to frame himself as an outsider and reformer when, in reality, his politics have strengthened the status quo and, hence, the interests of the establishment power elite. In chapter 7 I explain and critique the justice system, looking at the legal process and courts that are divided into two unequal parts: one system for the wealthy and another for the rest of us. This division reinforces inequality as a fundamental part of California—not to mention U.S.—politics. Local governments and how fear of taxes has been used to encourage still more urban development as local governments seek new revenue streams through the so-called fiscalization of land use are the subjects of chapter 8. When land use needs to be revitalized, redevelopment agencies serve as an arm of growth machines to funnel public money to private development interests.

The fear of taxation has created a kind of permanent economic crisis in California, the theme of chapter 9. Fearful that the governor and legislature will carelessly spend taxpayer dollars, voters have approved a series of ballot measures that have placed tight restraints on how money is to be spent and how it is to be collected via taxes. The problem, however, is not with runaway spending but with a federal government that is forcing state governments either to fund social programs with the help of state revenues or to get rid of "welfare" altogether. Since 2003 the governor's budgeting has relied on a new trick to pay for running these programs without creating new taxes: borrow the money and assume that things will sort themselves out over time. It might work, but it also leaves the state vulnerable to greater budgeting crises in the future, when those loans become due. Finally, chapter 10 focuses on the long-term outlook for the state, which includes the possibility that global warming might dramatically and suddenly change Californians' way of life completely.

Key Features

This is not a text for memorizing what each public official must do and how many legislators there are in the state assembly. (There are eighty, if you must know right now.) It does offer these basics, but, more important, the book goes another step in developing students' critical thinking skills. If democracy is ever going to become truly democratic, students need to be able to understand what real criticism entails. The pedagogical features used here are designed to help students acquire some new terminology and think critically about what they're learning. Key terms that are specific to this discussion appear in boldface type throughout the chapters, and the book features a glossary that further defines them. At the end of each chapter, readers will find a section called "Taking Stock" that encapsulates that chapter's analysis. These sections highlight the main themes of each chapter, integrating the parts of the story into a thematic whole. Discussion questions at the end of each chapter are intended to spark debate. Students will find a comprehensive list of research tools at the end of the book in an appendix called "For Further Research." These tools include books, articles, essays, online databases, blogs, and other kinds of scholarship and commentary, organized by type.

For faculty, I also offer a testbank of short and long essay-style questions that can be used for generating midterm or final exams, quizzes, or even study guides. Again, the emphasis is on presenting questions that encourage conceptual understanding rather than on requiring students to memorize facts.

Acknowledgments

Developing a critical approach that does not follow the standard textbook template involves some trepidation. But all the people at CQ Press have been incredibly supportive, helpful, and just plain nice! Thanks to Charisse Kiino for initially persuading me to draw up a prospectus for this little idea I had, and thanks to Elise Frasier and Talia Greenberg for their great editing help at CQ Press and to freelance copy editor Joanne S. Ainsworth. I'd also like to thank my reviewers, including Robert Benedetti, University of the Pacific; Michael Deaver, Sierra College; and Nicholas Dungey, California State University, Northridge, for their useful advice.

Aitäh (that's "thanks" in Estonian) to my family—Linda, Taavi, Priit, and Aivar—for putting up with me during my bouts of obsessive reading and writing. Thanks to my colleagues at California State University, Long Beach, for giving me an academic home. Finally, words can't express how grateful I am to all the students past and present at Cal State, Long Beach, who have given me energy and fired me up every time I walked into the classroom. They will see the footprints of a lot of different lectures and many different courses in this book. It's not just about California, and my students know that.

California Politics

Introduction

A couple of years back while searching for a California government textbook, I was struck by the similarities among the ones that crossed my desk. Almost universally, they focused on the institutions of California government without providing any context for what those institutions do and without broaching the issue of whose interests those institutions actually serve. Reading them, you would learn the astonishing facts that governors govern, legislators make laws, judges interpret the law, and interest groups play a pretty big part in both elections and day-to-day operations of these three branches of government. All pay homage to the diversity of California and make mention of its interesting geography but fail to analyze the way that our interactions with California's physical landscape figure into the state's political system.

The issue of federalism is an important case in point. Most texts approach the issue with a standard modus operandi in place: the federal government has gotten very large and powerful in the United States, whereas state and local governments have diminished in power and importance; it is thus almost natural or inevitable that some of that power be returned to the states following the model of governance prior to the 1930s. A turning point in American federalism was reached in 1937 with the Supreme Court decision in *National Labor Relations Board (NLRB) v. Jones and Laughlin Steel Corp.* That decision gave the federal government broader authority to regulate interstate commerce, setting off an evolutionary process that made the national level of government more powerful than that of the states. Beginning in the 1970s, the so-called Sagebrush Rebellion in western states demanded that the concept of federalism with a well-defined distribution of power between federal and state be strengthened and that power be returned to state hands. Originally the movement focused on federal administrative control of large areas of land in western states by the Bureau of Land Management, the U.S. Forest Service, National Park Service, and so on. As the Republican Party gained popularity in western states, however, by evoking the imagined independent spirit of the frontier and how that freedom had been taken away by heartless federal government bureaucrats, the Sagebrush Rebellion was eventually mainstreamed into the GOP platform in the 1990s. Implied in all this was that given a freer rein, state governments would make decisions fundamentally different from those made in Washington, D.C. But how would the political process be different? The answer is that not much at all would change. An

American political myth says that the closer politics is to us as individuals and communities, the more effect political decisions will have on us and the more aware we will be of those decisions and what occurs in the decision-making process. Are we more aware? Probably. Someone had to decide to limit parking on many streets in Santa Monica to those with residential permits only, and people feel the impact. Someone had to decide to create the redevelopment agencies in Long Beach that transformed a strip of downtown and waterfront from what it looked like twenty years ago. Awareness of how such decisions are made and who is responsible for them is another matter. Citizens' protests and complaints usually fail to change anything, thanks largely to a society that is both apathetic and antipolitical.[1] Even after the events of September 11, 2001, when, the cliché tells us, "everything changed," little has changed. The American public knows little about the context of global politics beyond what it is repeatedly told to believe by the mainstream media, now controlled by a handful of corporations. Its interest in local politics is even less informed, except in less populated rural areas. Unfortunately, that's not where most people live. In California the population is more than 90 percent urban.

People may claim to loathe the politics of Washington, but at least they turn out to vote in nominally democratic numbers during presidential election years. Still, in the 2000 and 2004 elections, which were projected to be very close races, turnout hovered around 50 percent nationwide, not much of an increase from midterm elections. When elections are held at the strictly local level, turnout drops dramatically. Without national or statewide offices in play, stand-alone local elections typically get voter turnouts below 20 percent. And if Jay Leno can have fun with people on the street unable to identify the picture of any national politician beyond George W. Bush, Dick Cheney, and maybe a few others, it is safe to say that practically no one in any local community would be able to identify a picture of their local mayor or city council members.

In democratic systems, the emphasis is often placed on elections—on who gets chosen to represent the interests of the people, and, of course, the election itself. In the United States, elections validate the notion that the country is a democracy, regardless of how weakly (or strongly) the interests of the public are represented in the process of governing. As long as elections are held, the system is—by definition—democratic. When many voices are represented within the institutions of government, it is said that this system is a pluralist system. But this kind of an approach is tautological. The system is democratic because there are elections, and there are elections because it is democratic. Moreover, in focusing on institutions, including the elections themselves, it is difficult to account for how political and economic processes shape the institutions of government and how power is inevitably distributed unequally within these institutions. Early in the twentieth century, the political psychologist Harold Lasswell came up with the simple definition of what politics is all about: "Who gets what, when, and how."[2] It is about the power and the deployment of power to make decisions over how resources are to be used and for what purposes. Put simply, California politics past and present must be analyzed in the context of a power elite that controls the decision making over who does get what, when, and how. To add to Lasswell's original formulation, we can include the geographical element of *where*, for California politics has always been driven by the spaces of production and how land and geographic resources (from gold to timber to water to oil) have been such a crucial part of generating wealth and, simultaneously, power. In a political sense, geographic location also involves the role of human beings. The social context is what gives places specific meanings, and human labor becomes necessary to make use of whatever the resource happens to be. The demand for labor in economic production has been the driving force in the continuous expansion of California's population from the 1840s into the present with only a few brief intervals in which population growth slowed but did not stop.

Although **elite politics**—by which we mean rule by the wealthy and influential, regardless of how "democratic" the system may appear—may explain the unequal distribution of power in the political sphere, this alone is still not sufficient to explain the patterns of decision making that can be seen over longer periods of time. In other words, not all elites make decisions in exactly the same way, not all benefit equally within this top-heavy system of governance, nor does government operate statically for 160 years of history.

California politics and its political institutions cannot be separated from the question of power. And although power takes many forms and practices, the primary focus in this book is on economic power. Lives have changed in countless ways in the past 100 years—from our dependence on the automobile to the impact of television on entertainment to the use of computers at work and home—but one thing that has not changed in society is that the United States remains a class divided society.[3] If anything has changed in that division in the post–World War II era, it is that the rich have gotten richer and the poor poorer. The sociologist C. Wright Mills argues for the presence of a power elite in the United States based primarily on socioeconomic class, whereas Michael Parenti, a political scientist, refers to the American system as a "plutocracy," a system by and for the wealthy.[4] Although this system "by and for the rich" has been able to hold onto power throughout American history, as the historian Kevin Phillips suggests, it may not be sustainable forever.[5] Edward Wolff, an economist, analyzes the concentration of wealth in America and concludes that such a "top heavy" system cannot ultimately hold together.[6] Unless relatively dramatic policy changes are implemented, the economist Robert Pollin sees sufficient economic instability emerging in the late 1990s and early 2000s that the system may be destined to collapse.[7]

California's development and the divisions that it has created need to be understood in the context of what have been called **growth machines.** Growth machines, comprised of those people who control the land and its resources, supported by local governments and a host of bureaucracies that bring together both private and public interests at local, state, and national levels, have been driven by an economic machine that has made and remade California several times over during the past two centuries. Land is not valuable in its own right; it must be put to use. Once land has been obtained, these growth machines have made sure that this is what happens, whether it is a real estate developer interested in building another subdivision, a manufacturer who requires a zoning variance in order to expand his or her business, or a farmer who needs water from a cheap (or free) source in order to irrigate crops that normally might not grow in the state's relatively arid climate. In turn, governments work to support the development of land by promoting the idea of growth as well as by making decisions clearing the way for land to be used in ways that create profit and wealth for its owners.

The operation of growth machines has a kind of internal consistency, because almost everyone simply accepts that if growth creates wealth, it must be good. But although the owners of land, resources, and power are supported in this logic of growth, there are others who stand to lose in this process; seldom, however, is much attention given to them. Smaller landowners may be forced to sell, zoning changes may lead to a decline in the values of adjacent properties, and all kinds of development may contribute to pollution and overcrowding that affect everyone in a community. The growth machines cooperate primarily on a local level, but both state and federal governments actively support the elite control of these machines by making sure that the infrastructure is in place to support this growth. Giant urban populations in Los Angeles, San Diego, and San Francisco, for example, would be unthinkable without enormous water projects built through the cooperation of state and federal bureaucracies. In a state vulnerable to any number of natural disasters, be it fires, floods, or the omnipresent threat of massive earthquakes, virtually all development depends on creating an insurance system designed to place values on the property risks all Californians must face. Again, although growth occurs locally, a broader governmental responsibility brings state and federal authorities into play too.

Growth machines generate wealth but they also generate and deepen social, economic, and political inequalities. As we will see, the distribution of wealth and income in California may be even wider than it is for the country as a whole, and we notice it in part because of the contrast geographically between pockets of extreme wealth and larger pockets of working poor. Areas of extreme contrast often coexist within short distances from one another. Fenced and gated estates reminiscent of feudal manors in Europe dot the fields around Bakersfield not far from farmworkers who still live in shacks built during the Great Depression in towns like Weedpatch, Lamont, and Arvin, unchanged from the days described by John Steinbeck in *The Grapes of Wrath*. The well-heeled, predominantly white enclaves of Oakland Hills look down upon an African American downtown Oakland blighted by abandoned warehouses and shuttered factories largely unchanged since the 1960s. The borders of the well-known 90210 zip code of Beverly Hills bump against the unknown zip codes of working-class neighborhoods of mixed ethnic origins, and these are only a few miles from African American areas like the Crenshaw District or Latino areas in Palms and MarVista (see table I-1 and map I-1).

Table I-1 Individuals and Families below the Poverty Level, by State, 2000 and 2003

| | Number below poverty | | | | Percent below poverty | | | |
| | Individuals | | Families | | Individuals | | Families | |
State	2000	2003	2000	2003	2000	2003	2000	2003
United States	**33,311**	**35,846**	**6,615**	**7,143**	**12.2**	**12.7**	**9.3**	**9.8**
Alabama	672	748	146	164	15.6	17.1	12.4	13.7
Alaska	55	61	11	13	9.1	9.7	6.8	8.0
Arizona	780	839	150	166	15.6	15.4	11.6	11.9
Arkansas	439	421	96	89	17.0	16.0	13.0	12.1
California	4,520	4,610	832	849	13.7	13.4	10.7	10.5
Colorado	363	433	64	88	8.7	9.8	5.7	7.3
Connecticut	254	273	51	58	7.7	8.1	5.8	6.4
Delaware	70	69	14	12	9.3	8.7	6.7	5.8
District of Columbia	94	105	17	21	17.5	19.9	15.4	18.5
Florida	1,987	2,174	387	422	12.8	13.1	9.3	9.7
Georgia	999	1,125	206	234	12.6	13.4	10.0	10.8
Hawaii	103	132	19	21	8.8	10.9	6.8	7.4
Idaho	144	183	26	35	11.4	13.8	7.7	9.8
Illinois	1,335	1,389	262	265	11.1	11.3	8.6	8.5
Indiana	592	633	113	119	10.1	10.6	7.1	7.5
Iowa	281	286	53	53	10.0	10.1	7.0	6.9
Kansas	247	284	43	51	9.5	10.8	6.2	7.1
Kentucky	640	696	148	159	16.4	17.4	13.5	14.2
Louisiana	862	882	182	191	20.0	20.3	16.0	16.6
Maine	124	133	22	26	10.1	10.5	6.6	7.6
Maryland	477	439	89	86	9.3	8.2	6.6	6.1
Massachusetts	586	582	110	118	9.6	9.4	7.1	7.5
Michigan	975	1,118	196	224	10.1	11.4	7.7	8.6
Minnesota	328	383	66	75	6.9	7.8	5.1	5.6
Mississippi	498	553	104	121	18.2	19.9	14.2	16.4
Missouri	606	646	118	133	11.2	11.7	7.7	8.6
Montana	117	126	23	24	13.4	14.2	9.5	9.9
Nebraska	158	182	28	36	9.6	10.8	6.5	8.2
Nevada	194	252	34	47	9.9	11.5	6.9	8.7
New Hampshire	63	96	11	17	5.3	7.7	3.5	5.1
New Jersey	651	704	126	145	7.9	8.4	6.0	6.6
New Mexico	320	340	64	70	18.0	18.6	14.2	14.8
New York	2,391	2,501	491	499	13.1	13.5	10.7	10.7
North Carolina	1,018	1,136	203	239	13.1	14.0	9.6	10.7
North Dakota	71	71	14	13	11.6	11.7	8.1	8.4
Ohio	1,216	1,343	246	280	11.1	12.1	8.4	9.4
Oklahoma	459	546	100	112	13.8	16.1	11.0	12.4
Oregon	439	481	84	88	13.2	13.9	9.5	9.7
Pennsylvania	1,240	1,296	247	260	10.5	10.9	7.8	8.2

(Continues)

Table I-1 (*Continued*)

	Number below poverty				Percent below poverty			
	Individuals		Families		Individuals		Families	
State	2000	2003	2000	2003	2000	2003	2000	2003
Rhode Island	108	117	23	22	10.7	11.3	8.5	8.2
South Carolina	557	563	123	121	14.4	14.1	11.7	11.3
South Dakota	83	81	16	14	11.5	11.1	8.4	7.2
Tennessee	745	780	158	164	13.5	13.8	10.5	10.6
Texas	3,056	3,508	639	712	15.1	16.3	12.3	13.1
Utah	192	244	40	43	8.8	10.6	7.2	7.6
Vermont	63	57	12	10	10.7	9.7	7.5	6.4
Virginia	630	642	124	126	9.2	9.0	6.8	6.6
Washington	667	654	127	121	11.6	11.0	8.6	7.9
West Virginia	327	326	72	76	18.6	18.5	14.7	15.5
Wisconsin	461	554	75	101	8.9	10.5	5.6	7.2
Wyoming	55	47	10	10	11.4	9.7	7.9	7.3

SOURCE: U.S. Bureau of the Census, American Community Survey, "Multi-Year Profiles 2003—Economic Characteristics"; www.census.gov/acs/www/products/profiles/chg/2003/acs/index.htm; revised June 28, 2005.
NOTE: The numbers and percentages for each year represent individuals below the poverty level in the previous twelve months; they are based on a sample and subject to sampling variability. The American Community Survey universe is limited to the household population and excludes the population living in institutions, college dormitories, and other group quarters.

Like a great many Americans, Californians do not trust government. Most believe that state government is run by a few big interests looking out for themselves.[8] They are right. Rather than employing poll numbers as an indication of just how alienated potential voters feel, I will focus here on the real consequences of having a political system that favors these "few big interests." Moreover, as we shall see, politics in California has historically been dominated by the elite, resulting in a landscape that reflects the concentration of wealth and power in the hands of relatively few people. California history treats the influence of the railroad's Big Four as a thing of the past, and yet, even today, Southern Pacific remains the largest landowner in the state, and railroad mogul Phillip Anschutz is emerging as one of the key developers in Southern California with interests in sports (Staples Center, Los Angeles Kings, and Major League Soccer) and movie theaters. To use a well-known saying, the more things change, the more they stay the same. This analysis of elite politics in California has a purpose. We expect this state and this country to be democratic. Although the system is designed to favor the wealthy and powerful, that is not to say that the system cannot be changed in some meaningful way. There is at least an entry-level understanding of and respect for democratic politics that provide opportunities for society to commit to social and political change. But as long as society remains mired in distrust so strong that it pushes people away from participating and as long as people are content to focus their interest and energy on the perceived values of a consumer society,

Map I-1 POVERTY RATE IN CALIFORNIA, 2000

SOURCE: © 2006 Fannie Mae Foundation. Printed from DataPlace—www.dataplace.org.
Reprinted with permission.

creating what Herbert Marcuse called a "one-dimensional" society, nothing will change.[9] Moreover, the warning signals from economists like Pollin must be taken seriously; the flaws and the contradictions inherent in this system will only become more troublesome as power and wealth accumulate into fewer and fewer hands. The year was 1929 the last time that inequality reached these levels.

The distribution of wealth has strongly affected both the geographic and political development of California. From its earliest days a gap has existed between rich and poor, and land use reflects this. Ranchos gave a relatively small number of property owners enormous holdings of land, the outlines of which are still seen today. They are especially evident in Southern California, where many of these holdings formed the basis for early subdivisions. Housing developments, streets, and various rights-of-way still mark out the outlines of many rancho lands. The names of the ranchos and their owners have become part of the landscape: Encino, Jurupa, Los Alamitos, Pico, Sepulveda. The railroads obtained huge amounts of land in the 1800s, and again, the railroads and the lands appropriated to them still exist today. Oil interests and the consolidation in the twentieth century of farmlands into tracts of agribusiness reflect the changing landscape of power in the state. Vast areas of the Central Valley appear almost barren of human existence, especially during the heat of summer. Farmworkers work the land for companies sometimes headquartered far away from the fields because the land holdings themselves are so immense in size. Most farms in California remain family owned, but most are family corporations with links to yet bigger agribusinesses further up the food chain. So as we look at political and economic processes, we will also keep an eye on the geography of inequality as well. Development is rooted in the land, the resources, and the people of California.

The Imagined West and the Mythical California

The words "American West" immediately conjure up a set of images: covered wagons, settlers trying to establish a homestead on the windswept plains, cowboys and Indians. An understanding of the "real West" must inevitably come up against those images that have been so ingrained in our minds; it is extremely difficult to think of the development of the West as anything other than an epic battle to challenge and then establish the frontier. The imagined West naturalizes a developmental pattern. First, at grave risk to life and limb, heroic explorers map the unknown (Meriwether Lewis and William Clark usually fill this role). Next, early settlers make tentative efforts to establish outposts of civilization by bringing their families to the West, not entirely certain of what natural elements they may have to face, ranging from extreme weather to poor soil to shortages of water to wild animals and bloodthirsty Indians. Other settlers in covered wagons go deeper into this great western abyss, which then turns into a flow of humanity after the discovery of gold in

California. The frontier is finally tamed and connected to the already developed East through construction of the railroads, after which the West is incorporated into a civilized world and the spatial expansion of the capitalist economy can now go about filling in all the blank spots yet to be filled on the western map.

The importance of the American frontier was first emphasized in the work of Frederick Jackson Turner, who argued that American identity was formed in and through this experience. Turner stated: "American social development has been continually beginning over and over again on the frontier. This perennial rebirth, this fluidity of American life, this expansion westward with its new opportunities, its continuous touch with the simplicity of primitive society, furnish the forces of dominating American character."[10] The frontier and especially the struggle to create something from what Turner sees as nothing summarize the American experience. One of the social consequences of this kind of an understanding of American history is that it has reinforced the importance of individualism in American culture. Rugged men did the exploring; rugged men struggled against nature to give their families all they could give; pious women tended to the farm and to the families, never complaining about just how difficult life was; in the meantime, men struggled against the savages and struggled against each other, as pursuit of wealth led to jealousy, greed, and violence. All these social and psychological processes are natural and we understand them to be part of human nature because American culture reproduces these stories on such a massive scale.

These images of the West have been produced and reproduced in art, literature, and mass media. One might think of the art of Ansel Adams, Albert Bierstadt, Georgia O'Keeffe, and Frederic Remington, but the images of the West that are so familiar are also to be found in Zane Grey and Louis L'Amour dime-store novels, and certainly in a long line of films and television dramas that have given us a relatively standard lineup of roles that we come to immediately recognize, be it the lonesome stranger, the school marm, the gunslinger, the town drunk, the diplomatic sheriff, the quiet doctor, the wild Indian, the stoic Indian, or the rugged man who has been wronged by society and is intent on doing things his way. The imagined West that we see as real is that of *Shane, High Noon, Stagecoach,* and many other films. And it is certainly the West of John Wayne. In the film *Stagecoach,* director John Ford transformed Wayne from movie star to American icon. He was America, a flawed figure (a Civil War veteran who fought for the South) who managed to remake himself on the western frontier by doing what he thought was right.[11] Determination and individualism defined Wayne's character, and they came to define what the entire western experience was about.

Turner's frontier hypothesis has recently been rethought and reevaluated. Led by Patricia Nelson Limerick and her groundbreaking book, *The Legacy of Conquest,* so-called New Western historians have looked more carefully and critically at the West as something more, something more diverse and certainly much messier than the Turnerian presentation suggests.[12] Western history is about development and changing the land to make it usable and profitable for those who have acquired it. It is also about the people of the West who have become the labor force working to transform that land into something far different from what it once was. More important, these historians have looked closely at how American culture has used the mythical West to paper over other parts of history that do not seem to fit into what the imagined West must be about. As Limerick points out, "The contest for property and profit has been accompanied by a contest for cultural dominance."[13] As a result, the culture reproduces an image of that romantically individualized West to mask the political and economic realities that must inevitably accompany such dramatic transformation. John Wayne rides in a Monument Valley untainted by the coal mining and high tension lines that crisscross the desert miles from where John Ford shot his epic westerns.

As always, the rugged individual makes the imagined West. The historian Richard White, however, reminds us that development was not just a process of individuals struggling against adversity. It was the state—the United States government—that supported and made possible the development of the West in the first place. It was the cavalry of the U.S. Army that engaged in bloody battle with the Indians, not courageous homesteaders plinking with shotguns. It was the U.S. government that also made construction of the railroads possible and later supported the further development of the West through water reclamation and eventual electrification. Moreover, the creation of the West was fostered by the mapping of the West as states and territories, giving the United States a presence above and beyond a sense of manifest destiny.[14]

Mention California today and a whole different set of images is likely to capture the imagination. Sand and surf, carefree days spent lounging in the warm sun humming along to the Beach Boys singing, "Catch a wave and you'll be sittin' on top of the world," on the radio. In tracing the entire trajectory of California history, the historian Kevin Starr returns time and again to the place that the "California Dream" has held in the minds of both Californians and those who can only dream of California.[15] From its earliest nonnative settlers on, this dream has powered the "imagineering" (with apologies to Disney) of California as a place of endless possibilities in a climate that is, as many a promoter has claimed, perfect. What that dream has meant, has, of course changed over time. Early visitors viewed the life of *californios* as paradise. Some, like the newspaper writer Hugo Reid, who was married to an Indian woman and wrote critically of the mistreatment of Indians under the mission system, and the New Englander Abel Stearns, who migrated to California and married into a family with huge landholdings, managed to find their own place among the Spanish landowning class. The Gold Rush generated its own kind of microclimate by bringing on a vast migration to the state. Even Karl Marx wrote approvingly of California's uniqueness, pointing out that the possibility of finding gold gave every worker an equal chance of escaping the grind of a working-class existence. As capitalist development (temporarily) bypassed much of the West between the Mississippi River and California, the social and political critic and historian Carey McWilliams called California "the great exception," not only because everything was literally built from scratch, but because that construction was fueled by that same dream of creating utopia.[16]

Later, the dream was shared through literature like Richard Henry Dana's *Two Years Before the Mast,* Helen Hunt Jackson's romantic *Ramona,* and many others. Charles Nordhoff wrote pamphlets widely distributed in the East praising the virtues of the California climate and its positive effects on health and well-being. And when California turned out not to be the dreamland that people imagined it was, it was transformed into one. The landscape of California became a pliable object that could be molded into paradise. Every real estate development, every promise of fertile land for the taking told settlers that California had become the place of dreams. The architectural critic Reyner Banham wrote lovingly of this same vision of Southern California as comprising four separate but interlocking ecologies, which by that time included the automobile as an important part of the California lifestyle.[17]

Long before the film *Field of Dreams* popularized the phrase "If you build it, they will come," Californians were saying the same thing. That dream guided the developer Abbott Kinney to build a Southern California version of Venice, it helped William Randolph Hearst imagine a Romanesque castle overlooking the central coast, and it helped William Mulholland imagine an aqueduct that would carry more water from Owens Valley to Los Angeles than the city at the time needed. The creation of a vision was repeated in thousands more examples, from vernacular architectural forms along the state's highways to suburban ranch homes with huge windows, overhanging eaves, lush gardens, and (naturally) a pool—a slightly more modest version of Frank Lloyd Wright's style of the times. "Local" architects like Richard Neutra and Rudolf Schindler (both were Austrian) repatriated California modern back into California and, unlike Wright, made the style livable, while magazines like *Sunset* popularized and extended it as a modern cultural style, making it the one that all Californians should live by—or at least aspire to.[18]

The 1960s surf music of groups like the Beach Boys and Jan and Dean, the Frankie and Annette beach blanket movies of that same era, and the ultimate dream-come-true of Disneyland's opening in 1955 created a utopia that still captures the imagination. Like all of these California dreams, this one was constructed during a time when the world was threatened by nuclear war and the state's economy was being reshaped to suit the needs of an ever-growing military-industrial complex. While the kids were expected to worry about how much tanning butter to put on, dad was at work designing airplanes and rockets, preparing for the possibility of a nuclear showdown with the Soviet Union. When the image of the wholesome California teenager was challenged by the 1960s demonstrations on the Berkeley campus and the Watts Riots in

Los Angeles, conservatives like future governor Ronald Reagan sought to keep that image intact in order to maintain the dream. Once Reagan moved to the White House in 1981, the dream became part of an imagined United States.[19] Ironically, it was Reagan's secretary of the interior James Watt who banned the Beach Boys from performing at the annual Fourth of July concert on the Washington Mall in 1983, because he felt that the Beach Boys would attract an "undesirable" rock and roll element to Washington. In a sense the imagined United States borrowed or revised images separated from where they actually came from.

But the other California—the dirty, kitschy, worn down, exploited California—is still there, and it too is a California made by and for the powerful. The historian and social critic Mike Davis introduces the world to this other California (at least the southern portion) in *City of Quartz* (1990) and goes on to rethink the perfection of California geography and climate in *Ecology of Fear* (1998).[20] As Davis reveals the fictions of utopia, he also chronicles the fictionalized emergence of dystopia in Southern California. The dream, as Davis suggests, finally turns on itself and with it disappears the landscapes of possibility.

Those who have lived their entire lives in California and are old enough to remember a time different from today are aware that that remembered time is now only a dream. There really was a time when there were orange groves and vineyards where today there is suburban sprawl. There was a time when rush hour started at five in the afternoon, not two. In her recent elegy to California, the writer Joan Didion comes to the rather mournful conclusion that California really wasn't what it was supposed to be.[21] Kevin Starr, who so thoroughly analyzes the dream of California as a place of hope and opportunity, similarly seems to question that dream in his recent *Coast of Dreams*, a history of California from 1990 to 2003.[22]

By the same token, what it was, is also not what it is today. And that is the problem. At what point does it all collapse under the weight of too many people, too much traffic, not enough fresh air, and not enough water?

Taking Stock

The political system in the United States is driven by a power elite that has successfully translated its economic wealth into political power. Although the exact composition of the power elite has changed over time, there is also remarkable continuity in regard as to who makes the decisions in this kind of system and who gains access to those making the decisions. The United States is defined as a democracy, but it is a democracy because it holds elections, not because the interests of the public at large have been adequately represented by those in power. In California the power elite system depends on the role of growth machines that bring together landed corporate interests, local political leaders, and bureaucratic structures crossing local, state, and federal categories to support development of land as a resource in order to generate profit and accelerate the growth of wealth for those within this power structure. The idea of growth in the state can be understood only by looking at history and the way that different groups of elites have managed to transform the state to what it is today. As this historical development has unfolded, society has been relegated to a supporting role, providing labor to make this transformation possible while having little say over what forms growth would actually take. The phenomenal growth of California is a key part of its history, and it is to this history that we now turn.

QUESTIONS FOR DISCUSSION

1. What makes a democracy a democracy? Is it majority rule? If so, what happens when the majority of those eligible to participate in elections do not? Is it still a democracy?

2. If people are as cynical about politics as described, and if they actually see economic inequality as a real part of California's landscape, why is it that this system has been so remarkably stable? If the majority sees that things are really so bad, why hasn't anything changed?

3. Is the imagined West strictly a thing of the past, or do the myths of the past still shape how we see the West today? Has the image of California changed? How has a changing political climate in the United States perhaps affected how California is perceived outside of the state?

NOTES

1. Carl Boggs, *The End of Politics: Corporate Power and the Decline of the Public Sphere* (New York: Guilford, 1999).
2. Harold Lasswell, *Politics: Who Gets What, When, How* (New York: P. Smith, 1950 [1936]).
3. Chuck Collins with Felice Yeskel, *Economic Apartheid in America*, rev. ed. (New York: New Press, 2005).
4. C. Wright Mills, *The Power Elite* (New York: Oxford University Press, 1956); Michael Parenti, *Democracy for the Few*, 7th ed. (New York: Wadsworth, 2001).
5. Kevin Phillips, *Wealth and Democracy: A Political History of the American Rich* (New York: Broadway Books, 2002).
6. Edward N. Wolff, *Top Heavy*, updated ed. (New York: New Press, 2002).
7. Robert Pollin, *Contours of Descent: The Changing Social and Political Landscape* (New York: Verso, 2005).
8. Mark Baldassare, *California in the New Millennium* (Berkeley: University of California Press, 2000), 46.
9. Herbert Marcuse, *One-Dimensional Man* (Boston: Beacon, 1964).
10. Frederick Jackson Turner, *The Frontier in American History* (New York: Holt, Rinehart and Winston, 1962 [1921]), 2.
11. See Richard Slotkin, *Gunfighter Nation: The Myth of the Frontier in Twentieth Century America* (New York: Atheneum, 1992).

12. Patricia Nelson Limerick, *The Legacy of Conquest* (New York: Norton, 1987).
13. Ibid., 27.
14. Richard White, *"It's Your Misfortune and None of My Own": A New History of the American West* (Norman: University of Oklahoma Press, 1991).
15. Starr's series of California history books includes the word "dream" in the title of each book. See Kevin Starr, *Americans and the California Dream* (New York: Oxford University Press, 1973).
16. Carey McWilliams, *California: The Great Exception* (Berkeley: University of California Press, 1999 [1949]).
17. Reyner Banham, *Los Angeles: The Architecture of Four Ecologies* (New York: Harper and Row, 1971).
18. For a discussion of California architecture, see David Gebhard and Robert Winter, *Los Angeles: An Architectural Guide* (Salt Lake City: Gibbs Smith, 1994), xiii–xxvi.
19. See Kirse Granat May, *Golden State, Golden Youth* (Chapel Hill: University of North Carolina Press, 2002).
20. Mike Davis, *City of Quartz: Excavating the Future in Los Angeles* (New York: Verso, 1990); Mike Davis, *Ecology of Fear: Los Angeles and the Imagination of Disaster* (New York: Vintage, 1998).
21. Joan Didion, *Where I Was From* (New York: Knopf, 2003).
22. Kevin Starr, *Coast of Dreams: California on the Edge, 1990–2003* (New York: Alfred A. Knopf, 2004).

Chapter 1 Capitalism, Inequality, and the Limits of Democracy
California, in Theory

A paradox arises in any political system claiming to be both democratic and capitalist. Although the principles of democratic rule emphasize equality of opportunity, an equal right to participate politically in the system, and equality before the law, capitalism as an economic system must create inequality. In a competitive system, there will be few winners and many losers. Sometimes the language of game theory is used to describe what is called a zero-sum game: the success of some must come at the expense of those at the bottom. So how can the United States be considered both democratic and capitalist?

In common, everyday usage, it is simply accepted that the United States is a democracy. There are, after all, free and competitive elections, more than one political party, and guarantees of something close to universal suffrage for its adult citizens. There is equal opportunity to vote, especially after the U.S. Supreme Court established the principle of "one person, one vote" in a 1962 ruling that gave minority voters equitable voting power.[1] There is nothing to prevent anyone from becoming a capitalist, an entrepreneur, and success stories like those of Bill Gates and Paul Allen have now supplanted the Horatio Alger stories of old. Similarly, we are told that "justice is blind," and statues of a blindfolded female figure holding the scales of justice stand in front of courthouses to prove it.

Democracy, Anyone?

In designating the U.S. system as a democracy, we ignore the history of this country and the reality that the Framers of the Constitution did not want a democratic system at all. A democratic system, as suggested in *The Federalist Papers,* was based on majority rule, potentially unstable, and subject to division and factionalization that might threaten the advantages that the owning classes of the country had acquired for themselves. Instead, the Framers put into place a republican form of government, one based on indirect democracy, in which the population elects members to represent their interests in the political institutions of the government, be it at the local, state, or national levels. Unlike a more pure form of democracy based on direct, participatory politics, this republican form was designed to limit popular power. Popular participation in decision making is a dangerous thing, as James Madison so eloquently puts it in *Federalist* No. 10: "Hence it is that such democracies

15

have ever been spectacles of turbulence and contention; have ever been found incompatible with personal security or of the rights of property; and have in general been as short in their lives as they have been violent in their deaths."[2] In *Federalist* No. 36, Alexander Hamilton reassures the reader that though the "door ought to be equally open to all," the people who will actually be elected will represent the ruling class. The Framers knew that the system would favor the wealthy, and state systems have followed the same formula.

With a few exceptions, the democratic system in California and the other forty-nine states emulates the institutions of indirect democracy established at the national level. The emulation is not a coincidence. Voters merely choose representatives, who are then free to interpret how they are to represent their constituencies, with the public relegated to a supporting and usually silent role until the next election cycle. Beyond that, the actual institutional set-up of American government at all levels ensures a powerful if not all-encompassing support system for keeping tight the status quo. Of the fifty state governments, all follow the same three-branch division between legislative, executive, and judicial duties to create a checks and balances system that guarantees stability by putting brakes on the possibility of drastic (or more radical) changes.

Therein lies the problem, for in any indirect system of government, it is the wealthy, the well-to-do, the elite, the ruling class—call it what you will— that dominates the political process. As with the rest of the United States, California's politics repeats and deepens the socioeconomic divide that sepa- rates this country into two unequal parts, a gap that has been widening in the past two decades or so.[3] While the rich were getting richer, the poor were staying about the same. Today, the inequality between the rich and the poor, the haves and the have-nots, is the most unequal that it has been since just before the Great Depression. Economic power is nearly always directly trans- ferable to the political realm, because political decisions focus on the author- itative allocation of values, as the political theorist David Easton so parsimoniously put it many years ago.[4] Seen in this light, politics is not about democracy at all; it is about the ruling class not only creating a system to pro- tect its economic interests in this society but also making sure that those with political power make "authoritative" decisions benefiting the elite's particular (and vested) interests. To the extent that the political process depends— increasingly so—on money in order to keep the system up and running through campaigns and elections, the influence of money on governance becomes ever greater. If democracy is defined as popular rule, majoritarian rule, or even participatory rule, there is no democracy here: this system, rather, is by and for the power elite of society.

In simplified form, a Marxist analysis of politics focuses on capitalism as the mode of production, generating the division between the owners, or bour- geoisie, and the working class, or proletariat. In a very general way, this analysis parallels what is described here. Because Marx wrote about nineteenth-century society, however, a more pure form of Marxist analysis misses the nuances of what occurs today. The divisions of owner and worker have been blurred considerably by corporate ownership structures, which may include a chief executive officer, chief financial officer, boards of directors, and the like, all of whom are extremely well paid (and usually overpaid) but are salaried employees and only partial owners when it comes to possessing shares of stock. On the other side of the scale, the working class no longer resembles the kind of factory worker or coal miner that seems to epitomize the proletarian of old. Although the control and the economic exploitation of such employees remain unchanged in regard to their wages not being equal to the worth of their labor, the lower class today is much more likely to include large numbers of so-called working poor, whose job is likely to be in the service sector, whether clerking in a retail store, working in a restaurant kitchen, or cleaning rooms in a hotel. The work seems cleaner and better than the back-breaking jobs of a century ago, although those who actually work these jobs may tell a different story.[5] And what has not changed in California is the role that the farmworker plays in this economy. Both the conditions and the relative salaries for this work remain much as they were 50, 75, and 100 years ago.

The Power Elite and Development

A more flexible definition seems to be in order. To that end, C. Wright Mills coined the term "power elite" in 1955, and his book seems as freshly descriptive of politics today as it did back then.[6] We will explore the idea in greater detail in the following chapter, but Mills's basic thrust is that although the wealthy (or the haves) of society firmly control economic and political power in this country, it is also the case that not all who enter into government and into the political process are necessarily themselves part of the economic elite. Those with political power, that is, the political elite, enter the power elite by reinforcing, supporting, and expanding the power of the economic elite upon whom their continued political life depends. (See figure 1-1.) In many instances the wealthy run for office themselves. The longtime U.S. senator Dianne Feinstein, for example, has family wealth into the many millions of dollars, and she is hardly alone in this millionaire's club. (See table 1-1.) In some cases those of more modest means may end up cashing in economically only after leaving office. As will be seen, term limits in California has created a growth industry out of professional lobbying, where huge salaries tempt officeholders who have been "termed out."

Mills discusses the role of celebrity in the power elite as well, and California has turned into a great example: Arnold Schwarzenegger was able to parlay his image as a tough-guy actor into election as governor of the state based on the fictional no-nonsense roles he played. In this way, the power elite become even more powerful and secure their hold on power. This is no longer about Barbra Streisand striking up a conversation with Gray Davis at a Hollywood cocktail party. In Schwarzenegger's political ascendancy the public has chosen to have

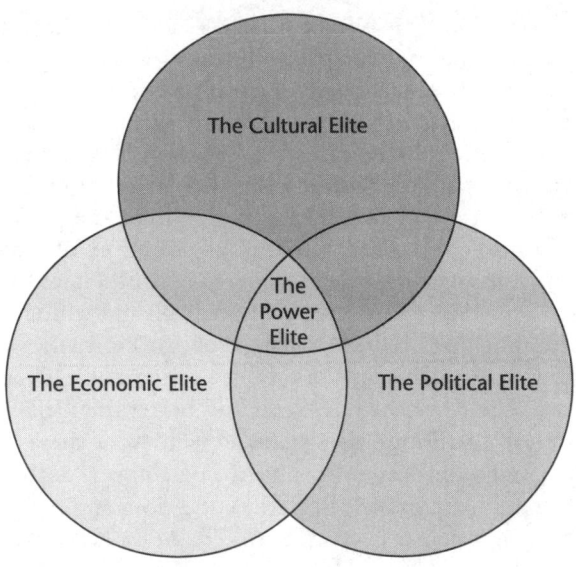

Figure 1-1 WHO MAKES UP THE POWER ELITE?

the image replace the substance of politics, and so has he. With a happy wink and nod, the "governator" liberally peppers his fund-raising speeches with canned phrases from his movies.

The development of the American West is emblematic of how the political system ultimately serves the interests of the power elite. As other countries colonized large swaths of Asia, the Middle East, and Africa in the nineteenth century (ironically, even as Latin America was largely being decolonized), the United States focused much of its colonization toward the West. The patterns

Table 1-1 Who's Worth What among California's Political Power Elite, 2005

Rank[a]	Name	Minimum net worth ($)	Maximum net worth ($)
2	Jane Harman (Dem., House)	168,651,649	289,045,000
4	Darrell Issa (Rep., House)	135,862,098	677,230,000
8	Dianne Feinstein (Dem., Senate)	43,343,464	98,660,021
14	John Campbell (Rep., House)	17,004,087	77,512,000
17	Nancy Pelosi (Dem., House)	14,746,108	55,085,000
22	Gary Miller (Rep., House)	12,013,065	51,750,000

SOURCE: Open Secrets, "Personal Financial Disclosures, Net Worth, 2005," www.opensecrets.org/pfds/overview.asp?type=W&cycle=2005&filter=C (accessed February 1, 2007).
NOTE: One-quarter of the nation's top twenty-five wealthiest congresspeople represent California.
a. Rank in Congress (House and Senate combined), based on personal financial disclosures.

of colonization closely resembled what was occurring in the rest of the world: local populations were displaced then, later, incorporated as wage labor; natural resources were identified and extracted; and land was occupied by the colonizers, who were protected by the military and subsidized via the Homestead Act of 1862. As government moved along with this "internal" colonization (a notion supported by the concept of Manifest Destiny and the need to expand from coast to coast), elite access to this land was consistently backed by governmental decisions that created an orderly distribution of scarce resources to those who already had some. Government was not in a position to follow the will or even the demands of a majority of the people. Instead, it presided over an epic transformation where the few decided and the few profited.

In California, development was initially powered by the discovery of gold in 1848. As Carey McWilliams notes, California became a **great exception,** because everything that capitalism required had to come in from outside sources, bypassing the rest of the West and making California ready immediately for statehood. As McWilliams puts it, "The Union is an exclusive body but when a millionaire knocks on the door, you don't keep him waiting too long; you let him in."[7] Karl Marx was fascinated by the idea that anyone could come to California and have a chance at striking it rich unencumbered by the looming threat of capitalist proletarianization. Miners had another name for this dream: they referred to it as "finding the elephant." Few, however, found that elephant because of the size of the rush and because of the rapid organization of development around business interests that captured for themselves the very best mining sites on the western side of the Sierras. California quickly became a place where landed interests constantly and dramatically altered the landscape for purposes of economic gain. Water was diverted from rivers and streams to support mining activities; enormous areas were transformed from grasslands, which had supported ranching going back to the Mexican and Spanish era of the late eighteenth and early nineteenth centuries, to irrigated farmlands; and later, huge urban areas were yet again reinvented as suburban sprawl. Were it not for the Pacific Coast Highway running too close to the waves in the north and the continued presence of Camp Pendleton to the south, all of Southern California would be a continuous strip of suburbanized development from Santa Barbara to the Mexican border. The Bay Area now extends well inland to San Ramon Valley and has worked itself into many of the communities across the Golden Gate Bridge, threatening with subdivision hallowed wine country. The cities of Sacramento, Fresno, and Bakersfield, once laughed at as cowtowns by coastal urbanites, are now among the fastest growing urban centers in the country. They too, are slowly starting to edge closer to one another.

It is the political process that has not only allowed the power elite to control so much of California geography but has required a kind of coordinated effort to constantly make and remake the landscape in an endless cycle of creative destruction, as the economist Joseph Schumpeter once called it.[8] Behind that political process lies an economic division between the haves and have-nots that ranks among the highest in the fifty states. As this gap grows, as statistics seem to suggest it is doing, the concentration of power manifests itself in the concentration of control over the use of physical space and in ordinary people's living their everyday lives in a map not of their own making.

Growth Machines

Inequality is thus seen in real space, that is, geographically. Indeed, as we look at California politics more closely, the elite power is defined through a structural relationship that the sociologists John Logan and Harvey Molotch call growth machines.[9] Logan and Molotch studied the role of land entrepreneurs and the ways in which government ultimately comes to accept the logic of growth as defined by these entrepreneurs who stand to gain the most from this growth. They noted:

> Places are not simply affected by the institutional maneuvers surrounding them. Places are those machinations. A place is defined as much by its position in a particular organizational web—political, economic, and cultural—as by its physical makeup and topographical configuration. Places are not "discovered" as high school history texts suggest; people construct them as a practical activity.[10]

These growth machines have an important social component. Groups of people, not abstract market forces, define the terms of growth, with the most significant group being these land entrepreneurs themselves. These are the landowners and the real estate developers who have been an enormous part of California's population growth from the 1880s to the present. Government at the local, state, and federal levels have played an active part in encouraging growth while also regulating the terms under which it is to occur. The historian Richard White incorporates the same model of growth machines to understand the development of the American West, emphasizing the interrelationship between cities, bureaucracies, and corporations, which have worked together as a triad to expand capitalism west of the Mississippi.[11]

Land use decisions flow primarily from the elite in urban centers, which determine not only how land in cities is to be utilized but also how land between centers is to be made productive. The landscape is dotted with cities and towns, but the "other" land is also valuable because of its function in supplying these urban nodes with what they need. In times past, this included dependent relationships in regard to lumber supplies, oil and mineral extraction, and water. Although water remains a crucial component of California politics, the complexities of global trade make the connections between city and country less direct today. Urban areas are, however, dependent on food supplies reaching their markets. This kind of urban-rural relationship formed the basis for **central place theory** in geography, which argues for a logical distribution of market centers based on size and market opportunities.[12] Urban politics—indeed all local politics—focus on decisions that will determine how specific places will be put to use to produce surplus value or profit. The growth machine accepts only the logic that growth is good and that growth must be continued regardless of what the consequences may be for some communities or for the environment. Growth assumes that at least some costs have to be incurred but that those costs will be offset by the generation of yet greater wealth over the long haul.

To understand the logic of political power in California, then, we need to understand the logic of growth and the imperative in capitalism to transform geographic space into usable property. A space can be put to many uses, but in a capitalist mode of production, that space must be first transformed into a commodity, which can then be bought, sold, or transferred as property, which, in turn, can become a place of production. It is from the use of space in production that rent can be derived from a location, but rent differs from other types of value in that it derives solely from the possession of space rather than from actual production occurring in that space.[13] The California political system is part of a global capitalist system, and decisions made within this state inextricably connect with political and economic processes across the globe. As the globalization analysts Janet Abu-Lughod and Saskia Sassen suggest, California and major urban centers like Los Angeles tie into a network of global cities.[14] Capitalist development of California is also part of a globalized expansion of the global system that effectively draws new land and new landscapes into the system. In the search for increased profits, capitalism must continue to expand spatially as well, and the entire state's history and the patterns of land use must be seen in the context of this never-ending pursuit. Just how, when, and why particular places are incorporated into a globalized system is a function of many factors at once. Interpreting the work of Henri Lefebvre, the urban geographer Edward Soja argues for the realization of a "thirdspace," where what he terms historicality, spatiality, and sociality combine to give being (and the space where being "exists") its meaning.[15] To put things only slightly less abstractly, how a place is seen, valued, and used is socially constructed over time and this relies as much on how one "sees" space in language and discourse as it does on the real, tangible space that is out there. What we think about a place determines how it is to be encountered and used, not the other way around.

Although the driving force of these growth machines is the interests of the power elite, the political process does provide at least some space for public participation as well. Growth machines must rely on the construction of what Logan and Molotch call **growth coalitions** in the community in order to support their idea of development. In this process it is often the case that anti-growth coalitions form in opposition to that growth. In other words, as elitist as California politics has been and continues to be, people do have a democratic role to play in trying to slow, stop, or alter the ways that economic growth takes place via these growth machines. No-growth coalitions surged in California communities in the 1980s, the most successful being the group fighting the development of the Ahmanson Ranch property along the border between Ventura and Los Angeles County. A revival of such coalitions appears to be going on today, evidenced by citizen groups demanding a moratorium on growth in places like Lake Tahoe, Half Moon Bay, and the Santa Inez Valley.[16]

Thus the power of the ruling elite is not total. Whether in support of development or against it, public participation is still part of the political process, and, to that end, the system may be defined as being democratic. But again, this version of democracy is far removed from typical textbook definitions of democracy in three ways. First, the role for the public in this system is relegated to either supporting decisions that have already been made elsewhere in the process or in fighting against these decisions, knowing that the growth machines will succeed far more often than not. Participation that makes this system at least partly democratic (and a very small part at that) is always reactive rather than proactive. Choices and decisions have been made and now the public is left to respond to it. Second, although formal institutions of government like legislatures, the courts, and the various departments and agencies of the executive branch are important venues for decision making to take place, the mechanics of how these structures work are far less important than their actual outcomes, which nearly always are endorsements of the positions of the ruling elite. It is important to understand how these institutions are organized because political struggle may actually occur there from time to time, but there should be no illusion that these struggles are fought fairly with all sides given an equal chance of winning. Finally, these institutions present a façade of formality when it comes to the wielding of power, whereas in reality power is to be found in a variety of social connections, some formally structured and some not.

The sociologist G. William Domhoff, for example, describes the kinds of interlocks that occur when the same people occupy directorships on many corporate boards at the same time; he also notes that this ruling class reinforces its hold on power through social interactions. The elite live together in gated enclaves, golf together, are members of the same clubs, and send their children off to the same preparatory schools and prestigious (because they send their kids there!) private universities; their elite status thus gets passed on to the next generation.[17] By buying into a notion of power that is formally distributed and therefore visible, people ignore the constant of power as part of institutional practices themselves and the spatial nature of power. Most Californians know that the Riviera Country Club and the Bohemian Grove are off limits to them; membership in such clubs is not a side effect of power: it is power.[18]

The function of growth machines and the ruling elite in California is hardly unique to this state. As White suggests, the history of the American West is a history of these growth machines. These machines have also played a major

SOCIAL NETWORKING AND INFORMAL COMMUNITY CONNECTIONS ARE AS IMPORTANT TO THE POWER ELITE AS WEALTH, CELEBRITY, AND POLITICAL POWER. THESE SOCIAL BONDS ARE BUILT AND MAINTAINED IN PRIVATE, EXCLUSIVE ENCLAVES LIKE THE RIVIERA COUNTRY CLUB.

part in the economic transformation of the United States as firms moved from the industrialized Rust Belt of the Northeast to the American South and Southwest. Sharpened competition within the global economy has also pitted different growth machines against each other. In order to create job opportunities they try to entice companies to locate their businesses in their own community, frequently by offering a host of incentive packages that results in a kind of bidding war. If anything, these growth machines and their ability to work the political process to get these advantages are more powerful than ever. Not surprisingly, their power has increased at a time when the distribution of income and wealth in American society overall has become lopsided. By the end of the twentieth century, the top 20 percent of the U.S. population took home 50.4 percent of total income, whereas the bottom 20 percent accounted for 5.2 percent of the total. The top 1 percent of people alone accounted for 12.9 percent of total income.[19] So of all the income earned in this country, one-fifth of the population earns more than half of everything. The distribution of wealth, including property, stocks, bonds, and other forms of investment, is still more disproportionate. As economic power grows, so does political power.

In California the unequal distribution of wealth corresponds to the unequal distribution of political power. A study by the Legislative Analyst's Office

(LAO) in 2000 concludes that based on adjusted income for tax purposes, the top 20 percent of California's population have been rapidly gaining in income while that of the bottom 80 percent has been decreasing. One of five people have been getting richer, four of five poorer.[20] As of 1998 the wealthiest 20 percent of Californians earned 56.7 percent of all taxable income in the state, with the bottom 20 percent taking in just 3.5 percent of total income. The middle 60 percent combined for a total of 39.8 percent of income.[21] The trend from 1975 to 1998 is clear: the rich were getting richer, the poor poorer. In 1980, for instance, the top 20 percent earned 44.6 percent of the total and the bottom, 6.3 percent; by 1990 the wealthiest quintile surpassed the one-half mark (50.6 percent), whereas the poorest earned only 5.1 percent. Overall, the total combined share of the top 20 percent rose from 1975 to 1998, whereas the combined share of the remaining 80 percent continued to fall. The bottom quintile share was halved during this period from 7.2 percent in 1975 to 3.5 percent in 1998.

Declining relative income becomes all the more troublesome given the cost of living in California, which perennially ranks among the highest in the country. In recent years, living costs have skyrocketed because of the rapid increases in gasoline prices in a car-dependent state (especially in Southern California, where most of California's population now lives) and because of the cost of housing, which increased dramatically in the real estate bubble of the 2000s. As of early January 2006, prices for homes in the state continued to spiral upward. The median price for a home in Southern California was $479,000, up 13 percent from a year earlier, and in the Bay Area it was $609,000; homes in the three largest Central Valley cities averaged more than $245,000. The price of homes in Kern County (the location of Bakersfield) had increased almost 45 percent in a year.[22] (See figure 1-2.) Rents tend not to increase as rapidly, especially in rent-controlled cities like San Francisco and Los Angeles, but they are still high, especially when new renters move in and pay at current market rates. The state minimum wage stands at $6.75 an hour, and assuming a forty-hour work week, an individual living alone would be hard pressed to find reasonable (that is, something above slum tenement levels) apartment living.

Although the numbers could use updating, what was true in the late nineties remains true today: the gap between rich and poor in California is likely to continue widening, given that almost 40 percent of employment growth is occurring in jobs that pay less than $10 an hour; the median wage in California of $11.96 in 1999 was actually 1 percent lower than the median wage five years earlier, despite an economy that was undergoing one of the longest periods of sustained growth ever. And the wealthy, in addition to earning more than half the total income in the state, also benefit from income sources that are nearly the exclusive purview of the upper and upper-middle class. The top 20 percent earn more than one-half of all the interest

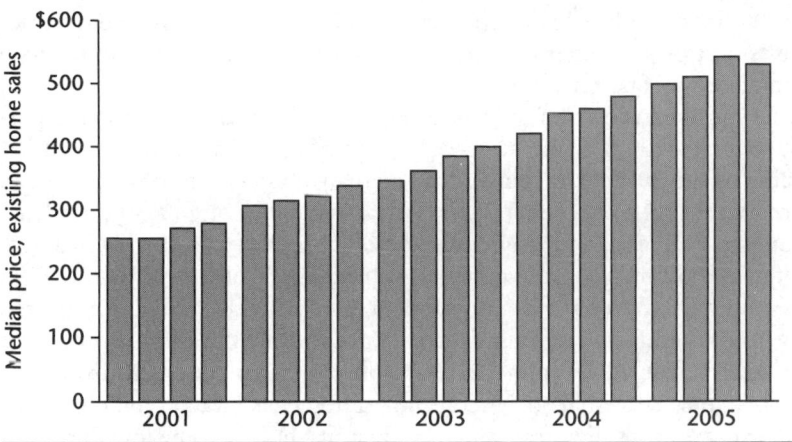

Figure 1-2 CALIFORNIA'S MEDIAN HOME PRICES, 2001–2005 (THOUSANDS)

SOURCE: California Legislative Analysts' Office, "Analysis of the 2006–07 Budget Bill, February 2006," www.lao.ca.gov/analysis_2006/2006_pandi/pi_02_anl06.html#Perspectives%20on%20the%20Economy%20and%20Demographics.

income in California, more than two-thirds of the earnings from dividends, and more than 90 percent of net capital gains.[23]

Adding to the momentum of socioeconomic disparity is the expanding population of the state. All of California history, as Carey McWilliams reminds us, has been shaped by rapid and unending population growth.[24] McWilliams was writing in the 1940s, but nothing has really changed. Population went from about 93,000 in 1850, when California gained statehood, to 1.49 million in 1900, 10.6 million in 1950, 23.8 million in 1980, and an estimated 36.5 million as of 2004.[25] Amazingly, the population grew by more than 10 million from 1980 to 2000 and beyond. Since the population of California was classified as 94 percent urban by 2000, most of this increase occurred in cities, at a time when urban areas already seemed desperately overcrowded. State population is currently projected to come close to 55 million people by 2050. About 60 percent live in Southern California. Roughly 50 percent live in metropolitan Los Angeles (which includes Los Angeles, Orange, and Ventura County plus the Inland Empire of San Bernardino-Riverside); another 8 percent live in metropolitan San Diego, and a further 2 percent reside in Santa Barbara and the Imperial Valley. The San Francisco Bay Area accounts for about 20 percent of the state's total population, and the Central Valley (including metropolitan Sacramento) for about 14 percent.[26] Population growth in the Sacramento and San Joaquin Valleys (referred to in combination as the Central Valley) has been particularly rapid and noticeable, because it has meant subdivision and primarily residential development on farmlands once considered to be the richest and most productive in the world. Vineyards and plum orchards have been replaced by neatly aligned stucco boxes in an array of pastel colors.

The ethnic dimension of California is legendary for its diversity but also perpetually overrepresented on the lower rungs of the socioeconomic ladder. According to the 2000 U.S. Census, the median annual household income in California of $47,493 is higher than the U.S. median of $41,994, and the medians across all racial and ethnic categories are higher than the comparative scores for the United States overall. However, much of the "advantage" in income that minorities have in California compared with the country overall is likely accounted for by the relatively high cost of living. When comparing median income for white (non-Latino) households to other groups in the state, it becomes clear that socioeconomic differences take on definite racial and ethnic dimensions. For example, median household income for whites was $53,734 compared with $48,650 for Pacific Islanders, $36,532 for Latinos, and $34,946 for black households. Only Asians, whose median income was $53,366, compared well with whites. Interestingly enough, median household income for Asians in California is higher than it is for whites in the United States as a whole. The poverty rate in California was also higher than it was in the country overall, with 13.7 percent living below the poverty line compared with 12.2 percent countrywide.[27] (See figures 1-3 and 1-4.)

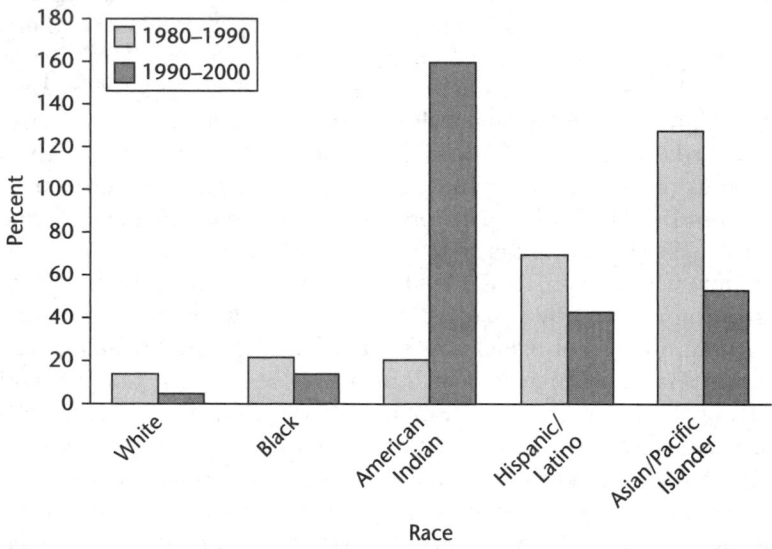

Figure 1-3 POPULATION GROWTH BY RACE, 1980–2000 (PERCENT)

SOURCE: Stanford University, Center for Comparative Studies in Race and Ethnicity, *Demographics of California Counties: A Comparison of 1980, 1990, and 2000 Census Data;* Race and Ethnicity in California: Demographics Report Series, no. 9, June 2002, http://ccsre.stanford.edu/publ_demRep.htm.

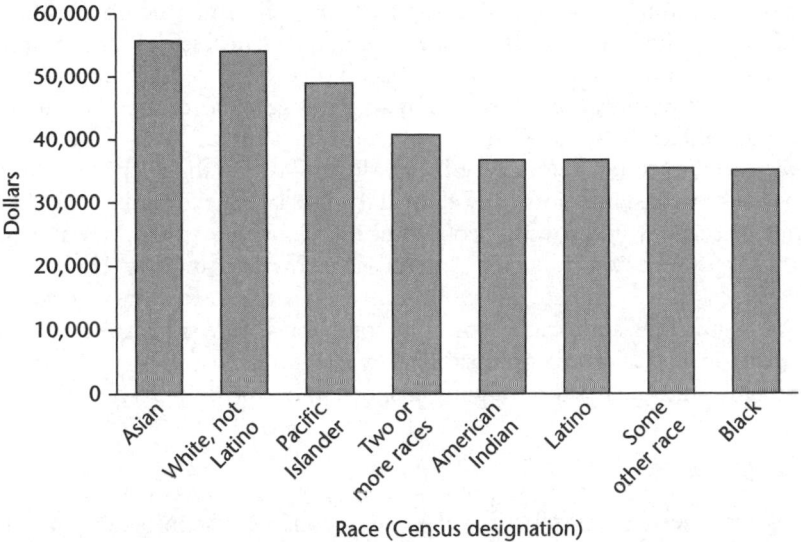

Figure 1-4 MEDIAN HOUSEHOLD INCOME BY RACE, 2000

SOURCE. Data from Stanford University, Center for Comparative Studies in Race and Ethnicity, *Race and Income in California: Census 2000 Profiles*; Race and Ethnicity in California: Demographics Report Series, no. 13, June 2003, http://ccsre.stanford.edu/publ_demRep.htm.

These differences are likely to become even more apparent as the ethnic profile of California continues to change. The white population dropped below the 50 percent line in 1999 for the first time in the twentieth century, and projections suggest that the Latino and Asian populations will continue to increase. A population that was 46.7 percent white, 32.4 percent Latino, 11.2 percent Asian/Pacific Islander, and 6.4 percent black in 2000 will be an estimated 44.8 percent white, 34.9 percent Latino, 13.3 percent Asian/Pacific Islander and 6.4 percent black by 2010. It is not just about haves and have-nots; the have-nots include large numbers of people of color. In California, especially, the growing Latino population will make it even easier for white society to blame social woes on the "illegal aliens" flooding the job market, even though the actual number of true illegals is surely exaggerated and often concentrated in agricultural employment, where they are paid less than the minimum wage. The rising Latino population has simultaneously created tensions between African American and Latino communities. In the relatively poorer neighborhoods of South Los Angeles, areas that were once overwhelmingly black (because black households were effectively kept out of white neighborhoods) are increasingly and in some cases majority Latino, contributing to tensions in an already crowded and underfunded Los Angeles Unified School District.

For the continued economic development of California, the power elite, whose interests the system must come to serve, must successfully incorporate these minorities into the wage system. This involves what Marxist economics refers to as commodification, a process by which wage laborers become inter-changeable objects or things in the production system. Land and other resources, too, must be commodified with similar success in order to create a system that can constantly form and reform itself as larger economic processes continue to evolve with growing profit in mind. Control by the power elite in California is hardly a new thing. The entirety of its history can be told by focus-ing on the role that this elite played in continuously transforming the state. Whether of missions and ranches, mining companies, railroad barons, or real estate developers, California political history is the story of the few deciding for the many, and the many struggling just for an opportunity to be heard.

Taking Stock

There is an inherited tension between the principles of democracy, which emphasize a value system based on various types of political equality, and capitalism, in which economic inequalities are large, inevitable, and necessary. In attempting to reconcile these contradictions, the Framers of the Constitu-tion created a form of indirect democracy and a system of checks and balances that vested power in representatives who would represent not the public will but the unequal distribution of property and wealth in American society. The emergence of an elite power structure—a power elite—stems from the very beginnings of American politics and is reproduced throughout state and local political systems as well. In California, economic development has been a product of elite politics, and the geography of the state today reflects the vested interests of the rich and powerful, who have organized around growth machines to take advantage of once-bountiful open land, natural resources, and labor to benefit most from this system. And over time, the rich have become much richer, the poor poorer. Layered onto these socioeconomic disparities are the fault lines of racial and ethnic divisions, with minorities overrepresented in the lowest segments of income and wealth. If we are to understand California politics, we need to look more closely at how the power elite works and what logic of growth has fueled California's perpetual development.

QUESTIONS FOR DISCUSSION

1. What is democracy? In answering this, think about what you have been taught about democracy in America. It is about free, competitive elec-tions, it is about majority rules, but are there other parts to democracy that are not discussed and debated?

2. Does public participation in a system dominated by elites matter at all? Is the public capable of creating a political agenda rather than responding to decisions already made by those in charge? Can you think of an example in California in which the people acted to set the political agenda?

3. What is meant by commodification, and how can it be that both land and human beings can actually be transformed into objects or things as part of an economic system?

NOTES

1. *Baker v. Carr* (1962) actually uses the phrase "one man, one vote."

2. Alexander Hamilton, John Jay, James Madison, *The Federalist Papers* (New York: Mentor Books, 1961).

3. Kevin Phillips, *Wealth and Democracy: A Political History of the American Rich* (New York: Broadway Books, 2002).

4. David Easton, *A Framework for Political Analysis* (Chicago: University of Chicago Press, 1979).

5. See Barbara Ehrenreich, *Nickel and Dimed: On (Not) Getting By in America* (New York: Holt, 2002).

6. C. Wright Mills, *The Power Elite* (New York: Oxford University Press, 1955).

7. Carey McWilliams, *California: The Great Exception* (Berkeley: University of California Press, 1999 [1949]), 48.

8. Joseph A. Schumpeter, *Capitalism, Socialism, and Democracy* (New York: Harper-Perennial, 1976 [1942]), 81–86.

9. John Logan and Harvey Molotch, *Urban Fortunes* (Berkeley: University of California Press, 1987).

10. Ibid., 43.

11. Richard White, "It's Your Misfortune and None of My Own" (Norman: University of Oklahoma Press, 1991).

12. Walter Christäller, *Central Places in Southern Germany* (Jena, Germany: Gustav Fischer, 1933).

13. See David Harvey, *The Urbanization of Capital: Studies in the History and Theory of Capitalist Urbanization* (Baltimore: Johns Hopkins University Press, 1985).

14. Janet Abu-Lughod, *New York, Chicago, Los Angeles: America's Global Cities* (Minneapolis: University of Minnesota Press, 1999); Saskia Sassen, *Globalization and Its Discontents: Essays on the New Mobility of People and Money,* new ed. (New York: New Press, 1999).

15. Edward Soja, *Thirdspace: Expanding the Geographical Imagination* (Oxford, UK: Basil Blackwell, 1996).

16. On the Ahmanson Ranch controversy, see William Fulton, *The Reluctant Metropolis* (Point Arena, Calif.: Solano Press, 1997), 175–199.

17. G. William Domhoff, *Who Rules America? Power, Politics, and Social Change,* 5th ed. (New York: McGraw-Hill, 2005).

18. Michel Foucault explores the discursive practices of power consistent with what is summarized here; see Michel Foucault, *Power/Knowledge* (New York: Pantheon, 1980).

19. Kevin Phillips, *Wealth and Democracy: A Political History of the American Rich* (New York: Broadway Books, 2002).

20. California Legislative Analyst's Office, *California's Changing Income Distribution*, Report (2000), www.lao.ca.gov/0800_inc_dist/0800_income_distribution. html. Hereafter cited as LAO 2000 report. Although the LAO has not completed a similar analysis to update the situation from 2000, other sources suggest that the trend toward greater inequality in the state has continued in the years since. The California Budget Project, for example, has issued a variety of briefs and analytical reports that draw the conclusion that the rich are getting richer, the poor poorer. See "A Growing Divide: The State of Working California 2005," www.cbp.org/publications/pub_workwagesinc.html; "Labor Day 2006," www. cbp.org/publications/0608_pp_laborday_001.pdf.

21. Based on adjusted gross income (AGI) in constant dollars. For an explanation of why AGI is used as a measure, see LAO 2000 report.

22. Data Quick, January 2006; Data Quick News updates housing prices monthly, posting the latest data on www.dqnews.com/.

23. LAO 2000 report, fig. 2.24.

24. McWilliams, *California*, 81–85.

25. See California Department of Finance, "An Overview of Californians," 2005, and "Population Projections," 2004, both at www.dof.ca.gov.

26. Based on Hans Johnson, "A State of Diversity: Demographic Trends in California's Regions," Public Policy Institute of California, www.ppic.org/content/pubs/ cacounts/CC_502HJCC.pdf.

27. U.S. Census data. Much of these data have been compiled in usable form by Alejandra Lopez, "Race and Income in California: Census 2000 Profile," Stanford University Center for Cooperative Studies in Race and Ethnicity (CCSRE), 2003, www.stanford.edu/dpt/csre/PUBL_publications.htm.

Chapter 2 **Elite Politics**
Individuals and Organizations

What makes someone part of the power elite? For example, does being a millionaire define the elite? If so, there are lots and lots of elites because the value of home ownership has created many paper millionaires in recent years. How about a billionaire? This probably gets us closer to the 1 percent who control nearly half of the wealth in this country.

Defining the Power Elite

Although it may be difficult to quantify who, precisely, belongs to the power elite of American society, there is at least a commonsensical awareness that such an elite does exist and has its hands on the levers of economic and political power. C. Wright Mills sums it up:

> The power elite is composed of men whose positions enable them to transcend the ordinary environments of ordinary men and women; they are in positions to make decisions having major consequences. Whether they do or do not make such decisions is less important than the fact that they do occupy such pivotal positions: their failure to act, their failure to make decisions, is itself an act that is often of greater consequence than the decisions they do make. For they are in command of the major hierarchies and organizations of modern society.[1]

In defining elite politics, the activist and author Paul Kivel distinguishes between a ruling class and a managerial class, which encompass about 20 percent of the population in the United States, adding that the power elite is but a small part of the ruling and managerial classes, who set and control the agenda of the owning class in America.[2] For Kivel, the ruling class includes only the top 1 percent of the top quintile (fifth) of the population, whereas the managerial sector takes up the other 19 percent. At the state level, few studies have looked at the uneven distribution of wealth and income. The most thorough one was issued by the Legislative Analyst's Office in 2000, showing that the top 20 percent of California's population collectively earned 49.4 percent of wages and salaries, an increase from 37 percent in 1975; earned 55 percent of interest income in the state, up from 48 percent in 1975; collected 66.8 percent of dividend income, compared with 67.2 percent in 1975; and netted 91 percent of earnings on capital gains, up from 74.9 percent in 1975.[3] As shown in table 2-1, the trend toward increasing inequality

Table 2-1 Distribution of California Income over Time

Percentile	1975	1980	1985	1990	1995	1998
0 to 20th	7.20%	6.30%	5.70%	5.10%	4.10%	3.50%
20th to 40th	12.2	10.0	10.3	9.6	8.9	8.1
40th to 60th	16.6	15.8	15.2	14.3	13.8	12.8
60th to 80th	22.4	22.4	22.1	20.5	20.1	18.9
80th to 100th	41.7	44.6	46.8	50.6	53.0	56.7

SOURCE: California Legislative Analyst's Office, *California's Changing Income Distribution*, Report (2000), www.lao.ca.gov/0800_inc_dist/0800_income_distribution.html (accessed February 1, 2007). NOTE: Income was adjusted gross income as it appeared on tax returns of selected income groups.

is also evident when adjusted gross income is considered, taking into account both salaries and investment income.

As one might expect, those at the highest rung of the socioeconomic ladder made more from investment earnings than did other Californians. But based on salary alone, one out of five people take home about half of all the money earned in the state. The lowest 20 percent earned only 3.5 percent of the total income. As the study states, "Over the past quarter century, the shift in California's overall income distribution reflects both a sizable increase in the real earnings reported at the high end of the income spectrum and declines in real incomes associated with lower income and middle-income returns."[4] Income in constant dollars increased by 66.3 percent for the top 20 percent; increased by 0.3 percent in the second quintile; decreased by 7.8 percent in the third group; decreased by 17.5 percent in the fourth 20 percent; and decreased by 24.8 percent in the lowest quintile. Note that together, the third and fourth quintiles would comprise what most would define as being the middle class.

The rich are getting richer and the poor poorer. Studies that draw upon data compiled during the 2005 census update reaffirm that this trend has continued.[5] The hourly wages (adjusted for inflation, but calculating real wages rather than income for tax purposes) of the top 20 percent of the population increased by 20.3 percent between 1979 and 2005, whereas wages at the bottom 20 percent declined by 3.7 percent. The median income, however, increased 2.3 percent. As the gap between rich and poor widened, so did their purchasing power, which declined among all lower wage categories. The biggest changes between 1979 and 2005 occurred in the lowest 10 percent, where purchasing power shrank 4.5 percent, and in the top 10 percent, where it increased 26.5 percent. Among the very wealthy in California—the top 1 percent—income increased 22.6 percent from 2003 to 2004 alone. More than one-third of that gain came from investment income (also referred to as capital gains), and very nearly all of it occurred among people whose incomes exceeded $100,000 a year.

The situation of those at the lower end of the socioeconomic ladder, though, obviously makes it tough to make ends meet. The jobless rate in California has hovered just above 5 percent in recent years, below the national average. Nevertheless, more than 13 percent of Californians live below the federal poverty line, and 18.5 percent of children live below the federal poverty line (as opposed to 17.6 percent in the United States overall). California is following the trend, apparent in other states as well, of increasing the number of working poor, that is, people who have jobs but still are categorized as poor. Because the minimum wage in California is not indexed, meaning that it is not automatically adjusted for inflation, the purchasing power of those earning the minimum wage has decreased by 11.5 percent since 2001 and as of 2005 was down a full one-third from 1968. The number of those without health insurance increases as salaries go down, so health care, too, is a concern among low-wage earners.

The trend toward greater inequality in the United States has deepened, helped along by a series of federal tax cuts in recent years, now making the United States the third most unequal country in the world among industrial states (behind Russia and Mexico).[6] Americans have also not been saving money; the average person now spends more than she or he makes in a year, thus, in effect, spending more while earning less. In California the large number of immigrants and their concentration at the lowest salary levels makes them especially vulnerable. Many of these people send some of the money they earn back to families living in other countries, a practice known as remittance (table 2-2).[7] Family members here subsidize the poor elsewhere while barely making ends meet themselves. The federal government estimated in 2003 that $25.5 billion of remittances were sent from the United States, much of it to Latin America, but a large portion probably also goes to Asia and India. In effect, the working poor of California are helping the poor in the rest of the global economy. No wonder that Mike Davis concludes that we are living on a "planet of slums."[8]

Table 2-2 Top Ten States with Largest Foreign-Born Populations, 2000 (percent)

Rank	State	Percent
1	California	26.20
2	New York	20.40
3	New Jersey	17.50
4	Hawaii	17.50
5	Florida	16.70
6	Nevada	15.80
7	Texas	13.90
8	Washington, DC	12.90
9	Arizona	12.80
10	Illinois	12.30

SOURCE: U.S. Census Bureau, Decennial Census, Summary File 3 sample data.

And as the poor help themselves, the wheels of commerce continue to turn profits, as evidenced by the increase in income by corporations in California. From 2001 to 2004, corporate income rose 369 percent in the state, compared with an overall increase of personal income of a little less than 11 percent.[9] That increase has helped to bring the state budget closer to being balanced, but a lot of it also slips through the system without being taxed, leaving the funding of state programs and services dependent on personal income tax increases.

Wealth in itself does not make one politically powerful, of course, but it helps. For one thing, those with wealth are able to gain access to the political system by making contributions to political campaigns. Those with more wealth, those whose earnings put them in the top 20 percent, are far more likely to contribute than those in the other 80 percent. Because of the high cost of campaigning and because they already have social connections linking them to others willing to support one of their own they are also more likely to run for office.

But the wealthy also control what some have called **private government,** that is, the decision-making process within the corporate world that stands outside public accountability. As corporations become more powerful, the decisions that their leaders make will have an impact, not only on their employees, stockholders, and themselves, but on the entire society. A decision to open a new big box "home improvement center" in a community, for example, will force smaller hardware stores to make a series of decisions with respect to the salaries they will pay their workers and the prices they will be able to charge for items that chains can purchase in large quantities. And exclusive contracts between suppliers and the chain stores may even prevent the smaller stores from carrying certain items.

Private government also extends into the rights of citizens. In the workplace, for instance, there is virtually no right to privacy. If a manager or boss wants to look through belongings or screen what Web pages have been browsed, there is nothing an employee can do about it. For most workers, then, the Bill of Rights gets checked at the door for about forty hours a week, possibly more if the company conducts drug testing.

These are decisions dealing with governance, but only the elite participate in them. The system is strengthened by the use of what G. William Domhoff calls **interlocks** of the same people sitting on many different boards of directors at the same time.[10] In this way, everybody in the power elite works together to make sure that the same corporate logic is maintained across this privatized system.

The power and privilege that this system brings is also maintained informally through social and cultural means. As mentioned in chapter 1, the wealthy live together, sleep together, eat together, and shop together; their children attend the same schools, preferably private prep schools and end up going to private universities together, with Stanford topping the list in

California, of course. Political party affiliation makes little difference. In an extremely rare glimpse into elite politics in Los Angeles, the "overlapping circles" include some people who are part of the political power structure (the former Republican mayor Richard Riordan, the current Democratic mayor Antonio Villaraigosa, the former U.S. secretary of state Democrat Warren Christopher), others who derive power from wealth (the supermarket buyout mogul Ron Burkle, the real estate developer Eli Broad), and those who support the political process with generous campaign contributions (such as the Univision executive Jerrold Perenchio.[11] Although the old elitism of private, men-only clubs like the Pacific Union, the California, and Jonathan Clubs is somewhat dated, the new elite can congregate in the luxury suites of the new sports stadiums and arenas in California with separate entrances and elevators to make sure that contact with the general public is minimized (figure 2-1).[12]

Growth Machines and Urban Development

The accumulation of wealth in the West has revolved around land and land use. The decision-making process, which involves both public and private government, drives the logic of growth of the growth machines.

The logic of growth accepts the following assumptions:

- Growth through the development of land is both necessary and good; land unused or underused by humans must be put to use.
- Unlike other commodities, the value of land (rent) is derived directly from its use; there is no substitute for it, and owners of any land inherently assume a monopolistic control over it.
- It is the responsibility of government to support and to organize growth.

Although the growth machine is first and foremost a local phenomenon, the support of government extends through local, state, and federal levels. As Logan and Molotch note, growth must be planned.[13] They add, "Intervention in land use has never been meant to replace the operation of the property marketplace, only to smooth out its functioning."

The growth machine is really a growth network, which is the term that the historian Richard White (1991) uses.[14] It encompasses cities, bureaucracies, and corporations, with each of these supported by the social, economic, and political networking of the power elite. Let's look at each of these components separately.

Cities. The logic of growth is supported by city governments, primarily city councils, planning commissions, and redevelopment agencies, which must approve land use and changes in land use in incorporated areas. Even a single visit to the local cable access channel broadcasting a city council meeting will quickly show what city politics is about: approving development, making zoning changes, allowing for variances, and so on. This is what city governments do. Increasingly, the task of making decisions about land use has been turned

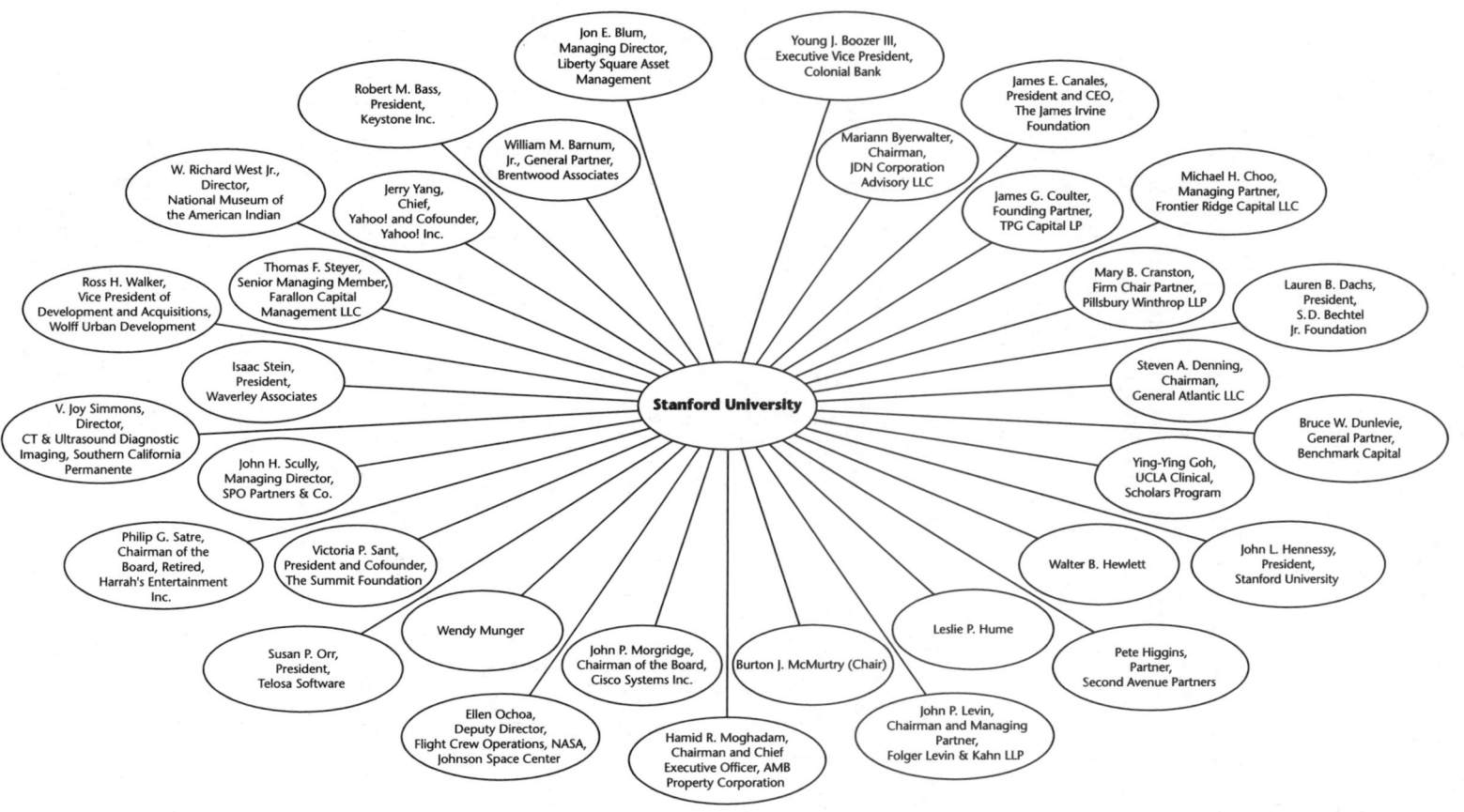

Figure 2-1 STANFORD UNIVERSITY'S BOARD OF TRUSTEES AS OF JANUARY 2007

over to redevelopment agencies, which operate separately from the city council (although councils and parts of councils frequently serve as redevelopment agencies) and with virtually no oversight. Redevelopment agencies can clear a direct path between government and private interests by offering a variety of incentives or subsidies for development to occur, as long as it is limited to a defined redevelopment zone. Until recently, redevelopment zones were employed in urban areas, but San Bernardino County approved a redevelopment zone in 2004 for Cedar Glen, a mountain resort community that was almost completely destroyed by fire in October 2003.

Bureaucracies. This includes the kinds of decisions being made in city government and its staff system, but it also includes other kinds of county, regional, state, and federal departments and agencies involved in any development decisions. Not all levels of government have exactly the same rules when it comes to allowing any land use to go forward, but as a general rule, the logic of growth acts as the default set of assumptions throughout these elaborate bureaucratic dances. Although rules on zoning, growth control, and the filing of Environmental Impact Reports (EIRs) may appear to impede growth, the objective is still to make sure that development of land is promoted rather than resisted. The federal government's Endangered Species Act (1973) is often cited by advocates of growth as an impediment.[15] In California, the act means limited growth in certain areas to preserve habitat of the desert tortoise, the kangaroo rat, red-legged frogs, and several other species. Although it does restrict how land is to be used (much as any zoning ordinance does), the bureaucratic system has coordinated development by negotiating critical habitat set-asides as the solution to allowing growth to go forward. As long as some land is surrendered to let the rats happily hop along, the subdivision can go forward.

Corporations. When it comes to suburbanization, tract housing is almost exclusively the domain of large corporate development groups. Companies like Lennar, KB (Kaufman Broad) Homes, and Centex can put together a development plan and begin construction in short order. But beyond this, corporations in general support any development that will bring additional business, labor, and consumers to urban areas. In some instances, however, corporate interests disagree on what development plan serves their particular interests best. A plan for an international airport to replace a closed air station in south Orange County, for example, pitted corporate interests who wanted the airport built (such as Disney and other corporations connected to the tourist industry) against others who did not want large jets landing over their corporate-owned residential properties (in Mission Viejo and Irvine). After a prolonged battle, the airport idea was scrapped.

Each part of this growth machine is supported by a network of elites, including those who are part of the social elite, those who serve as part of the corporate community via the interlocked board positions at the head of most corporations, and those who are a part of policy formation organizations, which reinforce the links between the private and public organization of power. These policy formation groups can involve any number of state committees and commissions, usually appointed by the governor, but can also involve less formal structures, such as blue ribbon panels, task forces, and business roundtables. The people who make up these latter groups might include a few "ordinary citizens," but they are dominated by those who have wealth, power, and are well-connected politically.

There is a democratic component in the functioning of growth machines too. These machines need to attract support within the community for specific projects that are planned. To that end, they must put together coalitions that support a particular development or development plan. When there is resistance to development, the growth machine must then engage in a public relations or marketing campaign in order to deter the public from resisting the objectives of modernity and progress. When local communities resist too much, some firms resort to the use of SLAPPs (Strategic Lawsuits Against Public Participation). SLAPPs are nuisance lawsuits filed against people who have used public forums, such as redevelopment hearings, city council meetings, and planning commission meetings, to criticize a corporation for its business practices. Although SLAPPs are illegal in California, they are still used to punish local community leaders who attempt to organize resistance to development by forcing them to pay an attorney to figure out that the action involves a SLAPP.[16]

The Hubs of Growth Machines

For most of the twentieth century, growth was organized by using a particular project as the hub for other development. Public universities are one example. The University of California at Los Angeles anchored the construction of Westwood Village around it in the 1920s and 1930s; UC Irvine helped secure development of the Irvine Ranch properties; more recent competition for what came to be UC Merced followed this same pattern. In the late 1960s and 1970s, the shopping mall was viewed as a hub for growth as enclosed malls replaced the traditional central business district. Today, growth machines continue to rely on shopping malls, now refined to "entertainment-retail complexes" and evolving into what are called "lifestyle malls," where retailing is combined with restaurant and entertainment facilities. They also depend on big box retailers to anchor redevelopment projects and to bring in revenues through collection of sales tax (see Chapter 8).

A recent innovation is the construction of new or drastically renovated sports stadiums and arenas to support these growth machines.[17] Owners of professional sports teams argue that they need new or upgraded facilities in order to stay competitive against other teams in regard to both team performance (the equation: good stadium = good team) and revenues. Threatening to move their team if public monies are not used to build a new venue, they argue that professional sports contribute jobs to the local community as well as lending prestige and name recognition to the city. And you can't put a dollar value on that, say construction supporters. Beginning with the success of Camden Yards in Baltimore, there has been a frenzy of stadium/arena construction throughout the country, mostly involving public funds to build so that private owners can make money with television packages, arena naming rights deals, and contracts giving them cuts of concession and luxury suite sales. In California, renovations and a lucrative ticket sales package for the National Football League (NFL) team Chargers led baseball's Padres to demand a new baseball-only park in downtown San Diego, which now expands the gentrified-chic Gaslamp District toward the waterfront. An economic carrot of a new stadium plus moving money led the NFL Rams out of California and to St. Louis. A reconfigured stadium with new luxury suites chased the Raiders football team out of Los Angeles and back to Oakland. A new arena anchors a redevelopment plan in Los Angeles dubbed the Figueroa Corridor; a new baseball stadium in San Francisco is to revitalize that side of the bayfront; noise has been made about a new basketball arena in Sacramento, bringing another NFL team to Los Angeles with a new stadium, and on it goes. Unlike other cities, where taxpayers have carried virtually the entire burden of construction, the deals brokered in California have required owners to share some of the costs. However, each of them does involve at least some governmental transfer of property or revenue (or both) to private hands. This is not unusual, because this is what growth machines are designed to do. What we are left with is a political system that continues to operate largely outside the boundaries of public accountability. It is a system in which the power elite decides what development will look like and who will benefit most from it. They will.

Taking Stock

Defining the power elite begins with identifying who has wealth and therefore power, but the actual implementation of power relies on a series of formal and informal networks. These interlocks connect business leaders through the hierarchical structures of the corporate world, across public institutions and government at state and local levels, and within private networks of social relationships and interactions. Growth machines are effectively growth networks, focused on urban development and relying on an elaborate set of linkages between city governments, bureaucracies at all levels of government, and corporations that are the driving forces of modern capitalism. The "traditional" hub of growth has been the construction of public institutions, such as the expansion of the University of California system. More recently, however, growth has been promoted through retail shopping centers and malls, and through public funding for sports stadiums and arenas that supposedly add status and prestige to urban communities. Although professional sports team owners argue that it is difficult to put a price tag on what a team brings to a city, its actual economic benefits are likely exaggerated at best, negligible at worst. Growth networks are not new to California. Some of the players have changed, but many have not. To understand California today, we need to take a look back in order to see how this interlocking system has operated for more than 150 years of state history.

QUESTIONS FOR DISCUSSION

1. What is meant by the "working poor" and how does this contrast with what is traditionally understood to be a poor person in American society? How are the working poor disadvantaged in regard to access to health care and how do the working poor among immigrant communities face additional economic burdens that others do not?

2. What is meant by "social networking," and how do the power elite rely on these networks to maintain power and wealth?

3. Even though local professional sports teams are privately owned and operated, does their presence in a city contribute to the prestige of a city and to a sense of "civic pride"? Should public taxpayer money be used to build stadiums for this reason? In answering this, think about the fact that the largest cities in California—Los Angeles, Oakland, Sacramento, San Diego, San Francisco, and San Jose—have all faced this same question recently and continue to face it today.

NOTES

1. C. Wright Mills, *The Power Elite* (New York: Oxford, 1956).
2. Paul Kivel, *You Call This a Democracy?* (New York: Apex, 2004).
3. California Legislative Analyst's Office, *California's Changing Income Distribution,* Report (2000), www.lao.ca.gov/0800_inc_dist/0800_income_distribution.html (accessed February 1, 2007).
4. Ibid., 5.
5. See California Budget Project (CBP), "A Growing Divide: The State of Working California" *Budget Brief,* September 2005, www.cbp.org/publications/pub_workwagesinc.html (accessed April 6, 2007); CBP, "New Census Data Show Few Gains for California," *Policy Points,* August 2006; CBP, "Labor Day 2006: Job and Wage Growth Lag Despite Economic Prosperity," *Policy Points,* September 2006, www.cbp.org/publications/0608_pp_laborday_001.pdf (accessed April 6, 2007); CBP, "Indexing Minimum Wage to Inflation," *Policy Points,* May 2006; all are available at www.cbp.org.
6. See Chuck Collins with Felice Yeskel, *Economic Apartheid in America,* rev. ed. (New York: New Press, 2005).
7. Congressional Budget Office, "Remittances: International Payments by Migrants" (Washington, D.C.: Government Printing Office, 2005).
8. Mike Davis, *Planet of Slums* (New York: Verso, 2006).

9. California Budget Project, "Labor Day 2006."

10. G. William Domhoff, *Who Rules America?* (Boston: McGraw-Hill, 2002).

11. Seldom do mainstream media consider the possibility of an elite-dominated political structure. The *Los Angeles Times* did, however, on one notable occasion: see Jim Newton, "The Other L.A. Leaders: They're Elite, Unelected," *Los Angeles Times,* November 28, 1999.

12. Not all of the old elitism is gone, though. A Web site describing the Flood Mansion, home of the Pacific Union Club, sums it up: "The Flood Mansion remains the home of the Pacific Union Club and is decidedly not open to the public. Not ever. Not under any circumstances. It is barely open to the wives of its members." See www.noehill.com.

13. John R. Logan and Harvey L. Molotch, *Urban Fortunes* (Berkeley: University of California Press, 1987), 153–154.

14. Richard White, *"It's Your Misfortune and None of My Own": A New History of the American West* (Norman: University of Oklahoma Press, 1991).

15. For a typical example from the Internet, go to www.grist.org.

16. See Lawrence Soley, *Censorship, Inc.* (New York: Monthly Review, 2002), 85–110.

17. Kevin J. Delaney and Rick Eckstein, *Public Dollars, Private Stadiums* (New Brunswick, N.J.: Rutgers University Press, 2003); Joanna Cagan and Neil deMausse, *Field of Schemes* (Monroe, Me.: Common Courage, 1998).

Chapter 3 The Historical Development of Elite Politics

The story of the California missions has served as a founding myth in state history and has long been a part of fourth-grade history lessons.[1] Beginning in 1769, the story goes, the benevolent Father Junípero Serra founded twenty-one missions, spaced a day's walk apart along the coast from San Diego to the Bay Area. The native populations were taught agricultural techniques not known among California's hunter-gatherer tribes, they were taught how to tan hides and make tallow to be used for trading. The missionaries brought Christianity, and many of the natives converted to Catholicism. Mission life was a mix of paradise amid lush green gardens of bougainvillea vines, elegant white arches, and church towers and of piety as the padres taught the Indians the ways of their church.

In recent years, this founding myth has been retouched. Indians were not always well treated. The "piety" of the missionaries also included out-and-out cruelty toward the Native Americans, including brutal beatings and torture. The Native Americans often tried to run away from the missions, only to be rounded up again. An Indian uprising allowed them to take over three missions on the Central Coast in 1824, and a larger movement against settlement that encompassed more than the mission system took place in the Central Valley in 1829. Even with these changes in the official story, however, the picturesque missions themselves, now popular tourist sites, have reinforced their positive imagery. Sure, the Indians were not always treated nicely, but it couldn't all be bad. Right?

Whether the story includes splashing fountains in a courtyard or beatings of Indians treated as slave labor, both stories reveal the essence of what California was and continues to be. Missions and the later ranchos comprised large landholdings that fundamentally changed the landscape. The Catholic priests and then the **californio** owners of the ranchos introduced a top-down power structure that forcefully remade the environment, a pattern that was to repeat itself over the next two hundred years of California history. This power was used to take advantage of cheap and plentiful labor, a necessary ingredient in economic growth. Although the faces have changed in California—from essentially enslaved Indians to Chinese railroad workers to Japanese horticulturalists to black cotton pickers to Okie fruit pickers to Mexican stoop laborers—the objectives of economic growth have always remained the same, and these workers have fueled the growth machines, especially in agriculture. Industrialization first attracted white factory workers into the relatively well paying and often unionized urban areas, and then these jobs too were largely turned over to minorities. By the end of the twentieth century, these industrial jobs also vanished, leaving what some have called a postindustrial economy built to a large extent on low-wage service employment.

From the Missions to the Ranchos (1770s–1840s)

California's missions are more important as founding myth than integral part of California economic development. Trade occurred on a limited basis because California was inaccessible, and conflict with the Indians kept any eastward movement of goods or population extremely dangerous. However,

CALIFORNIA RANCHO OWNER JUAN BANDINI (SEEN HERE WITH HIS DAUGHTER YSIDORA) WAS ONE OF THE LARGEST LANDOWNERS IN EARLY CALIFORNIA HISTORY. MANY OF THE RANCHO LANDS WERE SOLD OR SWINDLED AWAY FROM THE CALIFORNIOS WHEN CALIFORNIA JOINED THE UNION, BUT THE IMPRINTS OF THESE RANCHO LANDS REMAIN VISIBLE IN SOUTHERN CALIFORNIA TODAY. STREET AND PLACE NAMES STILL PAY HOMAGE TO THE EARLY LANDED CLASS.

the use of native populations as agricultural laborers does suggest that contrary to most stories of American conquest, the Indians were not just pushed off the land and killed but actually incorporated into a different system of production. Capitalism would later transform them again into wage laborers.

Mexican independence from Spain in 1821 marked the beginning of the end for the missions. The entire chain of missions was secularized by 1840. In its place rose the so-called **rancho system,** consisting of large land grants (not unlike the latifundio of South America) given to a handful of settlers who then dominated early economic and political development. In Southern California the names of the primarily Spanish rancho owners (among them Mexican California governors) can still be found in place and street names like Alvarado, Bandini, Pico, and Sepulveda. A few European and American settlers were integrated into the family-based californio society and power structure. For Abel Stearns, this meant marrying into the Bandini family and later gaining title to rancho properties covering a large portion of what was to become southern Los Angeles and much of Orange County. When Stearns later fell into debt and sold off this land, it became the model for subdivision as large parcels were bought, sold, and developed. A Swiss immigrant named Johan Sutter acquired property from a rancho to build a fort that served as a foundation for Sacramento and the gold trade that later flowed through this city.

After California gained statehood, the **California Land Act (1851)** required proof of ownership for these rancho properties. Faced with difficulties in proving title and manipulated by unscrupulous lawyers, some owners lost their properties during this transition, although a recent study suggests that in Southern California, about 80 percent of the owners were able to hold on to their lands.

The Gold Rush, Statehood, and the Power of the Railroads (1840s–1880s)

No other event has had the singular importance of James Marshall's discovery of gold in January 1848. Although American settlers, including the ill-fated Donner party, were starting to flow into California prior to this time, the military surveying expedition, led by John Frémont, had shown interest in claiming California for the United States. Even the so-called Bear Flag Revolt was primarily an ill-conceived attempt at American takeover, but the gold find at the American River guaranteed swift action on California statehood, granted in 1850. The gold rush brought huge numbers of people looking for opportunity in a growing capitalist system that did not offer many alternatives for entrepreneurship in either Europe or North America.

The gold rush also triggered rapid urban growth in San Francisco, because the gold supported a pyramid of development of a hinterland, or, as the social historian Gray Brechin calls it, a "contado," defined as a vast territory supporting the city's growth.[2] Although the legend of the gold rush suggests a free-for-all of mining claims and gold panners, the most lucrative areas for both placer gold and for mining ore were quickly acquired by companies that pushed individual miners (miners and placer panners were generically referred to as miners) to more marginal lands. Capital-intensive methods to divert stream flows into sluice systems and hydraulic mining of mountainsides brought the first large-scale water projects into California for purposes of making money rather than bringing drinking or irrigation water to the people of the state. As the historian Andrew Isenberg suggests, hydraulic mining also brought devastation to rivers and streams, which clogged with debris and carried huge amounts of mercury (needed to separate out gold) downstream from the mining sites.[3] Mining of all types also created a huge demand for timber, leading to massive deforestation (including very nearly all of the San Francisco peninsula) and the use of streams for floating logs to mills. Additional demand for wood for railroad ties contributed even more to the destruction of forests. Rivers that had supported runs of huge salmon could no longer do so because they did not run as deep as they once did. Overfishing made a bad situation worse.

As commercial mining took over, individual miners migrated to other areas, including the eastern side of the Sierra Nevadas and the Mojave Desert. Others moved east to Nevada with the hope, once the Comstock Lode was discovered, of mining for silver. The Comstock was quickly dominated by organized business interests, though, and other miners again had to move on.

Population growth and the need of access to California created demand for a railroad connection between the East and the West. The building of the transcontinental railroad and the large swaths of land given by the federal government to the railroad companies put the "Big Four," consisting of Charles Crocker, Mark Hopkins, Collis Huntington, and Leland Stanford, into a dominant economic and political position in California, which lasted for more than two decades. First among the Big Four was Stanford, who served as both governor and U.S. senator, providing a direct pathway of access between corporate and political power. The growth machine was the railroad industry, and the control it wielded over so much land allowed that power to play out long after the Union Pacific and Central Pacific teams met at Promontory Point, Utah, in 1869 (figure 3-1). Thus, growth in this early stage of California development was played out primarily between the railroads and the federal government. Local governmental functions were either nonexistent or wholly in agreement with the needs of the railroads. The understanding that a transcontinental line was necessary for the "good of all" found nearly universal acceptance. It was clear that this was part of a natural historical progression. Incidentally, the Union Pacific Railroad (which later merged with the Southern Pacific) continued to be the single largest landowner in California even at the turn of the twentieth century. Although the historian Richard Orsi has recently argued that the Southern Pacific was, in fact, a very good corporate citizen, none of the railroad companies hesitated to use and manipulate the political system for its own gain.[4]

Months.	1865.			1866.		
	Gross Earnings.	Operating Expenses.	Net Earnings.	Gross Earnings.	Operating Expenses.	Net Earnings.
January............	$11,040 89			$25,759 14	$10,793 19	$14,965 95
February...........	10,479 55			29,772 13	9,916 47	19,855 66
March	15,380 26			44,400 09	12,923 85	31,476 07
April..............	20,076 18			52,998 17	13,018 17	39,980 00
May	22,939 90	$93,447 77	$219,956 30	65,115 68	15,507 64	49,608 19
June	32,429 07			67,429 78	16,001 23	51,428 55
July	35,633 38			84,756 89	18,807 70	65,888 63
August	39,247 42			111,637 16	21,814 03	89,823 13
September	60,302 62			114,433 80	20,079 59	94,354 21
October	65,925 31			127,065 96	18,554 55	108,511 41
November	18,083 40	13,994 15	34,089 25	86,286 96	20,236 55	66,050 41
December..........	40,454 45	14,227 61	26,226 84	55,257 33	22,992 58	39,264 75
Total............	$401,941 92	$121,069 53	$280,272 39	$864,917 57	$200,710 61	$664,206 96

The business for the past year exhibits a remarkable increase upon the foregoing; although it has been kept greatly below its natural volume by the necessity of paying the high team-freights from Cisco to Virginia City—60 miles—averaging two cents per pound in Summer, and three and four cents as the season advanced. The four most active months afford a better basis for estimating what will be the ordinary traffic and the expenses of the road during the current year, between the steamboat wharves at Sacramento and Virginia Station. For July, August, September, and October, the totals are:

GROSS EARNINGS.	OPERATING EXPENSES.	NET EARNINGS.
$768,769 50	$135,067 24	$633,702 26

or, at the rate of (say) two millions and a half per annum per 100 miles worked, of which three-fourths are net earnings.

Figure 3-1 THE CENTRAL PACIFIC RAILROAD: COSTS AND REVENUES

SOURCE: Central Pacific Railroad Photographic History Museum, www.CPRR.org (accessed March 29, 2007).
NOTE: The actual cost of the CPRR is not easy to determine because the Contract and Finance Company, which built a majority of the railroad, mysteriously lost or destroyed its books. Estimates say the Contract and Finance Company received $47,000,000 to build the railroad. In an 1888 Senate Select Committee, it was determined that the price of the railroad should not have exceeded $36,000,000. The CPRR secretary, Edward H. Miller Jr., said that the actual cost was $46,989,320. Contract and Finance also received $54,000,000 in stock from the U.S. government. Of this stock, Stanford, Huntington, Hopkins, and Crocker each took away $13,000,000 when the company was dissolved.

The might of the railroads also helped create the political machines that came to dominate local politics in San Francisco and Los Angeles toward the end of the nineteenth century. The Southern Pacific dominated the politics of both parties in the state and the oligarchy dominated locally as well. Abe Ruef rose to prominence as head of the Union Labor Party, which was nothing more than a machine for distributing city contracts to companies willing to pay political graft. In Los Angeles the chief lobbyist for the Southern Pacific, William Parker, connected the local elite to the interests of the railroad. These machines were supported by compliant newspapers, which backed urban growth by any means necessary. The urban political scene in Los Angeles was controlled by the *Los Angeles Times* editor Harrison Gray Otis, whereas in San Francisco it was split by a conservative rivalry between the de Youngs at the *Chronicle* and the Hearsts at the *Examiner*.

Railroad construction created a demand for labor that was met with the importation of large numbers of Chinese workers, who cleared routes across the Sierras and through the deserts and were legendary for their stamina and work ethic. These "coolies" created resentment among the white working class, which viewed them as a threat in the job market. Under the leadership of Denis Kearney, the Workingmen's Party fomented hatred for the Chinese while simultaneously arguing for political reforms that even today look progressive: an eight-hour workday, government regulation of the railroads, and elections by secret ballot. The party's anti-Chinese racism, however, led to rioting and the burning of the Pacific Steamship Company wharf in 1877. The Workingmen's Party was also instrumental in rewriting the state constitution, including provisions that severely limited civil and property rights for the Chinese. As with immigrant workers before and after, the contribution that the Chinese made to the building of California was ignored.

The Progressive Era (1890s–1910s)

Rooted in midwestern middle-class values, the **Progressive movement** was directed primarily toward breaking the power of the railroad trusts by calling for radical political reforms. In California this included the introduction of nonpartisan offices (especially at the local level), primary elections to replace closed party conventions, and the three pillars of direct democracy in the state: the recall, the referendum, and the initiative process. The Progressives included a good deal of idealism to be sure in pushing for a more democratic system that would serve "the greatest good for the greatest number" and that would break the party machines so powerful in urban politics.[5] But this idealism also needs to be viewed through the lens of a changing capitalist system that had generated a group of economic oligarchs who had yet to match economic power with political clout. Progressivism provided a means by which the political structure could be opened to accommodate a new capitalist elite that was broader than the one dominated by the railroad interests. In San Francisco, the Progressives were led by Rudolph and John D. Spreckels (of sugar fame, though he later made greater fortunes in San Diego), the former mayor James Duval Phelan, and others, including Francis Heney (who prosecuted political boss Abe Ruef and was famously shot in a courtroom, many speculating that this was a hit ordered by Ruef or his supporters). The destruction caused by the 1906 San Francisco earthquake and fires was later blamed on the Ruef machine, which had tolerated shoddy construction in exchange for payoffs. Better construction would not have saved the city from devastation, however.

In Los Angeles the Progressives were led by Edward Dickson and supported in the press by the publisher of the *Express,* Edwin T. Earl. The Progressives' Lincoln-Roosevelt Republican League was successful in several parts of the state, and the Dickson-organized Good Government League was so successful in Los Angeles that Otis derisively nicknamed its followers the "goo-goos." Although the Progressives did have some impact in Los Angeles, the old guard oligarchs led by Otis and the Merchants and Manufacturers Association were able to keep them at arm's length until the need for water joined the two groups of oligarchs into a single power elite in 1913.

The most prominent Progressive was Hiram Johnson, who served as governor from 1911 to 1917, ran for vice president on the Theodore Roosevelt Progressive ticket in 1912, and later served multiple terms as a U.S. senator. Johnson's progressivism was typical of many in the movement: anticorporate, reform minded, but also firm in believing that change should be enacted by those in positions of power rather than by the public. Not surprisingly, most of the Progressives were intolerant or ignorant of rights for ethnic and racial minorities, although there were exceptions. The Progressives were primarily Republican, but their utilitarian philosophy attracted some Democrats and even some Socialists. In later years, Johnson at times crossed party lines to vote with the Democrats for New Deal legislation. This "nonpartisan" philosophy was to influence California politics for years to come.

Labor Unrest and the Great Depression (1910s–1930s)

The ancien régime and the Progressives shared disdain for organized labor, and so unions fought for workers' rights without significant political support. The **labor movement** relied on public protest and street demonstration because it lacked other venues to be heard. Harrison Gray Otis was a supporter of the open (that is, nonunion) shop both at the *Times* and elsewhere. Things came to a head when the *Times* building was bombed in 1910. Under a plea bargain the McNamara brothers, who had links to organized labor, pleaded guilty. The guilty plea came just before the election and probably prevented the Socialist Job Harriman from being elected mayor of Los Angeles. In San Francisco two labor supporters were framed for a bombing at a 1916 Preparedness Day rally. Although both were eventually pardoned, the event slowed the labor movement.

Beginning in the 1920s, the labor movement focused more on agricultural work. Farmworkers were poorly paid and suffered under oppressive summer heat (temperatures routinely top 90 degrees in the Central and Imperial Valleys) with little water and no shade. Workers were transient, moving with the harvest season for different crops and living in temporary camps that had no facilities for hygiene. Many farmworkers, however, received little union attention because they were ethnic and racial minorities. Chinese laborers had been excluded from the fields, replaced by Japanese, who were then discriminated against through the Alien Land Act of 1913, a law designed to prevent Japanese land ownership. Other farmworkers later took over, including Filipinos, Hindus, and Mexicans. In cotton-growing areas, blacks from the South filled a specific labor niche. A few attempts to make demands on behalf of farmworkers, such as the Industrial Workers of the World (IWW) protest at Wheatland in 1913, were met with violence as landowners sought help from police to stop union organizing.

During the Great Depression, the migration of Okies and Arkies (captured in John Steinbeck's *The Grapes of Wrath*) added yet more people seeking farm jobs. Although these workers were white, they were subject to discrimination. At one point, California posted guards on its borders to try to stop further migrants from coming in. The sheer mass of people eventually led to the construction of housing for some of these migrants, but not enough to take care of all.

Still, the people kept coming. In Los Angeles the first population boom had taken place in the 1880s, and a second acceleration occurred in the 1920s and 1930s. The extensive Red Car interurban train system allowed real estate developers to promote and sell properties across Southern California, creating the origins of urban sprawl. Los Angeles, however, lacked adequate water resources to support rapid development.[6] Led by the former mayor Fred Eaton and the chief engineer for the water system, William Mulholland, Los Angeles purchased large areas of land in Owens Valley to capture water drained eastward out of the Sierra Nevada range and then built an aqueduct from Owens Valley to its outfall in the northern San Fernando Valley. Residents of Owens Valley protested, sometimes violently by vandalizing or dynamiting the aqueduct, but there was little they could do to stop the theft. The project was supported by the Progressives, who decided that the greatest good in this instance was in Los Angeles. The completion of the aqueduct marked, too, a turning point in oligarchical power struggles. The weight of Harrison Gray Otis and the old guard of oligarchs was thrown behind the project when they were allowed to purchase shares in a company that would profit, first, by using the extra aqueduct water to irrigate the San Fernando Valley for agriculture and, later, for allowing that water to supply the valley's subdivision for residential use. As long as the old and the new elite were to share in the profits, the project was given its blessing. When William Hearst tried to reveal the duplicity in this, the power elite did the only thing it could do: it gave Hearst a cut of the investment and his criticism quickly disappeared.

For San Francisco the solution was to be found in the damming of the Hetch Hetchy Valley, a glaciated twin of Yosemite Valley. The Bay Area solved its water needs, but Los Angeles continued its drive to acquire yet more water, leading to the construction of the Colorado River Aqueduct; water was to be shared by a host of municipalities as part of the Metropolitan Water District. As the logic of growth would have it, it was impossible to conceive of putting any kind of cap on development in California; it was simply a technical matter of creating solutions to fit the needs of these growth machines.

The need for water supported the growth machines of the two largest urban centers, and in both cases, a fairly elaborate support system had to be developed linking federal, state, and local interests. In the case of Owens Valley, for example, the federal government ended up supporting Los Angeles's efforts by handing over its survey maps, completed a few years earlier, to Mulholland. President Theodore Roosevelt later declared large areas of Owens Valley to be national forest, thereby preserving the watershed for Los Angeles even though the "forest" was nothing more than scrub brush. With a water source, the growth machine of Los Angeles would be fueled for decades to come.

World War II and Postwar Suburbanization (1940s–Present)

World War II changed the growth of the state in several different ways. First, when war was declared, the internment of Japanese Americans followed the lines of discrimination and racial intolerance that had long been part of Californian (and American) culture. Lives were put on hold as people were shipped to **internment camps,** the most famous being Manzanar near Lone Pine in Owens Valley.

Second, war introduced to California what President Dwight D. Eisenhower was to call the **military-industrial complex**. Driven by the demands of war, industries dedicated to the making of armaments and other military hardware thrived, leading to the first real economic recovery since the Depression. War put people to work and turned the wheels of commerce. It brought naval shipbuilding to San Francisco Bay and airplane manufacturing to Southern California. After World War II ended, the cold war created a continued need for this war materiel, and airplane manufacturing spun off the aerospace industry (connected also to the space race against the Soviet Union) and many other kinds of so-called defense systems, which involved everything from missile weapons to laser targeting to advanced radar and sonar detection.

Third, the war changed the labor market. During World War II, the shortage of men brought women into industrial production on a large scale for the first time. The women's movement would be influenced by this temporary liberation, especially when contrasted with the return to domestic life that occurred after the war in the 1950s. A labor shortage also affected agriculture, leading the federal government to create the bracero program, which brought contracted temporary farmworkers from Mexico to work in the California fields. The Mexican became the new low-paid minority farmworker of choice, so much so that the program was extended several times after the war, ending finally in 1962. The **bracero system** worked, however, only as long as the federal government was willing to keep watch over the workers, who frequently left farmwork looking for less-backbreaking and better-salaried jobs.

The war in the Pacific brought large numbers of military personnel to California. A port city like San Diego, for instance, developed an entire economic sector around catering to servicemen and their families. Scores of military bases dotted the map. At war's end, many of these same people returned to California, enticed by job opportunities and cheap housing in the newly sprawling suburbs and helped along by the GI Bill, which made housing loans accessible to more people than ever. With still more people to deal with, the development of an entire freeway system (supported by the Interstate Highway Act) replaced public transit in Southern California, and more people migrating to the south meant that more water needed to be imported there. This time, it involved the Feather River project that created the California Aqueduct.

As suburban sprawl continued, businesses abandoned the city center in Los Angeles, leaving the underclass trapped in the city's heart. The power elite responded by promoting the first redevelopment of the city by evicting the poor, razing Bunker Hill, a poor neighborhood in the heart of the city, and starting on a forty-year remaking of this area anchored by the construction of the Los Angeles Music Center.[7] Not far away, the pattern was repeated in the working-class community of Elysian Park, where the voting public agreed to give away land to Walter O'Malley for purposes of building a stadium to bring the baseball Dodgers to Los Angeles. In San Francisco the Giants got a similar (though less lucrative package) to relocate from New York too.

Growth and the effect it was having on the state economically, politically, and socially did not go unchallenged. Students at the University of California at Berkeley were among the first to protest in the 1960s, in effect responding to the dead-end that the university president Clark Kerr suggested when he talked about students attending school to learn skills needed to fit into what he called a knowledge industry. These protests later evolved to include issues of civil rights, free speech on campus, and the Vietnam War. In 1965, blacks in the Watts section of Los Angeles violently demonstrated against how they were being treated, both by the police (the Los Angeles Police Department [LAPD] chief William Parker had, starting in the fifties, developed a militarized police force) and by the city, which focused on building infrastructure for the white suburbanization of the San Fernando Valley. The dissatisfaction leading to the protests and riots of the 1960s were never adequately addressed save for political leaders like future governor Ronald Reagan, who campaigned on restoring respect for law and order on the campuses and in the streets. Rather than treat the problems, the political establishment gave priority to controlling discontent, but the success of this approach is open to question. Years later, in 1992, when a trial failed to convict four LAPD officers for beating Rodney King, that anger again led to violence, rioting, looting, and arson. After this incident, the power elite of Los Angeles expressed "concern" about the lack of development in the inner city. Only some new development materialized, led primarily by retired Los Angeles Lakers star Earvin "Magic" Johnson, not coincidentally an African American. The numerous dirt lots that arson left in this area show that nothing has really changed.

Throughout the postwar era, the increasing population called for massive governmental investment to support the continuous growth. Although the growth machines encouraged private development, public funds had to be used to fuel the expansion. In the 1960s Governor Edmund G. "Pat" Brown helped push through a series of projects needed for California to keep growing, including public school construction, creation of a modern prison system, further expansion of the freeway grid, and the expansion of the development of a large state-run public university system. This growth and the government funding for it generated its own backlash. The people simply did not want to continue to pay for growth. By 1978, Proposition 13 was approved by voters, drastically reducing what had been a mainstay of local governmental funding: property tax revenues. Then, as now, the growth machine needed government to keep profits rolling in, so what changed was the pattern of support. Prior to Proposition 13, the government supported development directly through taxation. Now it promoted growth by encouraging the (often-subsidized) transfer of land from one set of private interests to another; the resulting reassessment of property based on changes in ownership and land use brought the government increased tax revenue. This process is referred to as the **fiscalization of land use,** described in detail later.

A 1990s stock market bubble brought rapid and large accumulation of wealth to the state, especially to the computer industry and the so-called dotcom companies of Silicon Valley near San Jose and to San Diego, also a center for the growing biomed industry. The collapse of stock prices triggered a second bubble in real estate, pushed by interest rates that were repeatedly lowered by the U.S. Federal Reserve in order to stimulate economic recovery. Development of land for residential and commercial use by growth machines has led to conflict over land and water use in the Central Valley, where farmlands are now being rapidly subdivided to accommodate the growing populations and water previously used for agriculture is now going in increasing volume to the watering of lawns and the filling of swimming pools. (See figure 3-2 for a comparison of California's population density versus the U.S. as a whole.) A similar push has been occurring in North San Diego County, where avocado, citrus, and flower growers have been replaced by the red-tiled roofs of Spanish revival suburban homes. In the larger, established urban areas, low interest rates have created housing demands pushing development in areas seemingly too far from the traditional central business district yet possible, given the different commuting patterns of what the author Joel Garreau dubbed **Edge Cities.** In the Los Angeles area, the low rates have led to a development boom as far as San Bernardino and Riverside Counties in the East and Ventura County in the North, as well as to the continuing development of South Orange County; all these areas still had sizable agricultural use as recently as the 1990s. In the Bay Area, the housing boom has continued to push development north into Napa and Sonoma Counties and has pushed as far east as Tracy, which has become a satellite bedroom community to San Francisco despite its considerable distance from the city.

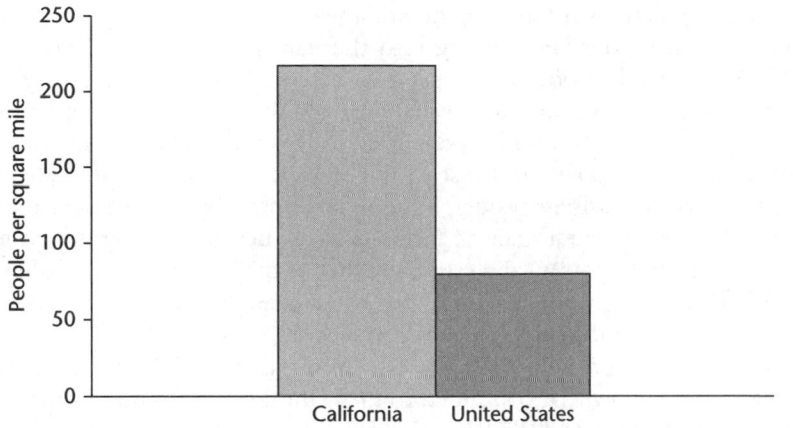

Figure 3-2 POPULATION DENSITY, CALIFORNIA AND THE UNITED STATES, 2000

SOURCE: U.S. Census Bureau, Decennial Census, Summary File 3 sample data.

Power Politics and Progressivism

Progressivism has had a lasting impact on California politics. The notion that government serves the needs of the people by defining what the needs of the people should be has allowed state and local government to support the interests of business and especially corporate business, which argues that government should do precisely that. Signs along Interstate 5 insist that cheap (subsidized primarily by the federal government) water should keep flowing to agribusiness because, after all, it does all Californians a service by providing cheaper food products at the supermarket.

Politically, the legacy of the Progressive era can be found in a politics of the middle, where antagonism between the two dominant parties has been muted and where the grand principle of bipartisanship has led to governors who have served more as managers of California than they have as strong executives. The middle-of-the-road position taken by Earl Warren in the 1940s and the 1950s has served as a model for many, although not all, governors since. Pure technocrats like George Deukmejian, Pete Wilson, and Gray Davis have had no discernible ideological attachments; even more blustery personalities like Pat Brown, Ronald Reagan, and Arnold Schwarzenegger have managed California more than politically steered it. To that end, the elite has had little trouble finding allies to support the fundamental truth of growth among the leading parties.

Taking Stock

The concentration of wealth and power predates the history of California as a state, beginning with the chain of Spanish missions, which took full advantage of native populations as forced labor, and the emergence of the rancho system, which put enormous landholding into the hands of the few. Although the gold rush seemed to offer hope that anyone could strike it rich at any time, the mining of gold was quickly mechanized and the best sites monopolized by private companies. The flood of people led to the construction of the railroads, shifting economic power not just to the so-called Big Four but, really, to a larger corporate business model, a move promoted by government itself as land was given to the railroads to facilitate construction. During the Progressive era, corporate power (and especially that of the railroads) was challenged and political reforms implemented, but these changes represented a rise of a new capitalist elite that had economic wealth but lacked political power. The Great Depression brought new waves of immigrants to California, providing a cheap labor supply that continued to grow until the very end of the twentieth century. After World War II, California's economic fire was stoked by the cold war and the growth of the defense industry, and the still-expanding population shifted growth to the suburbs. The unrest in the 1960s was directed toward demanding civil rights and opposing the war in Vietnam, but the underlying issues of the lack of economic development in poor and minority communities as well as the dominance of a war economy were ignored. Those same problems remained unresolved as California moved into the twenty-first century. The economic elite depends on connections to political leaders to get things done, and it is in the realm of party politics that the economic and political interests really begin to overlap.

QUESTIONS FOR DISCUSSION

1. What historic role have immigrants played in California, both those who have come from other countries as well as those who migrated from the East to the West across what was to become the United States? To what extent have these immigrants been commodified as laborers, as discussed in chapter 1?

2. How has government historically promoted economic interests in California, and can it be said that there has ever been a completely free market system in which capitalist interests stand entirely separate from those of government? If so, when?

3. How has progressivism had a lasting effect on California politics beyond the kinds of specific political reforms introduced during the Progressive era?

NOTES

1. This historical survey has been drawn from a number of sources. Kevin Starr's series of books (1973–2005) have no peer. See also Kevin Starr, *California: A History* (New York: Modern Library, 2005); James J. Rawls and Walton Bean, *California: An Interpretive History* (Boston: McGraw-Hill, 2002); Carey

McWilliams, *California: The Great Exception* (Berkeley: University of California Press, 1999 [1949]); Stephanie S. Pincetl, *Transforming California* (Baltimore: Johns Hopkins University Press, 1999); Mike Davis, *City of Quartz* (New York: Verso, 1990); Gray Brechin, *Imperial San Francisco* (Berkeley: University of California Press, 2001); Mike Davis, Kelly Mayhew, and Jim Miller, *Under the Perfect Sun* (New York: New Press, 2003).

2. Brechin, *Imperial San Francisco.*
3. Andrew C. Isenberg, *Mining California* (New York: Hill and Wang, 2001).
4. Richard Orsi, *Sunset Limited* (Berkeley: University of California Press, 2005).
5. George E. Mowry, *The California Progressives* (New York: Quadrangle, 1976 [1951]); Michael McGerr, *A Fierce Discontent* (New York: Oxford University Press, 2003); William Deverell and Tom Sitton, eds., *California Progressivism Revisited* (Berkeley: University of California Press, 1994).
6. Water has played a key role in the development of California. Many detailed studies have dealt with this specific topic. See Norris Hundley Jr., *The Great Thirst: Californians and Water, 1770s–1990s* (Berkeley: University of California Press, 1992); Marc Reisner, *Cadillac Desert: The American West and Its Disappearing Water* (New York: Viking, 1986); Donald Worster, *Rivers of Empire: Water, Aridity, and the Growth of the American West* (New York: Pantheon, 1985); William Kahrl, *Water and Power: The Conflict over Los Angeles Water Supply in the Owens Valley* (Berkeley: University of California Press, 1982); John Walton, *Western Times and Water Wars: State, Culture, and Rebellion in California* (Berkeley: University of California Press, 1992).
7. Don Parson, *Making a Better World: Public Housing, the Red Scare, and the Direction of Modern Los Angeles* (Minneapolis: University of Minnesota Press, 2005).

Chapter 4 Gaining Political Access
Parties, Campaigns, and Elections

The Secret Life of the Two-Party System

Ask someone about politicians or political parties and he or she will usually come back with some reply like, "Oh, it's all so corrupt, so who cares anyway?" A system dominated by a power elite will happily accept cynicism as long as it leads to alienation within the system instead of mobilization and action to demand a more democratic accounting of what the two major parties and their members actually stand for. Although Democrats and Republicans take great pains to outline differences between their parties for purposes of winning elections (and thus positioning their side to gain advantage in fund-raising), the two parties have far more in common than what they claim divides them. In fact, one would be hard pressed to slip a credit card between the two parties and the values they actually represent. With a few exceptions at the ideological fringes, both parties are firm believers in the kind of corporate-driven capitalist system that encourages growth and profit to benefit private interests while using public institutions and sometimes public funds to continue that accumulation of wealth and power into the hands of the few.

Some people fantasize about a third-party challenge to the dominance of the Democrats and Republicans. Many third-party alternatives have come and gone through the years, from the Peace and Freedom Party in the 1960s to more recent challengers like the Libertarian, Green, and Natural Law parties. But these third parties are just about doomed to failure because of the plurality system used for state elections as well as for congressional elections. The United States uses a plurality, or winner-take-all system, with single-seat districts, meaning that in order to gain seats in the legislature or in Congress, a small party has to win the election outright. This is not an easy thing to do, given the advantages that the two main parties have to start with: money, name recognition, and experience. But think also about what happens in this kind of a system come election day. The votes begin to be tallied, and exit polling already gives a strong hint as to who will likely win. The tally runs to 52 percent for, say, the Democrat, 48 percent for the Republican, and in the victory speech, the winner congratulates the opponent on a tough campaign, expresses regret for some of the harsh words exchanged during the campaign, and then talks about working for all the people in the district. The candidate has to make this kind of a speech. Why? From a party perspective, 48 percent of the people in that district will go unrepresented for that term. They voted for the other guy.

Some other countries use the plurality system. Great Britain and the remnants of its commonwealth employ this first-past-the-post system. Although some third parties do succeed in gaining seats (such as the New Democratic Party in Canada), all such systems tend toward a two-party system because the system puts other parties at a great disadvantage. For this reason, many developed countries use variations of proportional representation, a system in which the percentage of seats a party receives in the legislative body is roughly proportional to the percentage of votes it gets in the election. The simplest way to make such a system work is to increase the number of seats per district to allow smaller parties the chance to win some representation. If there are five or six seats per district, for instance, it is probable that a small party with 15 percent of the vote would get a seat; depending on the exact allocation rules used, even smaller parties could land seats. In contrast, the plurality system has a mechanical effect that leads to a two-party system. Political reform is often talked about in generalities; proportional representation would instantly revolutionize party politics. For this reason alone, it is not part of the "mainstream" discussion. The current system serves the ruling interests quite nicely.

Parties and Participation

Judging by party registration and by the current dominance of the Democrats in both houses of the California legislature, in statewide executive offices, and in the California congressional delegation, it seems that the state is overwhelmingly Democratic. Such a judgment assumes, however, that **party affiliation** really means anything beyond having a rooting interest for the Blue team (the Democrats) over the Red team (the Republicans) and goes against the old adage that nothing lasts forever. California was once a strongly Republican state, but the Democrats have had an advantage in the number registered since the 1930s, peaking at more than 60 percent in 1942. As of 2006 about 43 percent of registered voters in California were registered as Democrats, 34 percent as Republicans, and about 4 percent as members of other smaller parties. Although Democrats have held the edge in numbers in party registration, Republicans have been much more successful in getting their party loyalists to turn out and vote in elections, so the state has been competitive for the past seventy years, so successful, in fact, that it seemed that the Republicans were starting to take over in the late 1980s and early 1990s. The geography of party affiliation is also of interest: the coastal areas, especially the Bay Area and Los Angeles are Democratic, whereas the inland areas, extended suburbs, and San Diego are Republican strongholds (table 4-1). This mimics the Blue-Red divide nationwide, in which urban areas support one party, and rural areas and smaller cities the other.

The biggest change in party affiliation comes not in switching parties, but in the increasing number of voters who decline to state a party preference

Table 4-1 Red County, Blue County: Voting Patterns in the 2004 Presidential Election

	John F. Kerry	George W. Bush	Michael Anthony Peroutka	David Cobb	Michael Badnarik	Leonard Peltier
	DEM	REP	AI	GRN	LIB	PF
Alameda County						
Total votes	422,585	130,911	819	2,637	2,149	1,641
Percentage of total	75.4%	23.3%	0.1%	0.5%	0.4%	0.3%
Alpine County						
Total votes	373	311	2	7	1	5
Percentage of total	53.4%	44.5%	0.3%	1.0%	0.1%	0.7%
Amador County						
Total votes	6,541	11,107	56	47	70	28
Percentage of total	36.6%	62.1%	0.3%	0.3%	0.4%	0.2%
Butte County						
Total votes	42,448	51,662	312	506	518	289
Percentage of total	44.3%	54.0%	0.3%	0.5%	0.5%	0.3%
Calaveras County						
Total votes	8,286	13,601	98	110	152	59
Percentage of total	37.1%	60.9%	0.4%	0.5%	0.7%	0.3%
Colusa County						
Total votes	1,947	4,142	15	29	8	25
Percentage of total	31.6%	67.2%	0.2%	0.5%	0.1%	0.4%
Contra Costa County						
Total votes	257,254	150,608	760	1,229	1,606	682
Percentage of total	62.4%	36.5%	0.2%	0.3%	0.4%	0.2%
Del Norte County						
Total votes	3,892	5,356	47	30	55	41
Percentage of total	41.3%	56.9%	0.5%	0.3%	0.6%	0.4%
El Dorado County						
Total votes	32,242	52,878	220	358	406	174
Percentage of total	37.4%	61.3%	0.3%	0.4%	0.5%	0.2%
Fresno County						
Total votes	103,154	141,988	424	601	634	359
Percentage of total	41.7%	57.4%	0.2%	0.2%	0.3%	0.1%
Glenn County						
Total votes	2,995	6,308	27	31	47	27
Percentage of total	31.7%	66.9%	0.3%	0.3%	0.5%	0.3%
Humboldt County						
Total votes	37,988	25,714	191	832	381	404
Percentage of total	58.0%	39.3%	0.3%	1.3%	0.6%	0.6%
Imperial County						
Total votes	17,964	15,890	77	109	73	161
Percentage of total	52.4%	46.4%	0.2%	0.3%	0.2%	0.5%
Inyo County						
Total votes	3,350	5,091	35	36	51	37
Percentage of total	39.0%	59.2%	0.4%	0.4%	0.6%	0.4%
Kern County						
Total votes	68,603	140,417	499	308	634	397
Percentage of total	32.5%	66.6%	0.2%	0.1%	0.3%	0.2%

Table 4-1 (*Continued*)

	John F. Kerry	George W. Bush	Michael Anthony Peroutka	David Cobb	Michael Badnarik	Leonard Peltier
	DEM	REP	AI	GRN	LIB	PF
Kings County						
Total votes	10,833	21,003	71	55	69	62
Percentage of total	33.8%	65.4%	0.2%	0.2%	0.2%	0.2%
Lake County						
Total votes	13,141	11,093	109	124	117	79
Percentage of total	53.2%	44.9%	0.4%	0.5%	0.5%	0.3%
Lassen County						
Total votes	3,158	8,126	52	17	50	34
Percentage of total	27.6%	71.0%	0.5%	0.1%	0.4%	0.3%
Los Angeles County						
Total votes	1,907,736	1,076,225	6,565	10,749	11,855	8,517
Percentage of total	63.1%	35.6%	0.2%	0.4%	0.4%	0.3%
Madera County						
Total votes	13,481	24,871	98	126	127	77
Percentage of total	34.8%	64.1%	0.3%	0.3%	0.3%	0.2%
Marin County						
Total votes	99,070	34,378	178	474	620	199
Percentage of total	73.2%	25.4%	0.1%	0.4%	0.5%	0.1%
Mariposa County						
Total votes	3,251	5,215	58	41	39	34
Percentage of total	37.6%	60.4%	0.7%	0.5%	0.5%	0.4%
Mendocino County						
Total votes	24,385	12,955	133	267	224	215
Percentage of total	63.9%	33.9%	0.3%	0.7%	0.6%	0.6%
Merced County						
Total votes	24,491	32,773	142	174	171	194
Percentage of total	42.3%	56.5%	0.2%	0.3%	0.3%	0.3%
Modoc County						
Total votes	1,149	3,235	17	8	33	14
Percentage of total	25.8%	72.6%	0.4%	0.2%	0.7%	0.3%
Mono County						
Total votes	2,628	2,621	11	22	30	18
Percentage of total	49.2%	49.1%	0.2%	0.4%	0.6%	0.3%
Monterey County						
Total votes	75,046	47,789	299	453	475	236
Percentage of total	60.4%	38.4%	0.2%	0.4%	0.4%	0.2%
Napa County						
Total votes	33,666	22,059	177	190	238	135
Percentage of total	59.6%	39.1%	0.3%	0.3%	0.4%	0.2%
Nevada County						
Total votes	24,220	28,790	141	218	255	115
Percentage of total	44.9%	53.4%	0.3%	0.4%	0.5%	0.2%
Orange County						
Total votes	419,239	641,832	2,555	2,660	5,414	1,596
Percentage of total	39.0%	59.7%	0.2%	0.2%	0.5%	0.1%

(*Continues*)

Table 4-1 (*Continued*)

	John F. Kerry	George W. Bush	Michael Anthony Peroutka	David Cobb	Michael Badnarik	Leonard Peltier
	DEM	REP	AI	GRN	LIB	PF
Placer County						
Total votes	55,573	95,969	278	424	523	178
Percentage of total	36.3%	62.6%	0.2%	0.3%	0.3%	0.1%
Plumas County						
Total votes	4,129	6,905	30	42	49	23
Percentage of total	36.9%	61.7%	0.3%	0.4%	0.4%	0.2%
Riverside County						
Total votes	228,806	322,473	1,417	1,330	1,704	1,152
Percentage of total	41.1%	57.9%	0.3%	0.2%	0.3%	0.2%
Sacramento County						
Total votes	236,657	235,539	964	1,402	1,483	720
Percentage of total	49.6%	49.4%	0.2%	0.3%	0.3%	0.2%
San Benito County						
Total votes	9,851	8,698	47	41	54	34
Percentage of total	52.6%	46.5%	0.3%	0.2%	0.3%	0.2%
San Bernardino County						
Total votes	227,789	289,306	1,473	1,247	1,714	1,248
Percentage of total	43.5%	55.3%	0.3%	0.2%	0.3%	0.2%
San Diego County						
Total votes	526,437	596,033	2,129	2,551	4,660	1,774
Percentage of total	46.4%	52.6%	0.2%	0.2%	0.4%	0.2%
San Francisco County						
Total votes	296,772	54,355	380	1,854	1,401	1,167
Percentage of total	83.0%	15.2%	0.1%	0.5%	0.4%	0.3%
San Joaquin County						
Total votes	87,012	100,978	385	347	415	368
Percentage of total	45.9%	53.3%	0.2%	0.2%	0.2%	0.2%
San Luis Obispo County						
Total votes	58,742	67,995	335	684	665	226
Percentage of total	45.5%	52.7%	0.3%	0.5%	0.5%	0.2%
San Mateo County						
Total votes	197,922	83,315	392	899	1,142	407
Percentage of total	69.5%	29.2%	0.1%	0.3%	0.4%	0.1%
Santa Barbara County						
Total votes	90,314	76,806	272	676	885	272
Percentage of total	53.4%	45.4%	0.2%	0.4%	0.5%	0.2%
Santa Clara County						
Total votes	386,100	209,094	982	2,007	3,425	1,006
Percentage of total	64.1%	34.7%	0.2%	0.3%	0.6%	0.2%
Santa Cruz County						
Total votes	89,102	30,354	327	782	764	404
Percentage of total	73.2%	24.9%	0.3%	0.6%	0.6%	0.3%
Shasta County						
Total votes	24,339	52,249	264	185	290	244
Percentage of total	31.4%	67.4%	0.3%	0.2%	0.4%	0.3%

Table 4-1 (*Continued*)

	John F. Kerry	George W. Bush	Michael Anthony Peroutka	David Cobb	Michael Badnarik	Leonard Peltier
	DEM	REP	AI	GRN	LIB	PF
Sierra County						
Total votes	646	1,249	16	10	17	7
Percentage of total	33.2%	64.2%	0.8%	0.5%	0.9%	0.4%
Siskiyou County						
Total votes	7,880	12,673	71	58	121	60
Percentage of total	37.8%	60.7%	0.3%	0.3%	0.6%	0.3%
Solano County						
Total votes	85,096	62,301	285	327	429	308
Percentage of total	57.2%	41.9%	0.2%	0.2%	0.3%	0.2%
Sonoma County						
Total votes	148,261	68,204	569	1,133	1,246	664
Percentage of total	67.4%	31.0%	0.3%	0.5%	0.6%	0.3%
Stanislaus County						
Total votes	58,829	85,407	342	294	333	309
Percentage of total	40.4%	58.6%	0.2%	0.2%	0.2%	0.2%
Sutter County						
Total votes	9,602	20,254	83	64	86	56
Percentage of total	31.9%	67.2%	0.3%	0.2%	0.3%	0.2%
Tehama County						
Total votes	7,504	15,572	105	66	96	62
Percentage of total	32.1%	66.5%	0.4%	0.3%	0.4%	0.3%
Trinity County						
Total votes	2,782	3,560	41	17	41	38
Percentage of total	42.9%	54.9%	0.6%	0.3%	0.6%	0.6%
Tulare County						
Total votes	32,494	65,399	188	239	228	191
Percentage of total	32.9%	66.2%	0.2%	0.2%	0.2%	0.2%
Tuolumne County						
Total votes	10,104	15,745	82	86	126	45
Percentage of total	38.4%	59.8%	0.3%	0.3%	0.5%	0.2%
Ventura County						
Total votes	148,859	160,314	767	1,031	1,381	557
Percentage of total	47.6%	51.2%	0.2%	0.3%	0.4%	0.2%
Yolo County						
Total votes	42,885	28,005	164	452	316	187
Percentage of total	59.6%	38.9%	0.2%	0.6%	0.4%	0.3%
Yuba County						
Total votes	5,687	12,076	69	73	69	46
Percentage of total	31.6%	67.0%	0.4%	0.4%	0.4%	0.3%

SOURCE: California Secretary of State, "Statement of Vote," www.ss.ca.gov/elections/sov/2004_general/formatted_pr.
NOTE: Dem = Democratic Party; Rep = Republican Party; AI = American Independent Party; GRN = Green Party; LIB = Libertarian Party; PF = Peace and Freedom Party.

Table 4-2 Registration by Political Party, 1992–2004

Year	Democratic (%)	Republican (%)	Other (%)	Declined to State (%)	Democratic Counties (no.)	Republican Counties (no.)
2004	43.0	34.7	4.6	17.7	21	37
2000	45.4	34.9	5.3	14.4	25	32
1996	47.2	36.4	5.1	11.3	32	26
1992	49.1	37.0	3.6	10.3	45	13

SOURCE: California Secretary of State, "Historical Voter Registration Statistics," www.ss.ca.gov/elections/ror/reg_stats_10_18_04.pdf (accessed March 21, 2007).

(table 4-2). By 2006 about 18 percent of voters registered as independent voters, officially designated in California as "declined to state," a big jump from 1978, when just under 8 percent did so. This should not be altogether surprising for three reasons. First, California has had a relatively weak party system and a tradition of ideological centrism going back to the Progressive era (see figure 4-1 for the organization of California's Democratic Party). The Progressives broke through the dominance of the party machines by introducing primary elections to choose party candidates for the general election. In these primaries California also allowed for cross-filing, meaning that members could register for other parties' primaries as well. In 1946 Republican Earl Warren ran unopposed in the general election by winning the Republican, Democratic, and Progressive Party primaries. California tried to resurrect a version of this open primary system with the blanket primary, which allowed voters registered with any party to vote for other party candidates in the primary election, but this was ruled unconstitutional by the U.S. Supreme Court in June 2000. The primary process was changed in 2002, permitting decline-to-state voters to vote in party primaries (in the party of their choice) instead of being limited to voting on ballot measures alone. The trend toward nonpartisanship was already there, but this change in law made it easier for voters not to register with either of the two dominant parties.

Last, the decline in party affiliation indicates disenchantment with the status quo. More people are starting to recognize that the two-party system does not serve their political interests. California has made it progressively easier to register to vote since 1993; still, less than half of those eligible to vote (citizens over age eighteen) are registered. This shift to decline-to-state voters is also indicative of this trend.

In the 2000 presidential elections, discrepancies and out-and-out manipulation with the results in Florida helped push through reforms that would bring in e-voting (electronic voting) to replace the punch card systems typically used in California elections.[1] These new systems, also called direct recording electronic (DRE) devices, use some kind of touch-screen voting with computer linkage to the registrar or optical scan methods, not unlike those used on multiple-choice exam forms. Because of problems with these

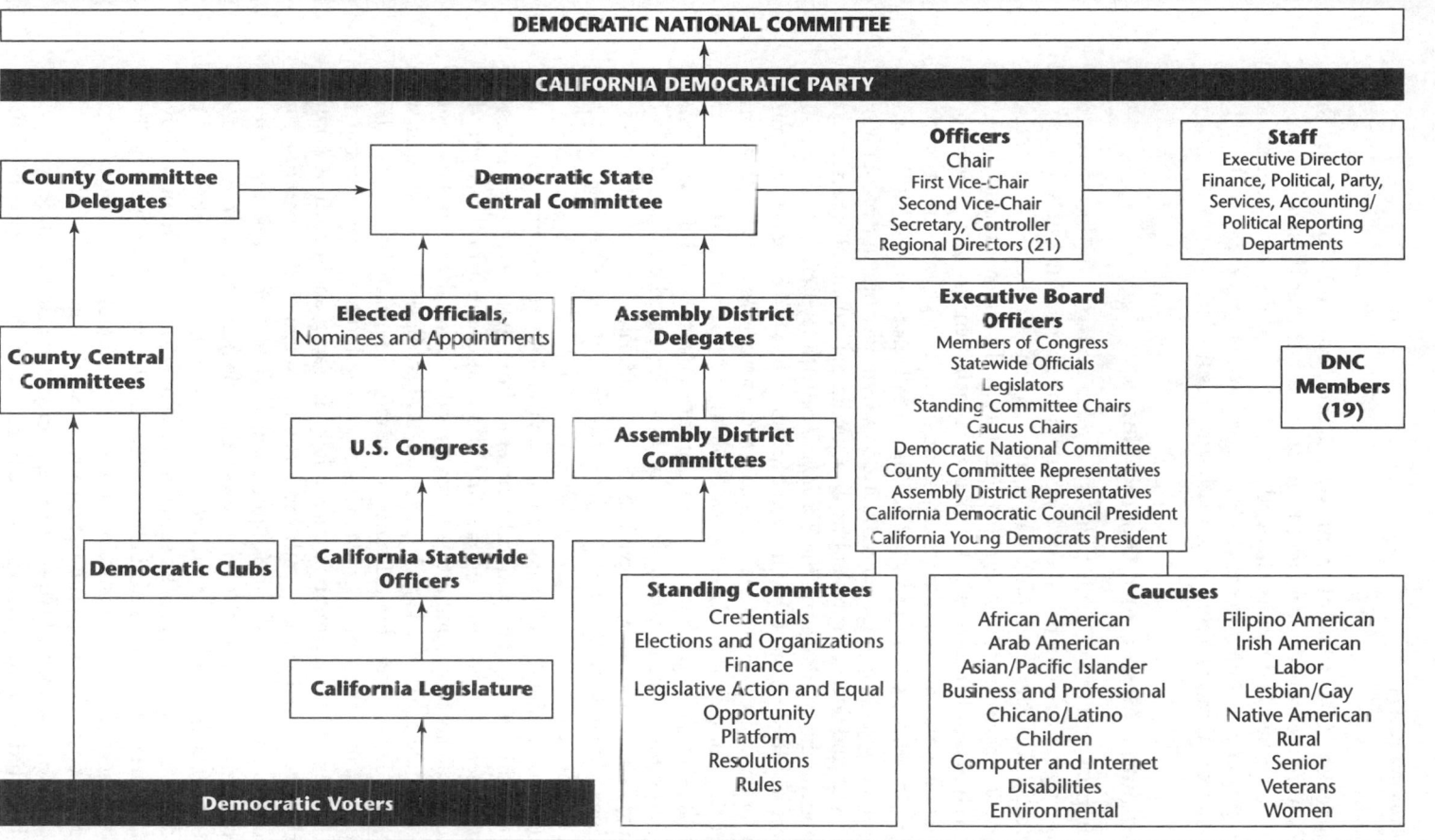

Figure 4-1 CALIFORNIA'S DEMOCRATIC PARTY ORGANIZATION

SOURCE: California Democratic Party, "California Democratic Party Structure," www.kintera.org/site/pp.asp?c=fvlrk7o3e&b=33603 (accessed March 29, 2007).
NOTE: The Republican Party follows a similar organizational pattern.

machines in 2004, some of them were decertified. In 2006 some of these DREs were recertified, but critics have pointed out that these machines can easily be hacked and results changed. In addition, the software for some of these products include internal codes that allow programmers to "key" back into the vote totals and thus potentially alter results.[2]

Candidates, Media, and Getting Elected

The normal path to a career in politics has been to start at the local level, such as running for a school board or city council, then working one's way up the political ladder by developing name recognition and networking through the party. This is still the general pattern, but the last decades have also given rise to **citizen politicians,** who try to finance their own way into political office by spending enormous amounts of personal wealth to bypass this traditional route. In running for governor in the recall election of 2003, Arnold Schwarzenegger had money and the added advantages of name recognition as a film star and access to the public as a media personality, characterized by announcing his candidacy on the *Tonight Show* with Jay Leno in August 2003. Others have been part of the elite establishment but lacked name recognition without dedicating money to developing that identity, as Richard Riordan did in running for mayor of Los Angeles. Still other "citizens" have spent wealth to build both connections and recognition. Michael Huffington spent huge amounts of money to gain a seat in Congress, then narrowly lost to Dianne Feinstein in an expensive U.S. Senate campaign in 1994. In 1998 the unknown Al Checchi spent $38 million running in the Democratic primary for governor and lost.

Elite power depends on being able to translate economic control into usable political form. The political process is about getting those elected who will represent the interests of that elite, and campaigning in the twenty-first century is all about gaining access to mass media, through which the image of the candidate can be packaged, marketed, and sold. Media coverage of state politics today is almost nonexistent. For a state with 36 million people, fewer than 100 daily newspapers survive. Cities that used to have several competing papers now are dominated by a single daily; in San Francisco, the *Chronicle,* which once shared the city with the Hearst newspaper the *Examiner,* now dominates. A buyout of the Knight-Ridder chain (including the *San Jose Mercury News*) by the McClatchy newspapers, owners of the *Sacramento Bee,* in 2006 further complicates the picture. Because the new owners have indicated a desire to sell off at least some of these new properties to other buyers, it is not certain what will remain under McClatchy control and what will not. Newspaper chains have drastically cut back coverage of state politics because it is more cost effective to run national news stories that can be standardized across the entire chain. Investigative reporting dedicated to state politics has also been reduced. In Los Angeles, the purchase of the *Times* by the *Chicago*

Tribune has led to a reworking of that paper's priorities to a national agenda too. In late 2006, the *Tribune* company announced that it was interested in selling some of its media holdings, including the *Times,* so the picture may change again soon. For example, George Skelton's column, which covers state politics, has been pushed back into an inside section of the paper and is published only twice a week.

Corporate media ownership places a priority on selling advertising in order to turn a profit; consequently the news content acts as a wrapper around the advertising itself. This is particularly true in Sunday editions where advertising inserts and coupons often outweigh the news by a wide margin. As people abandon newspapers as an information source, television takes priority. Here, too, daily coverage of events in Sacramento is missing. Local news also becomes a wrapper for advertising, for feature stories with minimal substantive information, and, in Southern California, for live coverage of police car chases. Corporate media in the United States is now dominated by five multinational corporate conglomerates: Viacom/CBS (although technically, on paper, the two companies have split), NBC/GE, Disney/ABC, NewsCorp/Fox, and Time Warner. Another ten to twenty, including the Tribune Company, McClatchy, and Clear Channel radio, make up a second tier of media. The vast majority of all media holdings in this country, ranging from newspapers to television, radio, and magazine and book publishing, are controlled by these corporate giants.[3]

For candidates for public office the use of paid advertising in the media to sell themselves and the issues with which they are concerned takes money. In a big state with large districts that need to be covered, the most widely used method of advertising continues to be direct mailings. Campaigns that obtain marketing information about the people being sent this mail can send specific messages to different households. For statewide campaigns, television and radio spots are more practical, but these can be extremely expensive: a single thirty-second television advertisement in prime time in the larger urban markets can run $100,000 or more plus production costs. Modern campaigning and the coordination needed to get the message out has turned political consulting as an offshoot of public relations and marketing into what must easily be a multibillion dollar industry. In the near future, computers and the Internet are likely to play a more important part in the campaign process, both in regard to getting the "right" message out to potential votes as well as using Web pages to solicit campaign donations. Although the Internet has already been used with some success, notably at the national level in the 2004 presidential campaign and in the 2006 congressional elections, its full potential has yet to be tapped. When it is, it may lead to a complete shift in how campaigns are structured around Internet messages, blogs, e-mail reminders, spam, and so on. Some argue that it could open up the electoral process and democratize it, but this seems unlikely. The ability to use the Internet will still require a substantial commitment of resources to adequately focus campaign messages to target audiences. This, like all traditional campaigns, requires money. The more money, the better.[4]

Campaigns and Regulating Money

State Assembly Speaker Jesse Unruh once famously declared, "Money is the mother's milk of politics."[5] The amounts of money pouring into elections today continue to grow with each campaign season. In the 2002 gubernatorial race, the incumbent governor, Gray Davis, beat back a late challenge by Bill Simon, a Republican, by outspending him $78 million to about $36 million. The total amount spent on that gubernatorial election cycle alone came to about $130 million. Davis introduced a new campaign strategy as well, running negative campaigns against Republican Richard Riordan prior to the primary election so that he would face a weaker opponent heading into the general election. Only a year later, Schwarzenegger and groups backing the recall of the governor spent about $26.4 million, with Schwarzenegger spending about $8.6 million of his own money, and Gray Davis spent $17.4 million to oppose the recall; the closest challenger to Arnold Schwarzenegger, Cruz Bustamante, spent about $14.4 million. The total spent for all candidates was $83.6 million, about what was spent on the general election a year earlier. In this case, though, the entire campaign was compressed into three months.[6] In the 2004 election cycle, total campaign contributions across the state exceeded half a billion dollars. Although the totals have not been completed, contributions for the 2006 election exceeded $717 million (table 4-3).[7]

Many attempts have been made to limit the amount of money that can be contributed to campaigns. At the federal level, the Federal Election Campaign Act of 1971 (revised 1974) set hard limits on how much money individuals and organizations were allowed to contribute to individual campaigns. This was the beginning of regulating **hard money contributions.** Very quickly, however, the two parties and their wealthy supporters developed **soft money** means to get around these rigid rules. These means included the following:

- Political action committees (PACs), which are organizations that originally could take in unlimited amounts of contributions and distribute them to campaigns of their choice. In 1974 there were just over 600 registered PACs; today, there are more than 4,000. PAC contributions are now regulated by the Bipartisan Campaign Reform Act (2002), better known as the McCain-Feingold Act, which placed limits on individual and organizational contributions. However, the act does not substantively restrict the creation of new PACs nor does it limit the amount of start-up funding that goes into any PAC.
- Unlimited contributions made to the national parties earmarked for voter mobilization activities. Again, this loophole has been closed and the size of contributions limited.

Table 4-3 Top Twenty Contributions to Candidates for the 2006 California Election

Contributor name	Amount
Steve Westly	$25,150,000
Candidate self-finance	
Poizner Family Trust	$12,731,458
Candidate self-finance	
Steve Westly	$10,000,000
Candidate self-finance	
California Democratic Party	$3,815,969
Party committees	
Arnold Schwarzenegger	$3,500,000
Candidate self-finance	
Phil Angelides	$2,517,305
Candidate self-finance	
California Republican Party	$1,426,824
Party committees	
Sacramento County Democratic Central Committee	$1,382,900
Party committees	
California Republican Party	$870,315
Party committees	
AT&T	$790,538
Telecom services & equipment	
California Teachers Association	$764,055
Public sector unions	
San Diego County Democratic Party	$745,150
Party committees	
Pacific Gas & Electric (PG&E)	$564,872
Electric utilities	
Grace Hu	$525,000
Candidate self-finance	
California Building Industry Association (CBIA)	$512,549
General contractors	
Stanislaus County Democratic Central Committee	$500,000
Party committees	
Monterey County Republican Party	$490,000
Party committees	
Pechanga Band of Mission Indians	$476,047
Tribal governments	
John A. Dutra	$463,808
Candidate self-finance	
California Correctional Peace Officers Association/CCPOA	$440,700
Public sector unions	

SOURCE: "California 2006: State at a Glance," Follow the Money, www.followthemoney.org/database/state_overview.phtml?si=20065#top20_cand (accessed March 29, 2007).
NOTE: In addition to special interests making large campaign contributions, Steve Westly used his personal wealth to run in the Democratic gubernatorial primary and lost. Running as a virtual unknown, however, Steve Poizner was elected insurance commissioner.

- The nonprofit organizations called 527s, named after the section of the federal tax code that defines their nonprofit status. These 527s may not endorse a candidate or campaign, but they can run election advertising for purposes of providing "information" to voters.

All three of these soft money alternatives are nothing more than forms of money laundering. New mechanisms are developed to get around the law and to allow money to flow into the election process. The desire to augment (or defeat) specific campaigns has also given rise to what are called issue advocacy advertising and independent expenditures. The law does not allow advertising to specifically support a campaign, but issue advocacy advertising usually makes it clear enough what candidate is to be supported. Through the use of independent expenditures, organizations can run advertising separate from the campaign proper, hence allowing "attack ads" to be used without the candidate's having to claim responsibility for them.

In the past three decades California voters have passed several campaign finance reforms that have been ruled unconstitutional by the federal courts. The main attempt to regulate financing was the **Political Reform Act** (passed as a proposition in 1974), which established rules for the public disclosure of all donors and campaign expenditures. Today, lists of these donors and expenditures are accessible through the secretary of state's Web site at www.ss.ca.gov. The transparency of the campaign finance system should, in theory, limit contributions by exposing individuals, unions, and other groups to the public. In practice, few voters bother or care enough to access this information.

Proposition 34 (2000) establishes hard caps on contributions to individual campaigns as well as to PACs in California. However, it, too, leaves many loopholes. The number of PACs can continue to increase, and contributions made from political parties to specific candidates or campaigns are still unlimited. In other words, as long as money can be filtered to the parties, they can, in turn, get it to candidates with no further restrictions. Limits on contributions to the party are much higher than they are to individual candidates.[8] Politicians may also continue to contribute to their own campaigns in unlimited amounts. A candidate with a large personal bankroll and a willingness to spend it can have a definite advantage.

The Coopting of Direct Democracy

Progressivism brought to California a series of democratic reforms, none more crucial than the three primary mechanisms of direct democracy: the initiative, the referendum, and the recall processes. In theory, each of these tools gives the public direct access to the political system. In practice, each has been coopted by organized interest groups that have been able to turn these participatory forms of government into specialized engines for serving their particular interests.

- **Initiative.** Twenty-four states allow initiatives to be put on the ballot. Californians can directly take the initiative to write laws, change laws, and amend the state constitution by gathering a specified number of signatures to qualify that measure for the ballot. The legislature may later amend the initiative, but this is also subject to voter approval unless designated otherwise. The initiative is pure direct democracy, for it allows voters to make law when elected officials are unwilling or unable to take action.
- **Referendum.** There are two types of referenda. A compulsory referendum is placed on the ballot when the legislature approves constitutional amendments and when most bonds are issued. Both of these referenda must be passed by a two-thirds majority in both houses of the legislature and must be approved by a majority of voters to go into effect. A petition referendum can be thought of as a recall of a law already passed by the legislature. After a statute has been passed, voters usually have ninety days to gather signatures and request that voters approve it before it goes into effect. Petition referenda are rare. One did appear on the 2004 ballot.
- **Recall.** Made famous by Governor Gray Davis's recall in 2003, the recall of an elected official can be accomplished by gathering petition signatures and putting the candidate back on the ballot with a two-part ballot. The first question asks whether the person should be recalled (decided by simple majority), the second asks who should replace the elected official (elected by plurality vote). Eighteen states provide for the recall of elected officials. Davis was recalled by a 55.4 to 44.6 percent margin, with Schwarzenegger prevailing on the second part of the ballot by a comfortable 48.6 to 31.5 percent margin over the runner-up, Lieutenant Governor Cruz Bustamante.[9]

All three of these mechanisms have been largely taken over by organized interests, who hire clipboard petition companies to gather signatures. These companies hire people, sometimes students, to stand in front of supermarkets or the nearest big box store asking people to sign these petitions. As a petition gatherer (and former student) once confided, some companies pay based on the total number of signatures the gatherer obtains, and others base pay on the number of valid signatures. The three processes for reform are no longer about "concerned citizens" demanding change or taking action into their own hands; they are all about groups who have enough money to hire clipboard companies to get the job done for them. Davis's recall required a large number of signatures (12 percent of votes cast in the last election) to be gathered in a very short time.

The initiative has been used to qualify a variety of issues for the ballot with the expectation that the advertising campaign to follow will persuade voters to approve the proposition. This does not always succeed as planned. In 2005

Schwarzenegger and his allies qualified four ballot initiatives for a special election that included a total of eight propositions. Proposition 74 proposed to make it more difficult to give tenure to teachers, and Proposition 75 sought to require unions to get membership consent before spending money for political purposes. Another proposed a state spending cap, and the final Schwarzenegger initiative offered to establish a redistricting panel. The election campaign was another costly one: approximately $220 million was spent by all sides combined. All four of the Schwarzenegger "reforms" were rejected by voters. The defeat was helped along by the huge contributions to the opposition campaign from unions that opposed the measures and Schwarzenegger's seemingly antiunion stance.

The coopting of the referendum process is a bit more complicated. In recent years, the insurance industry has allowed stricter regulation to be passed by the legislature and then has used petition referenda (supported by huge ad campaigns) to defeat these measures. The industry has apparently used this method to show that voters do not want a regulated business environment. In effect, to benefit themselves, these insurance companies have orchestrated the initial passage of regulations and their subsequent defeat by referenda.

The state constitution does not require that cause be established for recalling an official. One of the problems with this is that the recall has been used as a political bludgeon rather than as a means to remove corrupt, incompetent, or inept politicians from office. Prior to the Davis recall, several recalls were mounted in California by Republican Party operatives working in coordination with Assemblyperson Curt Pringle in order to punish members of their own party who were apparently viewed as disloyal because they had cooperated with the Democratic Speaker Willie Brown. The recalls of Republican assembly members Doris Allen and Paul Horcher in 1995 were orchestrated by their party. These recalls seemed to stretch the spirit of what the mechanism is supposed to be about: rather than about citizens taking action, they were about party leaders using the system to get political payback.

Securing Two-Party Dominance: A Second Look

In a single-seat, plurality system, the geographic and demographic composition of districts is of paramount importance. Draw the district boundaries one way, and one party may win; draw them another way, and the other may prevail. This is much different from proportional representation systems, where net gains or losses in a specific district may not matter, since overall proportionality is what matters most. In American politics the politicization of this process is referred to as **gerrymandering,** named after a nineteenth-century salamander-shaped election district in Massachusetts and the state's governor at the time, Elbridge Gerry. The redrawing of district boundaries must take place in California after every U.S. census. Following the U.S. Supreme Court cases of *Baker v. Carr* and *Reynolds v. Sims* in the 1960s, California's forty districts for the state senate and eighty districts of the assembly have to be of equal population. Up to that point, California had used a districting system based on geographic divisions for the senate, which overweighted less populous, mostly rural seats in the north.

The process of **reapportionment,** or redistricting, is vitally important in determining who is likely to win elections in that district for the next decade, that is, until the next reapportionment takes place. The gerrymandering that goes into this process can be a highly politicized matter, such as it was between 1981 and 1987, when Republicans challenged the Democratic-led plan for redistricting in the courts and tried to get voters to approve a nonpartisan panel to oversee the process. These days, however, computer programs make the drawing of boundaries simpler, and modeling allows the respective parties to project what is likely to happen demographically in any district over ten years' time. The two parties have consensually agreed to the creation of as many safe seats as possible, where known party affiliation is likely to place Democrats or Republicans at an advantage, at least until the next census occurs. Very few truly open, or contested, seats are left on California's political map. Of the 120 legislative seats, probably no more than 5 can be considered contestable seats. So although term limits regulate how long a specific member stays in office, party affiliation and the demography of a district will determine who gets in next.

If safe seats make life easier for candidates and their parties, the benefits of being an incumbent should not be overlooked either. Incumbents come into any election with name recognition and ready-made connections to campaign fund-raising. Not surprisingly, current officeholders win reelection campaigns well over 90 percent of the time, following the pattern for the rest of the country. Money begets stability, and stability begets money.

Taking Stock

The two dominant political parties, the Republicans and the Democrats, certainly have some philosophical differences, but they also have a lot in common, especially when it comes to the day-to-day policymaking that is part of California's political system. It is there that their belief in continued corporate prosperity and continued economic growth pushes them together toward policy decisions that continue to concentrate wealth and power into fewer and fewer hands. A handful of other parties compete too, but they stand little chance of making any impact in a winner-take-all, single-seat electoral system. Elections are driven by money, and lots of it. To get that money, candidates must be wealthy themselves or well connected to those willing to pay for campaigns that increasingly rely on television and radio advertising to reach voters in such a big state. Attempts have been made to regulate the amount of cash flowing into the campaign process, but politicians have found loopholes in virtually every limit created. It may be that voters in California are expressing their discontent with this system by registering in increasing numbers as nonpartisan voters, but will this really change anything? The links between the two parties in the legislature and the interest groups that support them financially are as strong as ever. And what happens when these same groups then turn to the elected legislators whose campaigns they supported and ask for favors?

QUESTIONS FOR DISCUSSION

1. Proportional representation would drastically change the electoral process and would give more representation to smaller parties, but are there any potential drawbacks to having this kind of a system?

2. Is there any way to get money out of politics? Should money play less of a role in the electoral process? How have legislators and voters tried to limit its impact, and how successful have they been?

3. What are the three mechanisms of direct democracy in California and how have organized groups coopted them to serve their particular interests in the political process?

NOTES

1. BBC investigative reporter Greg Palast was the first to uncover problems with purges of voters from registered voter rolls, but others have documented many additional problems with the 2000 election. See Greg Palast, *The Best Democracy Money Can Buy* (New York: Plume, 2003); see also Douglas Kellner, *Grand Theft 2000* (Lanham, Md.: Rowman and Littlefield, 2001); John Nichols and David Deschamps, *Jews for Buchanan: Did You Hear the One about the Theft of the American Presidency?* (New York: New Press, 2001).

2. For more on DRE devices and problems related to them, see BlackBoxVoting. org, www.blackboxvoting.org; see also http://blackboxvoting.com.

3. Robert McChesney, *The Problem of the Media: U.S. Communication Politics in the Twenty-First Century* (New York: Monthly Review, 2004); Ben Bagdikian, *The New Media Monopoly* (Boston: Beacon, 2004).

4. Joe Trippi, who ran Howard Dean's campaign and later helped John Kerry's presidential campaign in 2004, is seen as a guru of Internet campaigning. Trippi insists on the democratic potential of computer technology, also used in the 2008 John Edwards presidential campaign. See Joe Trippi, *The Revolution Will Not Be Televised: Democracy, the Internet, and the Overthrow of Everything* (New York: Regan Books, 2005).

5. Jackson K. Putnam, *Jess: The Political Career of Jesse Marvin Unruh* (Lanham, Md.: University Press of America, 2005), 150.

6. Larry N. Gerston and Terry Christensen, *Recall! California's Political Earthquake* (Armonk, N.Y.: M. E. Sharpe, 2004), 108.

7. There are two excellent resources for tracking the amount of contributions made to state campaigns and candidates, both of which include searchable databases for all states: the National Institute on Money in State Politics and its Web

site, www.followthemoney.org, and the Center for Responsive Politics, www. opensecrets.org. The former includes data for all political contributions, whereas the latter focuses on donations to campaigns, candidates, and political action committees. California's secretary of state office also posts contributions and amounts spent, available at www.ss.ca.gov.

8. As of January 1, 2007, individual limits for contributions to a candidate for the state legislature are capped at $3,600 per election, statewide offices at $6,000, gubernatorial candidates at $24,100, and contributions to the party at $30,200. For more information see the Fair Political Practices Commission Web site: www.fppc.ca.gov.

9. Gerston and Christensen, *Recall!*, 130–131.

Chapter 5 The Legislative Process and the Role of Interest Groups
The Road to a Professional Legislature and Back Again

In 1966 California professionalized its legislature by making the legislative positions full-time. Legislators now had a full-time salary, perks, and a full-time professional support staff. Progressives like Hiram Johnson had railed against the role of special interests in the legislative process some fifty years earlier, but the relationship between lobbyists, the interest groups they represented, and the legislators had deepened over the years. With members of the legislature usually holding jobs outside of government and meeting only for limited sessions, lobbyists found it rather easy to peddle influence by wining and dining officials to get them to vote the way they wanted them to. The pre-eminent lobbyist, arguably in the entire United States, was Artie Samish, who posed for a *Collier's* magazine photo holding a marionette symbolizing how California was really governed: "Mr. Legislature," as he called the senate and assembly, was his puppet.

The drive to professionalize the legislature was led by the assembly Speaker, Jesse Unruh, the man who was to benefit most from the change. Although the guarantee of a full-time salary did sever one of the strings connecting lobbyists to government, lobbyists merely shifted their money to the election process. In order to win influence, it became important for interest groups to make sure that sufficient campaign funding would flow to those candidates who supported those interests. It is here also that party affiliations often blurred, because relatively little of what any legislative body does, then or now, has a direct and visible effect on how people lead their lives. What matters most are pieces of legislation—bills—that change the rules by which the process of capital accumulation is made easier either for large swaths of businesses that stand to benefit or, in some cases, for a relatively small group that gains advantage when its competitors must make some large or costly change to their operations. More than anything, the power elite seeks consistency and continuity, allowing a political status quo that lets the machine continue to operate.

A **professional legislature** did just that. The power elite could ensure the status quo by supporting incumbent candidates whose voting records revealed how they were likely to vote on a given issue and what it would take to get them to change their minds. That incumbency could then create a class of

Table 5-1 Compensation of California's State Legislators, Then and Now

	Amount paid	Contingent expenses	Transportation
1879	$8/day	$25/session	$0.10/mile
1908	$1,000/term	$25/session	$0.10/mile
1924	$100/month[a]		$0.05/mile
1949	$300/month[a]		
1954	$500/month[a]		
1966	$16,000/yr		
1988	$40,816/yr		
2005	$110,880/yr		$0.31/mile[b]

SOURCE: Data from State of California, Legislative Council, *California's Legislature*, pp. 93–94, www.leginfo.ca.gov/pdf/Ch_07_CaLegi06.pdf (accessed March 29, 2007).
a. During their terms.
b. Only applicable when legislator is traveling privately—not on a common carrier.

professional politicians who could be voted repeatedly back into office, further professionalizing them as "pols" and making them evermore dependent on cash flows to support the next reelection campaign. Nicknamed Big Daddy, Unruh was further able to capitalize on his speakership by having campaign contributions flow to him, in turn distributing funds to Democratic allies willing to vote consistently as he wished them to. Unruh and later Speakers to follow, including Leo McCarthy and, especially, Willie Brown, used what amounted to a patronage system within the Democratic Party to hold on to power for more than two decades (table 5-1).[1]

By the 1990s this patronage system seemed to have run its course, and the power that Willie Brown had wielded over the assembly from 1980 to 1996 had rubbed Republican colleagues the wrong way, much of their disgruntlement having to do with Brown's over-the-top style. In 1990, voters in California approved Proposition 140, which established **term limits** of three two-year terms for assembly members and two four-year terms for state senators. It brought into the vernacular a new phrase, "termed out," to describe elected officials who could no longer run for that office as a result of the limits in place. Professionalization solved one set of problems and created new ones, and the same can be said for term limits. Setting limits on how many times a person may run for the same office is promoted on the idea that it opens up the system to more competition and clears the way for new faces to enter the political system. It also, however, deprofessionalizes the system to a point where lobbyists and interest groups play a much more powerful role in the legislative process than ever before.

In a nationwide survey of state legislators, an overwhelming number did not support term limits (see figure 5-1), believing that they make the legislature less efficient and committees less effective while making the executive branch as well as legislative staff more powerful. Most telling of all, however,

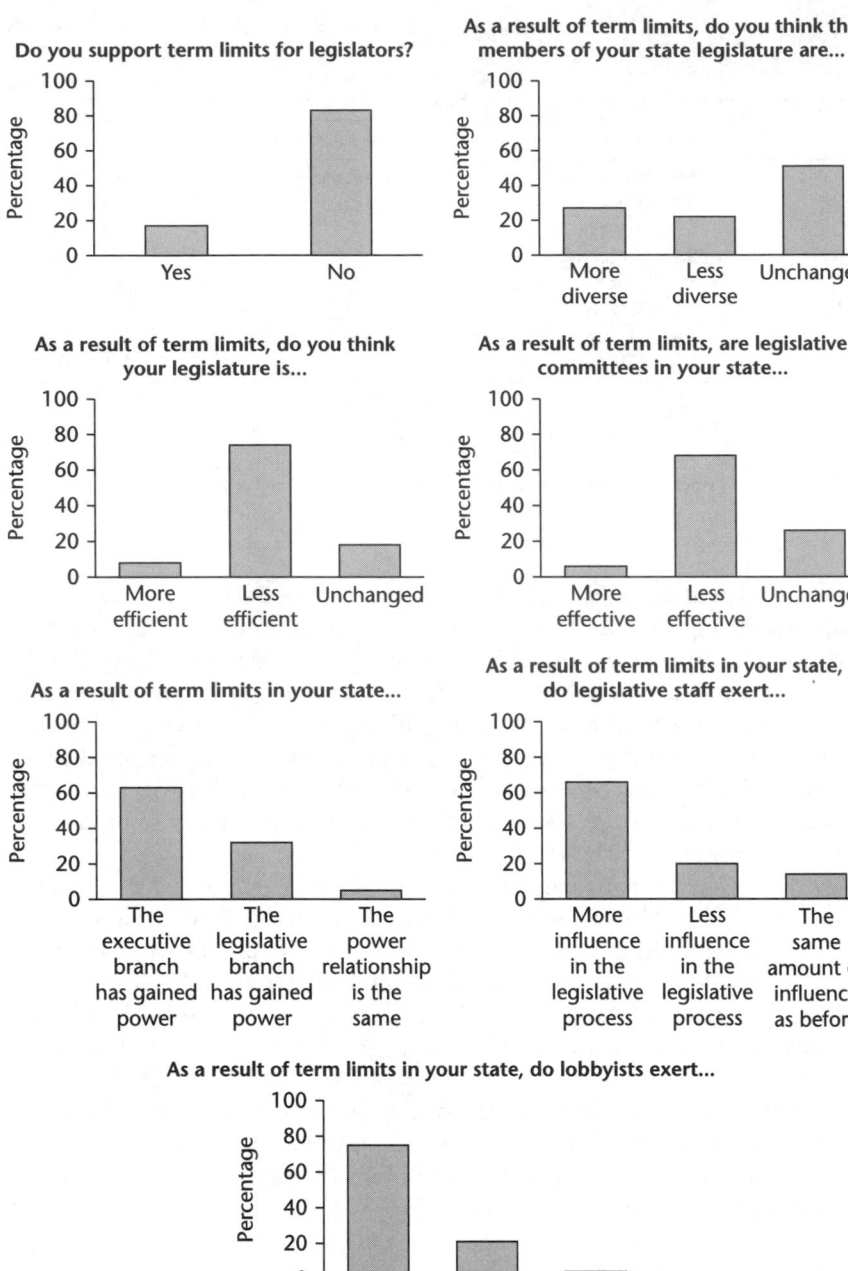

Figure 5-1 NATIONAL COUNCIL ON STATE LEGISLATURE'S TERM LIMITS POLL: SURVEY RESULTS

SOURCE: National Conference on State Legislatures, "Term Limits Survey Results," www.ncsl.org/programs/legismgt/ABOUT/Termlimit.htm (accessed March 29, 2007).

was that three of four polled believed that limits had given lobbyists more influence over the legislative process.

As members are termed out, new legislators enter office as novices at this level of the government, although in many cases, termed-out assembly members then seek to extend their political careers by running for the senate, and newly out-of-work senators run for the assembly. At most, then, members have a political lifespan of fourteen years in the legislature. Brown, by contrast, was in the assembly for thirty-one years, and this length of service was not uncommon. As newcomers have come into office, the role of interest groups and the lobbyists who do their bidding has strengthened because the real professionals in this term-limit system turn out to be the lobbyists and not the legislators. The lobbyists are the ones who understand the inner workings of the system; many lobbyists have themselves served in public office earlier in their careers and they have a shared collective memory of how these institutions function. To exaggerate only slightly, the legislators are the amateurs, the lobbyists the professionals, reversing the roles so carefully realigned in the 1960s. In order to have the best chance at reelection and thus make their brief careers in public life as lengthy as possible, legislators remain dependent on campaign contributions made by individuals, interest groups, PACs, and 527s. And those campaign supporters have the same aim.

California's legislature remains a professional legislature because the average salary, staffing levels, and length of legislative sessions rank at or near the top among the fifty states.[2] Some states still have part-time legislatures, that is, the sessions are limited in length (Kentucky, Nevada, and Texas), salaries are minimal (New Hampshire and Wyoming; New Mexico pays no salary but does cover expenses), and the size of staffs is small (Delaware, Idaho, Wyoming). Most legislatures in the United States today, however, are far more professional than they were prior to the 1960s. Still, the pendulum is swinging in the opposite direction. As of 2006 sixteen states have adopted term limits, and as the political scientist Thad Kousser strongly suggests, the effect of term limits has been to undo the positive benefits that professionalism brought to state governments in the previous thirty years.[3]

Interest Groups and Lobbying

An interest group can be defined as any group that shares common political beliefs and values and organizes in an attempt to gain access to the political process. There is nothing inherently wrong with interest groups. In theory, any group of concerned citizens can band together to try to get a law passed or changed, and we glorify this in American political lore as the essence of grassroots politics. The problem, however, lies in the fact that some interest groups consistently dominate the system by being well financed and well organized, the latter nearly always being a function of the former (table 5-2). In a political system that decides who gets what, when, where, and how, the same

Table 5-2 Money In, Money Out: Expenditures and Receipts of California's Top Lobbying Organizations, 2005

	Rank lobbying organization	Cumulative expenditures ($)
1	California Teachers Association	9,456,813
2	AT&T and its affiliates	4,065,146
3	Western States Petroleum Association	3,130,034
4	California Chamber of Commerce	2,570,516
5	California State Council of Service Employees	2,014,715
6	Edison International & Subsidiaries	1,873,265
7	BHP Billiton LNG International	1,765,541
8	California School Employees Association	1,570,845
9	Blue Cross of California (Wellpoint Health Networks)	1,566,508
10	Consumer Attorneys of California	1,549,113

		Cumulative payments received ($)
1	Kahl/Pownall Advocates	4,706,161
2	Nielsen, Merksamer, Parrinello, Mueller & Naylor LLP	4,129,228
3	Aaron Read & Associates	4,013,465
4	Sloat Higgins Jensen & Associates	3,990,225
5	Capitol Advocacy, LLC	3,229,195
6	Governmental Advocates, Inc.	3,100,552
7	Lang, Hansen, O'Malley, and Miller Governmental Relations	2,985,242
8	Public Policy Advocates, LLC	2,850,516
9	Platinum Advisors, LLC	2,777,529
10	Manatt, Phelps, & Phillips, LLP	2,775,950

SOURCE: California Secretary of State, *Lobbying California State Government,* lobbying report, 2005, www.ss.ca.gov/prd/Lobreport2005/Lobbyist_Report_2005.pdf.

groups get their way far more often than not. Even when they do not, they have the financial means to be able to continue the same cause and to repeat the same demands over and over again. As these words are being written a phone call is received with a recorded message asking for support of an initiative to require parental notification of an abortion in California if the girl is a minor. Virtually identical legislation was turned down by voters in a special election in 2005. But with financial and organizational support, the same issue can go on even after Californians have made their opinions known.

Politicians, especially those who like to think of themselves as conservatives, are skilled at slurring together the words "big-business-and-big-labor." The California Teachers Association (CTA), which represents teachers in the public K–12 schools, has been an extremely powerful interest group in the state, contributing generously to the campaigns of Democratic candidates. The CTA was also instrumental in defeating the propositions put on the ballot by Arnold Schwarzenegger in the 2005 special election, primarily because

Schwarzenegger had reneged on a promise to restore K–12 funding after a $2.4 billion temporary cut in 2004.[4] The California Correctional Peace Officers Association has also been a powerful political player among unions and a large campaign contributor, especially during Gray Davis's term as governor. But business interests far outweigh the influence of a relatively few (but admittedly powerful) labor unions. The power of business interests has been augmented by the decline of organized labor in the state. Union membership in the United States as a whole fell to 12.5 percent of the workforce in 2005, compared with 20.1 percent as late as 1983; in California 16.5 percent of workers were unionized, higher than the national average but helped to a great degree by high rates of union membership among public employees (somewhere close to 50 percent).[5] Labor interests concentrate among a few unions, but business interests are spread across a wide array of groups. These groups can range from real estate development to insurance to agricultural and farming organizations, all of them with a considerable overlap of interests, given the kind of vertically integrated production that present-day capitalism relies upon.

Interest groups try to influence the political process in many ways. The most prominent ones are discussed in the following paragraphs.

Campaign Contributions

Huge amounts of money flow through campaigns in order to make sure that those in power stay in power. Although term limits create some uncertainty in regard to the individual elected, this uncertainty is counterbalanced by a system stabilized by the increasing number of safe seats and by locktight two-party dominance.

Lobbying

Lobbying is the mainstay of interest group politics. Although the largest corporations and unions may have lobbyists in-house, other groups may have to rely on larger organizations or associations to represent their interests. Business interests are represented by a range of groups, such as the California Chamber of Commerce, the California Association of Realtors, the California Medical Association, and the California Small Business Alliance. Unions are represented by such groups as the CTA, the California State Employees Association, and the United Farm Workers. Local governments, too, must lobby to get their voices heard, and they do so through groups like the League of California Cities and the California State Association of Counties. Public interests are collectively represented by such organizations as the League of Women Voters and the Sierra Club (national organizations with state chapters) but also include groups like The Utility Reform Network (TURN) and the California Taxpayers' Association. TURN played a key part in revealing the role that companies like Enron, Duke, and Sempra had played in manipulating electricity supplies to create rolling blackouts and drive up costs in 2000.[6] The taxpayers' association is a continuation of the group that originally supported the idea behind Proposition 13, which rolled back property taxes in 1978 and now continues to resist all efforts to increase taxes in the state.

Rather than rely on these umbrella groups or pay for staff lobbyists, California politics has increasingly made use of **contract lobbying.** Combining public relations with a legal background, contract lobbying companies specialize in providing lobbyists who can be hired on a temporary, contractual basis, to argue any position that the client needs. They are, in effect, hired guns. Among the best-known and most powerful contract lobbying firms are Kahl/Pownall Advocates; Carpenter, Snodgrass, and Associates; Platinum Advisors; and the group Nielsen, Merksamer, Parrinello, Mueller, and Naylor LLP. So although the number of lobbyists registered in California has gone down since the late nineties, the amount spent on lobbying has increased and continues to grow every year. According to the public interest group Center for Public Integrity, $228 million was spent in 2005, up from $213 million in 2004 and an increase from $155 million in 2003 (not in constant dollars).[7] Among the states the ratio of lobbyists to legislators in California ranks sixth highest at ten to one. Interest groups who want to get heard can do so for a price. They can get lobbyists who are professionals at what they do and who may have some experience working in government; this may be a cost-effective way to buy influence in the system. Lobbyists themselves often insist that what they do is provide information to elected officials to allow them to make decisions based on the merits of the legislation being considered. In practice, it may go well beyond this, including the actual writing of legislative proposals or making specific suggestions as to bill wording.[8]

Successful lobbyists must be able to influence legislation. To do so, they must have direct or even indirect access to legislators and their staff, be knowledgeable and influential enough to be called to testify before committees considering a bill and provide additional written analysis to them (described below), or work in collaboration with other lobbyists to develop a "united front." Again, term limits makes a lot more former legislators available for lobbying purposes, and old friendships can be used to strengthen the lobbyist's hands.

Public Relations, Advertising, Propaganda

Whether one chooses to call it public relations, advertising, or mass persuasion, the techniques used to influence and to create public opinion rely on a well-known array of propaganda techniques that have evolved over the years.[9] Lobbying groups work through mass media by providing press releases and other information to "assist" reporters doing their job; holding press conferences; coordinating letter-writing and e-mail campaigns to targeted legislators; and organizing rallies, demonstrations, or other events to draw attention to some particular political cause. As public relations techniques continue to be refined, the organized events may not even appear to be directly connected to any particular piece of pending legislation. Instead, it might create an atmosphere of support for an issue. A relatively new and often-used technique involves the organization of so-called **astroturf lobby groups,** which have the appearance of real grassroots community political movements but are organized and funded by larger, often corporate, interest groups. A group known as Californians for Schools supported the passage of bonds for school construction but was really a front organization set up by the construction industry. The California Restaurant Association created "public events" to support Governor Schwarzenegger's push to change lunch break rules for union workers in 2003–2004.[10]

Litigation

In recent years, it seems that any proposition approved by California voters has been immediately challenged in a court of law, sometimes the very next day. Organized special interests have the financial means to litigate, are prepared (in advance) to argue that a law is unconstitutional, and at the very least, may be able to get the court to stay implementation of a law pending a full hearing. Challenges to the constitutionality of withholding services to illegal immigrants, bilingual education, and the use of medical marijuana are among the many cases that have been filed. Not all are successful, but they do keep particular issues alive regardless of the outcome.

The Legislature: Lawmakers?

California has a bicameral legislature, meaning it has two houses, a feature shared with forty-eight other states. The exception, trivia fans know, is Nebraska, which has a unicameral legislature. There are eighty seats in the assembly, forty in the upper house, the senate. Following the U.S. Supreme Court decision of *Reynolds v. Sims* (1964), the senate was reorganized to make the districts equal in population. Today, each assembly seat represents 462,500 residents, whereas each senate district includes about 925,000 people. With the number of legislative seats fixed, the effective representation of each constituent will continue to be diluted as the population increases. This dilution supports the notion that democratic representation takes a backseat to the institutional structures that give the power elite sufficient space to be able to continue to use the system to serve their vested interests.

The Progressive legacy has left a relatively weak party system. Although a tradition of cooperation and "bipartisan spirit" shapes the work of the legislature, the two major parties in both houses must depend on their leadership and at least some party discipline to determine the legislative agenda and steer specific pieces of legislation through the process (figure 5-2). The respective

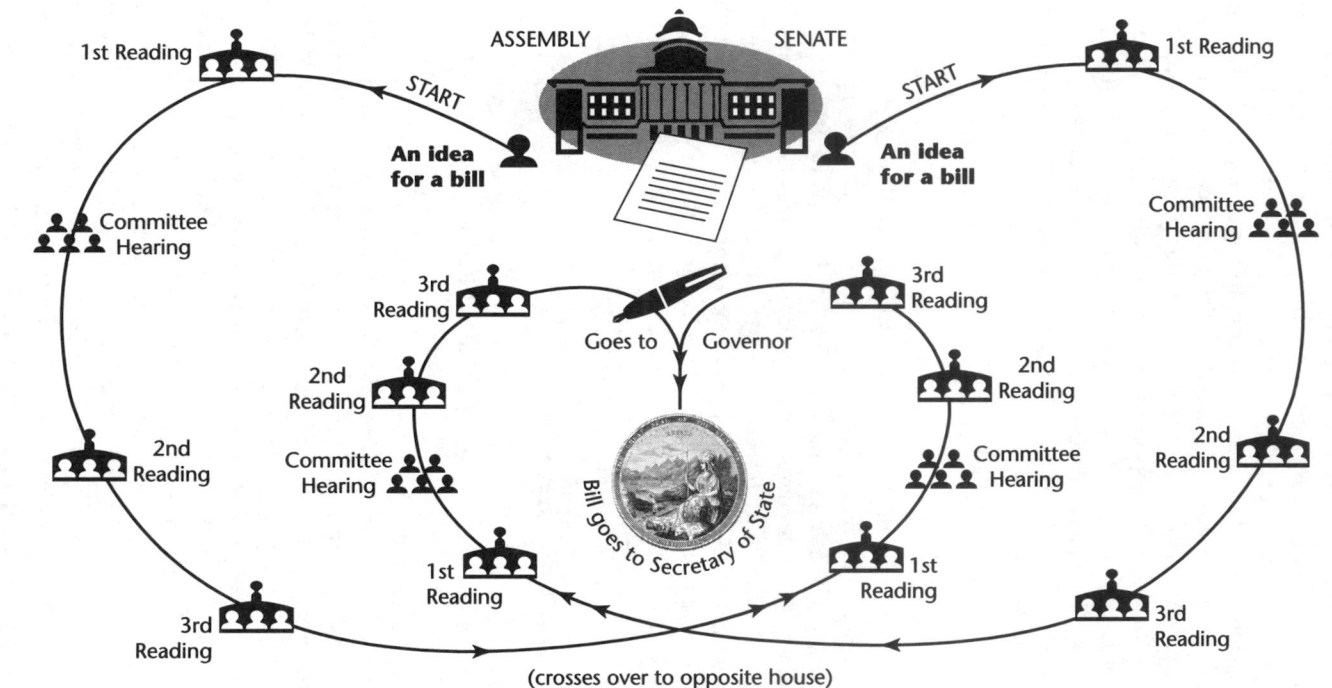

Figure 5-2 THE LIFE CYCLE OF LEGISLATION: FROM IDEA INTO LAW

SOURCE: State of California, Legislative Council, *California's Legislature*, 104, www.leginfo.ca.gov/pdf/Ch_09_CaLegi06.pdf (accessed March 29, 2007).

party leaders also determine committee assignments and chair positions; in this, the majority party has the advantage in that it can put its most important "stars" onto the most powerful committees and into chairperson status. Leaders also can influence the favorable or unfavorable treatment of a particular bill by suggesting how the rank-and-file members of the assembly should vote on it. Party members who do not respect the leaders' wishes may jeopardize their chances for choice committee assignments as well as endorsement for future public office. In this way the leaders maintain party discipline. Still, given that the Progressive spirit does live on, there is not nearly the same kind of arm-twisting that occurs in the present-day U.S. Congress. Discipline was comparatively stronger when the assembly Speaker was able to make committee assignments that could be held by the same person for decades if he or she abided by the party leader's wishes. With term limits, no one can serve for very long on any committee.

Similar to Congress, the assembly tends to work more quickly than the senate because the leadership structure is more hierarchical and less discipline is tolerated. The senate is more deliberative. The senate also has the responsibility of confirming some gubernatorial appointments, as the U.S. Senate does. The assembly is led by the Speaker, who is chosen by the majority party. Party leadership and discipline are enforced (again, relatively weakly) by the majority leader (from the majority party), the minority leader (from the minority party), and the whips, who are responsible for letting party members know how the leadership wants them to vote and when votes are scheduled so that they can be there to participate.

In the senate the most powerful leader is the president pro tem, who is chosen by the majority party; majority and minority leaders and whips provide additional partisan leadership support. The pro tem also presides over the Rules Committee in the senate. The rules committees in both houses are powerful because they determine to what committee a bill will be sent. If it is sent to a friendly committee, the bill stands a better chance of making it through the process; if it is sent to a more hostile committee, it may never make it out of committee or may be amended beyond recognition. Here again, the tradition of party discipline and bowing to the bosses is important.

On the odd occasion that the media pay attention to what is going on in state politics, news anchors like to use the phrase, "lawmakers in Sacramento." Legislators, however, are not really lawmakers; to paraphrase the film director Quentin Tarantino, they "kill bills." In an average two-year session, about 6,000 bills are introduced. About one-fourth to one-third of the bills actually make it to the floor for a vote. This is a much higher percentage than in Congress, where perhaps 5 percent make it to a vote, but it shows that the road for a bill to become a law is still a dangerous one.

The legislative process (assuming for our purposes, from senate to assembly) looks like this: A legislator authors a bill and puts it into proper legal form with the help of the legislative counsel. It is introduced and numbered, said to be the first reading of the bill. It then goes to Rules for assignment to a committee. In committee, hearings are held, testimony is given, and lobbyists are given an active role in being able to influence the fate of the bill. Not all who participate are lobbyists, of course, but although American folklore glorifies the grassroots image of a grandmother in sneakers appearing before a committee, most of this business is conducted by professional lobbyists, technical and legal experts, and various government officials who are asked to appear before the committee. If the bill makes it out of committee (rather than being held there, which effectively kills it), it is reported out with a recommendation: "do pass," "do pass as amended," or "amend and re-refer." The bill is read a second time and amendments offered; it then goes to the third reading, which opens floor debate, and a final roll-call vote is taken. The infamous filibuster of the U.S. Senate is not possible in either house. If approved, the bill then moves to the second house (here, the assembly), where, with a few minor exceptions, the same process occurs. If there are differences between the version of the bill as passed by the senate and that passed by the assembly, the bill goes to a conference committee comprised of three senate and three assembly members, who attempt to compromise on the substance of the bill. If the bill reported by the conference committee is not accepted by the respective houses, the bill can be re-referred to the committee a maximum of three times. As in Congress, most bills end up in a conference committee, so the committee is very powerful. Bills must pass by absolute majority, that is, the majority of total members, not just of those present. Urgency bills (bills that go into effect immediately), budget and appropriation bills (where money is to be spent), constitutional amendments, and veto overrides must pass by an absolute two-thirds majority in both houses. Constitutional amendments are then put on the state ballot for voter approval. The governor has twelve days to decide whether to sign the bill or to veto it. Any bill not signed in twelve days will become law. At the end of a session, the governor is given thirty days to sign.

There are some interesting differences between the California legislature and the U.S. Congress. First, the **author system** in California means that the author of a bill is responsible for seeing it through the process. In Congress many bills are introduced but forgotten by those who sponsor them. California legislators are limited to fifty bills per two-year session in the assembly and sixty-five in the senate, so a member does not want to waste opportunities. Second, a **weak party system** means that committee chairs are not necessarily assigned according to seniority and some committees may be chaired by minority members, although these are typically less powerful committees, to be sure. In Congress, committee chair assignments have been returned to a seniority-based system after an attempt to change this in the 1990s, and the majority party controls all chair positions. Third, there are three **nonpartisan independent bureaus** that support the work of the legislature: the legislative counsel, who drafts wording for bills; the Legislative

Analyst's Office, which offers advice on any and all matters pertaining to the budget and fiscal matters, including the publishing of detailed reports on the governor's proposed budget; and the state auditor, who conducts oversight and investigations of state agencies and issues reports on the efficiency of government. Fourth, the *flow of legislation* usually goes from one house (due to the author system) to the other. In congress, legislation in this era is introduced concurrently in both houses. Finally, *direct democracy* allows citizens to effectively nullify the work of the legislature via referendum or to bypass the legislative process entirely through the initiative. No such options exist at the federal level.

Power Politics, Insider Trading, and the Apathetic Public

"Democracy," as the political theorist Joseph Schumpeter reminds us, "means only that the people have the opportunity of accepting or refusing the men who are to rule them."[11] It's not about giving power to people; it's about deciding who will have power over them. To follow Schumpeter, we can extend the democratic process in California today to include many more people of color, ethnicity, and gender diversity (including many more women as well as gay and lesbian legislators), reflective of the state's diverse culture. Beyond the self-satisfaction of outwardly showing diversity (to whom and for what purpose, we might ask), however, the legislative process remains as closed as ever. Interest groups and the lobbyists who work for them are as influential as they have ever been. Once proposed legislation begins going through this process, the insider trading of votes, commonly known as logrolling, becomes a means by which the political building of support for passage of a bill takes priority over the actual merits of a bill. The logic of "vote for mine, I'll vote for yours" replaces the very notion of a system supposedly constructed to represent the interests of the electorate. Moreover, legislative pork (a derivation of what used to be called pork-barrel legislation) in the form of bills or portions of bills that bring direct benefit to specific constituents in a member's district are not about serving the public good but about delivering the goods to campaign supporters so that those in power can stay in power.

The frantic circular motion of money and legislative pork can be best viewed in the final days of a legislative session, when legislators have to make decisions about pending bills, knowing that elections are upcoming and that some members may not be back come January. Those running either for reelection or another public office have a keen interest in pulling in campaign contributions that could help their political careers. Those not returning to politics need to act on bills that they have sponsored that might involve a "debt" owed to a particular constituent, perhaps a specific organization or an entire industry. At the end of California's two-year legislative session in August 2006, at least $3.5 million worth of donations were made to members of the legislature, led by contributions of $1.1 million from organized labor and nearly $1 million from real estate and construction interests. A total of $193,000 in contributions came in on the Monday of the final work week alone. It repeated the pattern from the end of the last days of a session prior to a general election in 2004, when $3.2 million worth of contributions were made, and 2004, when $2.1 million came in. Not everybody gets exactly what they want in exchange for this cash, but money at least gives them an opportunity to get laws passed in their interests, whereas those without these resources have to sit it out and hope for the best. This movement of money in exchange for political favoritism has been referred to as "pay to play." It is certainly part of California politics. It is certainly not democratic.[12]

The system is transparent. Campaign contributions must be posted on the secretary of state's Web page, lobbyists must be registered and their biographies and photographs can be found on the Internet, and bills up for consideration can all be accessed from any computer. All of this is meaningless when the public does not care and no one cares that they do not care. The very openness of the system is the ultimate manifestation of power. And as the public roots for the Blue team or the Red team, the machinery of development continues to turn. The logic and inevitability of growth is the one thing that both teams agree on, and we are left to wonder which legislators will do a better job of bringing home the bacon to their local power elite. If there is one thing that has changed, though, it is that California's financial crisis limits the amount of pork that can be spread around. Unwilling to raise taxes and unable to secure additional finances from Washington, D.C., which also finds itself following an extreme laissez-faire economic policy, the legislature has been left to try to manage a government with limited resources. Only some Californians understand the scope of the problem. For most, getting rid of a leader, Gray Davis, was the solution, and now the machine can resume normal operation.

Taking Stock

The close relationship between special interest groups, their lobbyists, and state lawmakers was a problem seemingly addressed by the professionalization of the California legislature in 1966. Over the next several decades, however, party leaders in the legislature used their positions not only to wield power over the potential passage of bills but to make sure that those loyal to the leaders would hold on to the best committee assignments and that their bills would be given priority treatment. In turn, voters of California at least partially deprofessionalized the legislature by introducing term limits to keep legislators from becoming career politicians. But this has created other problems: interest groups that are willing to spend money by making lavish campaign contributions in the hopes of influencing political outcomes, and hired lobbyists, who are often more experienced in politics than the legislators themselves. Special interest groups, professional organizations, corporations, and labor unions have a voice in the legislative process because they have the resources—money—to try to influence the decisions that legislators ultimately have to make. But members of the assembly and the state senate are not alone in this game of "pay to play." When Arnold Schwarzenegger was elected governor in 2003, he promised to clean up Sacramento and insisted that his political influence could not be bought, because he was "plenty wealthy" himself. Four years of California under the governator suggest that nothing really has changed.

QUESTIONS FOR DISCUSSION

1. What did professionalization of the legislature hope to accomplish and what did it actually accomplish? Do you think that those pushing for a full-time legislature at full salary really sought to clean up the California political system? If not, why not?

2. Is it possible to influence the political process without substantial financial resources? How might this be done?

3. Does greater representation for different ethnic, racial, and gender groups really represent a change in terms of how the legislature works in California? Could it make a bigger difference in the future? If so, how?

NOTES

1. Dan Walters, "Broken Promise: The Rise and Fall of the California Legislature," in *The California Republic: Institutions, Statesmanship and Policies*, Brian P. Janiskee and Ken Masugi, eds. (Lanham, Md.: Rowman and Littlefield, 2004), 127–134; Jackson Putnam, *Jess: The Political Career of Jesse Marvin Unruh* (Lanham, Md.: University Press of America, 2005).

2. Keith E. Hamm and Gary F. Moncrief, "Legislative Politics in the States," in *American States: A Comparative Analysis*, ed. Virginia Gray and Russell L. Hanson (Washington, D.C.: CQ Press, 2004).

3. Thad Kousser, *Term Limits and the Dismantling of State Legislative Professionalism* (New York: Cambridge University Press , 2005).

4. See Peter Schrag, *California: America's High-Stakes Experiment* (Berkeley: University of California Press, 2006).

5. See United States Bureau of Labor Statistics, "2006 Union Member Summary," www.bls.gov/news.release/union2.nr0.htm; see also California Labor Federation, "2004 Biennial Review Policy Statements," www.calaborfed.org/pdfs/Political/FinalPolicy.pdf (accessed May 2, 2007).

6. Kevin Starr, *Coast of Dreams: California on the Edge, 1990–2003* (New York: Alfred A. Knopf, 2004), 588–603; Diane Renzulli, *Capitol Offenders: How Private Interests Govern Our States* (Washington, D.C.: Public Integrity Books, 2002), 109–130.

7. Center for Public Integrity, "Hired Guns: A Comprehensive Look at Lobbying in the 50 States," www.publicintegrity.org/hiredguns/. This includes constantly updated information on money going to state politics, including comparisons of all fifty states. The original 2003 Public Integrity report, "Hired Guns: Lobbyists Loads of Money to Influence Legislators—and in Many States, with Too Little Scrutiny," www.publicintegrity.org/hiredguns/report.aspx?aid=165 (accessed May 2, 2007).

8. Alan Rosenthal, *The Third House: Lobbyists and Lobbying in the States* (Washington, D.C.: CQ Press, 2001), 79–107; Diane Renzulli, *Capitol Offenders: How Private Interests Govern Our States* (Washington, D.C.: Public Integrity Books, 2002).

9. Anthony Pratkanis and Elliot Aronson, *Age of Propaganda: The Everyday Use and Abuse of Persuasion,* rev. ed. (New York: W. H. Freeman, 2000).

10. Christian Berthelsen, "Documents Show Clout of Lobbyists with Governor—Records of Effort to Weaken Workers' Right to Meal Breaks Reveal Influence of Business," *San Francisco Chronicle,* September 7, 2005.

11. Joseph Schumpeter, *Capitalism, Socialism, and Democracy* (New York: Harper-Perennial, 1976 [1942]), 284–285.

12. Dan Morain, "Checks Roll In as Laws Roll Out," *Los Angeles Times,* August 31, 2006.

Chapter 6 **California's Governor and Challenges to the Plural Executive System**

Gubernatorial Competence and Political Personality

Because of California's size and economic heft, the governor of the state is a political leader of national importance. Ironically, recent governors have been elected on their reputations as being competent managers of government rather than as leaders with strong personalities who might draw political attention to themselves. This was true of Gray Davis, whose name was entirely appropriate, and the two men who preceded him, Pete Wilson and George Deukmejian.

Arnold Schwarzenegger seems to fall outside the more recent pattern, for everything about Schwarzenegger's campaign and his years in office have accentuated his Hollywoodness and over-the-top personality. Beyond the glitz, Schwarzenegger pitched a traditional set of political ideas that appealed to voters and to a power elite that ultimately endorsed him. For the voters, it was a message of government waste and mismanagement, and for the elite, it was an assurance that despite enormous budget deficits, the wealth they had amassed would not be threatened by taxes that could be used to try to rebalance the ledger. The elite could rest assured that one of their own would protect their economic interests. Schwarzenegger has done that. By the same token, the supposed political "enemy," the Democrat dominated legislature has done nothing to force the issue, thus falling in line with the neoliberal, laissez-faire interpretation of capitalism that today dominates all facets of economic theory, planning, and policymaking. With few exceptions, both governor and legislature agreed that a tax increase could not help resolve the budget crisis that continues in California, even though this would appear to be the easiest road to balancing a budget still dealing with large deficits.

Formal and Informal Powers of the Governor

Progressive reforms have also left their mark on the relatively weak powers delegated to the governor. Early in his tenure, Schwarzenegger often spoke of a need to strengthen the duties of the governor if he was to carry out needed reforms and break the legislative impasse on reducing government spending.

ARNOLD SCHWARZENEGGER ON THE CAMPAIGN TRAIL IN 2004, SUPPORTING PASSAGE OF PROPO-
SITIONS 57 AND 58 IN A SPECIAL ELECTION HE HELPED ORGANIZE. PROPOSITION 57 ALLOWED
CALIFORNIA TO SELL $15 BILLION WORTH OF BONDS TO PAY OFF ITS BUDGET DEFICIT. IN SO DOING,
CALIFORNIA EFFECTIVELY BORROWED MONEY TO PAY OFF BORROWED MONEY. PROPOSITION
58 CREATED AN EMERGENCY RESERVE FUND IN THE STATE BUDGET, A FUND THAT THE STATE HAS
ALREADY DIPPED INTO.

Compromising with the Democratic legislature, Schwarzenegger was able to
qualify two linked propositions for a place on a March 2004 ballot: Proposition
57 authorized California to sell $15 billion of bonds in order to pay short-term
debts, and Proposition 58 required the legislature to set aside 3 percent of revenues into a fund each fiscal year beginning in 2006 to provide a cushion in the
event of a budgetary emergency. Both propositions were approved by the
voters. Fueled by this success, Schwarzenegger decided to push "reform" further still with the special election of 2005. That ballot included Proposition 74,
which rolled back tenure for teachers to five years; Proposition 75, which
required unions to get members' consent for political spending; Proposition 76,
which set a state spending cap; and Proposition 77, which put redistricting under
the control of a panel of retired judges. By using the mandate of the popular
vote, Schwarzenegger was hoping to gain political power at the expense of the
powerful unions (especially the CTA) and the Democrats, who stood to be
weakened by the redistricting plan. All four measures were turned down by
voters, weakening, perhaps fatally, Schwarzenegger's grab for power.[1]

There are, of course, formal powers delegated to the governor. These constitutionally defined duties encompass the following:

- **Director of finance.** The governor is responsible for preparing and presenting a budget, which is proposed in January and must be approved by July 1, the start of the fiscal year.
- **Veto.** The governor has a line-item veto on appropriations or can use a general veto against an entire bill. With the line-item veto power, the governor can veto a particular section of a bill without having to reject the entire bill. Forty-three states have some form of line-item powers. As does the federal government, California requires a two-thirds majority in both houses to override a veto. Such an override rarely occurs. None of the last four governors (Schwarzenegger included) has had a veto overridden.
- **Appointments.** The power of appointments is usually downplayed by scholars, but it has an important impact on cycling elites and the well-connected through political service. Although 98 percent of state employees are subject to civil service selection, the governor appoints about 2,500 persons to fill various executive departments and cabinet agencies. Another 2,000 or more appointments are made to various commissions, committees, and panels. Most of these positions are unpaid or nominally cover expenses. But they are important because they allow elites to rotate through the system, retain name recognition, and further their contacts within elite circles. It is the political equivalent of the interlocks described by G. William Domhoff.[2] Governor Schwarzenegger has been criticized for abusing his appointment power by using it to distribute state jobs to his friends, supporters, and political cronies, this after running for governor on the argument that many of these state commissions were unnecessary and a waste of taxpayer money. In some cases, he also used his authority to assign former staff members to high-paying positions in state government, leaving the impression that he was granting them favors in gratitude for past service and loyalty.[3] In addition, the governor makes appointments when vacancies occur in other elected offices. Most often these appointments are of judges, who are replaced because they move to other jobs, retire, or die in office.
- **Executive orders.** Technically, executive orders interpret law within the executive branch, but in practice they have the force of law. For instance, in a state where natural disasters like earthquakes, fires, and floods are all too common, executive orders declaring a state of emergency authorize state agencies to bypass normal administrative procedures in order to deal with a crisis situation. One of the first orders signed by Schwarzenegger, however, was a repeal of the vehicle license fee, the "car tax," as it was named during the recall campaign.
- **Special sessions.** The governor can convene the legislature, usually to discuss one particular issue or pending crisis.

- **Military.** The governor is commander in chief of the state National Guard and can order deployment when disasters occur or in times of social unrest, during the 1992 riots in Los Angeles, for instance.

The governor's informal powers, however, are much more important in regard to governing California than the formal powers.

- **Symbolic leader.** The governor is the symbolic leader of the state and of the party that she or he represents. Both recent governors, Davis and Schwarzenegger, have had fairly cool relationships with their respective party leaders, creating considerable discontent. Beyond that, the election of a film star fueled the continued mythology surrounding California craziness and the extremes of social and political culture that the state seems to generate, as recounted in glorious detail by Carey McWilliams, Mike Davis, and Kevin Starr. As the media culturists Michael Blitz and Louise Krasniewicz note, "The national pastime of watching California make a fool of itself had entered the championship playoffs."[4]
- **Agenda setting.** Despite the dearth of information on state and local politics in the mass media, the governor is still able to draw attention to himself and to define the political agenda for California. Over the past forty years or so, a handful of issues have filled the agenda for a period of time, reform measures have been contemplated and sometimes applied, and then new issues have taken over. The reformist template for agenda setting should not be underestimated as a tool for attracting attention. It reinforces the notion that government is doing its job and also creates circumstances in which attention can be diverted from the division between the elite and the rest of the people that is at the core of political behavior. Crime, education, and taxes have functioned as the most popular issues in recent generations, and illegal immigration made its way onto the scene in the 1990s (after a brief debut in the 1980s), reappearing in a big way in 2006. In response to congressional bills that would make it difficult if not impossible for illegal immigrants to gain permanent residency or citizenship status, hundreds of thousands of people demonstrated in various cities in March 2006, including Los Angeles, where the crowd may have reached 250,000 individuals or more. The immigration question had been a peripheral part of the national political agenda since the attacks of September 11, 2001, but found a new life in both state and country after Governor Schwarzenegger vetoed a law that would have allowed illegal immigrants to obtain driver's licenses. In addition he endorsed the work of the Minutemen, a militia organization that sent people out to the desert to catch illegal migrants crossing the United States–Mexico border.[5] The governor later backtracked by making his endorsement more ambiguous, but the agenda was set just the same. (See table 6-1 for a list of California's governors.)

Table 6-1 California's Governors: A Timeline

Governor	Party	Years
Peter Burnett	Democrat	1850–1851
John McDougall	Democrat	1851–1852
John Bigler	Democrat	1852–1856
J. Neeley Johnson	American Party	1856–1858
John Weller	Democrat	1858–1860
Milton Latham	Democrat	1860
John Downey	Democrat	1860–1862
Leland Stanford	Republican	1862–1863
Frederick Low	Republican	1863–1867
Henry Haight	Democrat	1867–1871
Newton Booth	Republican	1871–1875
Romualdo Pacheco	Republican	1875
William Irwin	Democrat	1875–1880
George Perkins	Republican	1880–1883
George Stoneman	Democrat	1883–1887
Washington Bartlett	Democrat	1887
Robert Waterman	Republican	1887–1891
Henry Markham	Republican	1891–1895
James Budd	Democrat	1895–1899
Henry Gage	Republican	1899–1903
George Pardee	Republican	1903–1907
James Gillett	Republican	1907–1911
Hiram Johnson	Republican	1911–1917
William Stephens	Republican	1917–1923
Friend Richardson	Republican	1923–1927
C. C. Young	Republican	1927–1931
James Rolph	Republican	1931–1934
Frank Merriam	Republican	1934–1939
Culbert Olson	Democrat	1939–1943
Earl Warren	Republican	1943–1953
Goodwin Knight	Republican	1953–1959
Edmund G. "Pat" Brown	Democrat	1959–1967
Ronald Reagan	Republican	1967–1975
Edmund G. "Jerry" Brown	Democrat	1975–1983
George Deukmejian	Republican	1983–1991
Pete Wilson	Republican	1991–1999
Gray Davis	Democrat	1999–2003
Arnold Schwarzenegger	Republican	2003–

Total no. of governors: 38
Total no. of Republican governors: 22
Total no. of Democratic governors: 15
Total no. of American Party governors: 1

Percentage of Republican governors: 58
Percentage of Democratic governors: 39.50

SOURCE: From Kevin Starr, "Governors of California," www.californiagovernors.ca.gov/h/biography/index_party.html.

The Plural Executive System

Unlike the federal government, California has a **plural executive system,** meaning that statewide executive offices are elected separately by the voters rather than being appointed by the chief executive, the governor (figure 6-1). This Progressive era reform was intended to make those in these positions directly accountable to the voters and to dilute the power of the governor.

The plural executive positions are lieutenant governor; attorney general; secretary of state; treasurer; controller; insurance commissioner; superintendent of public education; plus the four members of the state board of equalization, who are elected on a district basis, and the controller, who sits on the board. The governor's cabinet includes the directors of seven state agencies and the governor's executive secretary, but the cabinet serves almost exclusively in an advisory capacity. So the real decision-making power resides in the statewide elected offices and not in the cabinet per se. Each office conducts business autonomously from the governor, thus limiting the governor's institutional powers. These statewide positions are also used as political stepping-stones to other public office. The limits on the governor's institutional powers mean that the informal powers become even more important: they are the only way he or she can really make an impact.

Politics at the End of Reality

For years, the French social theorist Jean Baudrillard has claimed that reality has been replaced by an endless series of simulations and simulacra, copies that have no originals. We happily accept the simulation and the fake for the real thing, never stopping to contemplate exactly how fictional this world may be. Baudrillard writes, "The absence of things from themselves, the fact that they do not take place though they appear to do so, the fact that everything withdraws behind its own appearance and is, therefore, never identical with itself, is the material illusion of the world."[6]

For every problem there is a new image or screen to conceal what is really at stake. Society seamlessly blends together the imagery of film, television, literature, art, into the lived experience, where real life becomes the stuff of movies and the other way around. The recall of Gray Davis as governor of California in October 2003 and the election of Arnold Schwarzenegger cannot adequately be explained only by public attraction to celebrity. True, we obsess over actors and their personal lives, as any *People, US,* or *National Enquirer* reader knows, but Schwarzenegger's political ascent is different. This was a candidate who not only announced his candidacy on a talk show but constantly alluded to his film characters in campaign speeches; named his campaign buses for his movies; accepted and used the nickname "Governator," based on his *Terminator* film character; and even used phrases from the *Saturday Night Live* parody characters of Hans and Franz to refer to his political enemies as "girly men." Schwarzenegger ran for office neither as himself nor even by trading on his public persona. He ran as a cardboard movie cut-out of himself, and each time that image was mentioned, used, even ridiculed, his image was enhanced.[7] People wanted the cut-out and got it. Schwarzenegger was elected with 48.6 percent of the vote, a comfortable margin over the runner-up, Democrat Cruz Bustamante, in an open field of 135 candidates.[8]

The "problem" leading to the recall effort was equally contrived. Gray Davis had been reelected by a surprisingly narrow margin after a large early lead in the 2002 election over the Republican challenger, Bill Simon. Politically, Davis was seen as vulnerable and was not particularly well liked even among his fellow Democrats, who did not like his micromanaging style and were unhappy that he did not share his fund-raising skills or his coffers with other party candidates.

More important, Californians had experienced several rounds of rolling blackouts going back to 2000, caused by the self-interested manipulation of energy supplies to California by corporations, who were now free to operate in a deregulated energy market with virtually no oversight by the Federal Energy Regulatory Commission. Davis and the legislature had bought into the idea that privatization of public utilities would lower costs but failed to recognize that the lack of oversight allowed these companies to make up their own rules as they went, including the invention of spot markets for electricity by Enron and its corporate chief Kenneth Lay, whom President George W. Bush affectionately called Kenny-Boy. Already faced with budget deficits that were growing rapidly in a system in which political officials refused to raise taxes in order to balance the budget, more money was borrowed to pay for the needed but now more expensive electricity. By January 2003 the budget deficit had reached an estimated $34.6 billion.[9]

The budget crisis itself was real and continues to be, even as the annual deficits are a fraction of what they were in 2003–2005. The budget as a political issue, though, was the stuff of pure fiction, as Schwarzenegger repeatedly referred to the out-of-control spending in Sacramento, insisting that there was unimaginable waste in how the state government spent money. The blackouts themselves contributed a visual aid to symbolize the collapse of the system, although it is likely that few citizens actually recognized how the energy crisis had been a product of corporate greed. Helped financially by the millionaire Republican congressman Darrell Issa, clipboard petition companies were able to quickly gather enough signatures through the summer of 2003 to force the recall election. The rest is history.

In 2005 and into 2006, Governor Schwarzenegger's approval rating went into a steady downward spiral. He had forced a special election in 2005 that included four reforms for which he campaigned vigorously, but all four failed to pass. Campaign promises of reform were attractive to voters, but once they were put into concrete terms as ballot measures, they appeared less appealing,

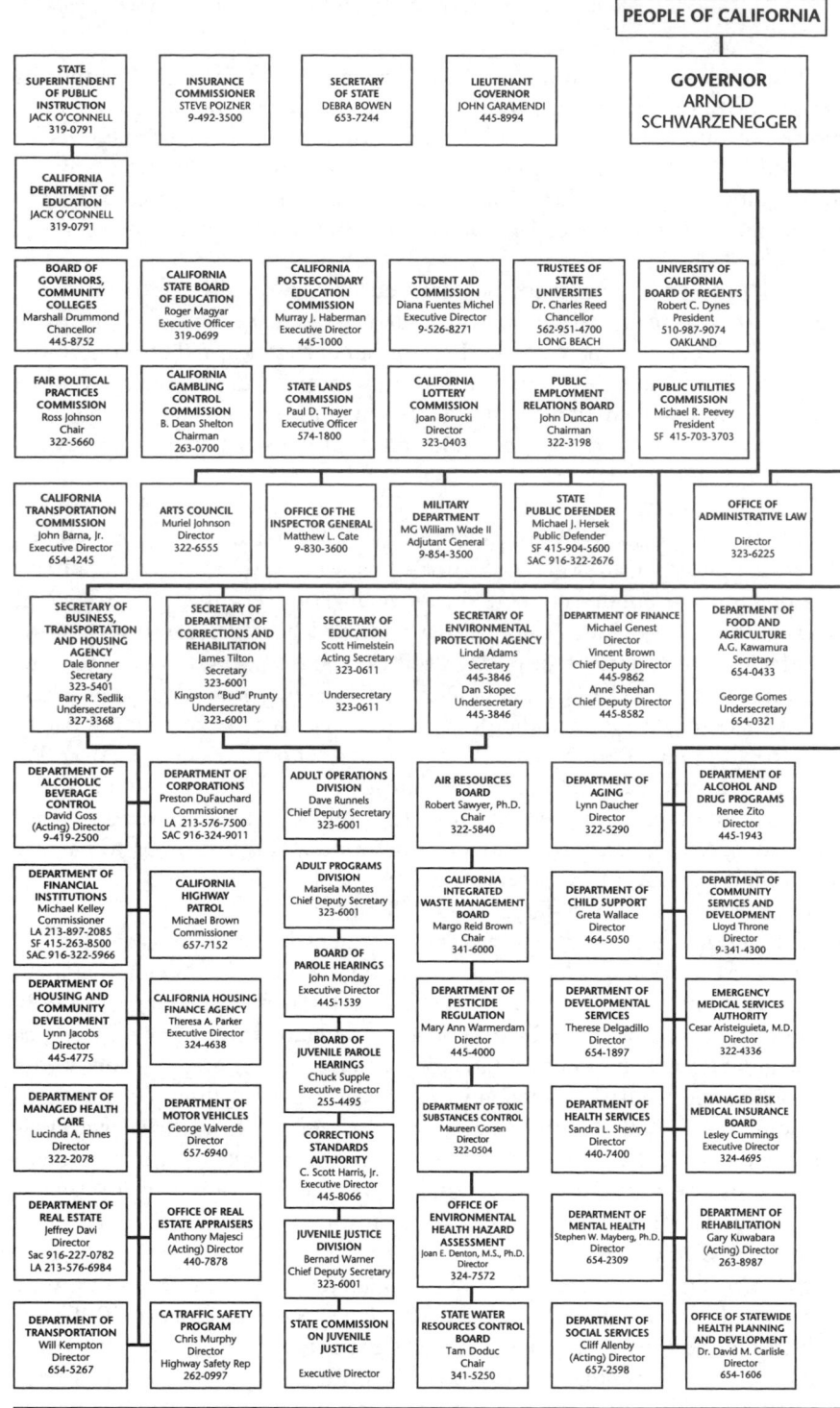

PEOPLE OF CALIFORNIA

GOVERNOR ARNOLD SCHWARZENEGGER

STATE SUPERINTENDENT OF PUBLIC INSTRUCTION JACK O'CONNELL 319-0791

INSURANCE COMMISSIONER STEVE POIZNER 9-492-3500

SECRETARY OF STATE DEBRA BOWEN 653-7244

LIEUTENANT GOVERNOR JOHN GARAMENDI 445-8994

CALIFORNIA DEPARTMENT OF EDUCATION JACK O'CONNELL 319-0791

BOARD OF GOVERNORS, COMMUNITY COLLEGES Marshall Drummond Chancellor 445-8752

CALIFORNIA STATE BOARD OF EDUCATION Roger Magyar Executive Officer 319-0699

CALIFORNIA POSTSECONDARY EDUCATION COMMISSION Murray J. Haberman Executive Director 445-1000

STUDENT AID COMMISSION Diana Fuentes Michel Executive Director 9-526-8271

TRUSTEES OF STATE UNIVERSITIES Dr. Charles Reed Chancellor 562-951-4700 LONG BEACH

UNIVERSITY OF CALIFORNIA BOARD OF REGENTS Robert C. Dynes President 510-987-9074 OAKLAND

FAIR POLITICAL PRACTICES COMMISSION Ross Johnson Chair 322-5660

CALIFORNIA GAMBLING CONTROL COMMISSION B. Dean Shelton Chairman 263-0700

STATE LANDS COMMISSION Paul D. Thayer Executive Officer 574-1800

CALIFORNIA LOTTERY COMMISSION Joan Borucki Director 323-0403

PUBLIC EMPLOYMENT RELATIONS BOARD John Duncan Chairman 322-3198

PUBLIC UTILITIES COMMISSION Michael R. Peevey President SF 415-703-3703

CALIFORNIA TRANSPORTATION COMMISSION John Barna, Jr. Executive Director 654-4245

ARTS COUNCIL Muriel Johnson Director 322-6555

OFFICE OF THE INSPECTOR GENERAL Matthew L. Cate 9-830-3600

MILITARY DEPARTMENT MG William Wade II Adjutant General 9-854-3500

STATE PUBLIC DEFENDER Michael J. Hersek Public Defender SF 415-904-5600 SAC 916-322-2676

OFFICE OF ADMINISTRATIVE LAW Director 323-6225

SECRETARY OF BUSINESS, TRANSPORTATION AND HOUSING AGENCY Dale Bonner Secretary 323-5401 Barry R. Sedlik Undersecretary 327-3368

SECRETARY OF DEPARTMENT OF CORRECTIONS AND REHABILITATION James Tilton Secretary 323-6001 Kingston "Bud" Prunty Undersecretary 323-6001

SECRETARY OF EDUCATION Scott Himelstein Acting Secretary 323-0611 Undersecretary 323-0611

SECRETARY OF ENVIRONMENTAL PROTECTION AGENCY Linda Adams Secretary 445-3846 Dan Skopec Undersecretary 445-3846

DEPARTMENT OF FINANCE Michael Genest Director Vincent Brown Chief Deputy Director 445-9862 Anne Sheehan Chief Deputy Director 445-8582

DEPARTMENT OF FOOD AND AGRICULTURE A.G. Kawamura Secretary 654-0433 George Gomes Undersecretary 654-0321

DEPARTMENT OF ALCOHOLIC BEVERAGE CONTROL David Goss (Acting) Director 9-419-2500

DEPARTMENT OF CORPORATIONS Preston DuFauchard Commissioner LA 213-576-7500 SAC 916-324-9011

ADULT OPERATIONS DIVISION Dave Runnels Chief Deputy Secretary 323-6001

AIR RESOURCES BOARD Robert Sawyer, Ph.D. Chair 322-5840

DEPARTMENT OF AGING Lynn Daucher Director 322-5290

DEPARTMENT OF ALCOHOL AND DRUG PROGRAMS Renee Zito Director 445-1943

DEPARTMENT OF FINANCIAL INSTITUTIONS Michael Kelley Commissioner LA 213-897-2085 SF 415-263-8500 SAC 916-322-5966

CALIFORNIA HIGHWAY PATROL Michael Brown Commissioner 657-7152

ADULT PROGRAMS DIVISION Marisela Montes Chief Deputy Secretary 323-6001

CALIFORNIA INTEGRATED WASTE MANAGEMENT BOARD Margo Reid Brown Chair 341-6000

DEPARTMENT OF CHILD SUPPORT Greta Wallace Director 464-5050

DEPARTMENT OF COMMUNITY SERVICES AND DEVELOPMENT Lloyd Throne Director 9-341-4300

DEPARTMENT OF HOUSING AND COMMUNITY DEVELOPMENT Lynn Jacobs Director 445-4775

CALIFORNIA HOUSING FINANCE AGENCY Theresa A. Parker Executive Director 324-4638

BOARD OF PAROLE HEARINGS John Monday Executive Director 445-1539

BOARD OF JUVENILE PAROLE HEARINGS Chuck Supple Executive Director 255-4495

DEPARTMENT OF PESTICIDE REGULATION Mary Ann Warmerdam Director 445-4000

DEPARTMENT OF DEVELOPMENTAL SERVICES Therese Delgadillo Director 654-1897

EMERGENCY MEDICAL SERVICES AUTHORITY Cesar Aristeiguieta, M.D. Director 322-4336

DEPARTMENT OF MANAGED HEALTH CARE Lucinda A. Ehnes Director 322-2078

DEPARTMENT OF MOTOR VEHICLES George Valverde Director 657-6940

CORRECTIONS STANDARDS AUTHORITY C. Scott Harris, Jr. Executive Director 445-8066

DEPARTMENT OF TOXIC SUBSTANCES CONTROL Maureen Gorsen Director 322-0504

DEPARTMENT OF HEALTH SERVICES Sandra L. Shewry Director 440-7400

MANAGED RISK MEDICAL INSURANCE BOARD Lesley Cummings Executive Director 324-4695

DEPARTMENT OF REAL ESTATE Jeffrey Davi Director Sac 916-227-0782 LA 213-576-6984

OFFICE OF REAL ESTATE APPRAISERS Anthony Majesci (Acting) Director 440-7878

JUVENILE JUSTICE DIVISION Bernard Warner Chief Deputy Secretary 323-6001

OFFICE OF ENVIRONMENTAL HEALTH HAZARD ASSESSMENT Joan E. Denton, M.S., Ph.D. Director 324-7572

DEPARTMENT OF MENTAL HEALTH Stephen W. Mayberg, Ph.D. Director 654-2309

DEPARTMENT OF REHABILITATION Gary Kuwabara (Acting) Director 263-8987

DEPARTMENT OF TRANSPORTATION Will Kempton Director 654-5267

CA TRAFFIC SAFETY PROGRAM Chris Murphy Director Highway Safety Rep 262-0997

STATE COMMISSION ON JUVENILE JUSTICE Executive Director

STATE WATER RESOURCES CONTROL BOARD Tam Doduc Chair 341-5250

DEPARTMENT OF SOCIAL SERVICES Cliff Allenby (Acting) Director 657-2598

OFFICE OF STATEWIDE HEALTH PLANNING AND DEVELOPMENT Dr. David M. Carlisle Director 654-1606

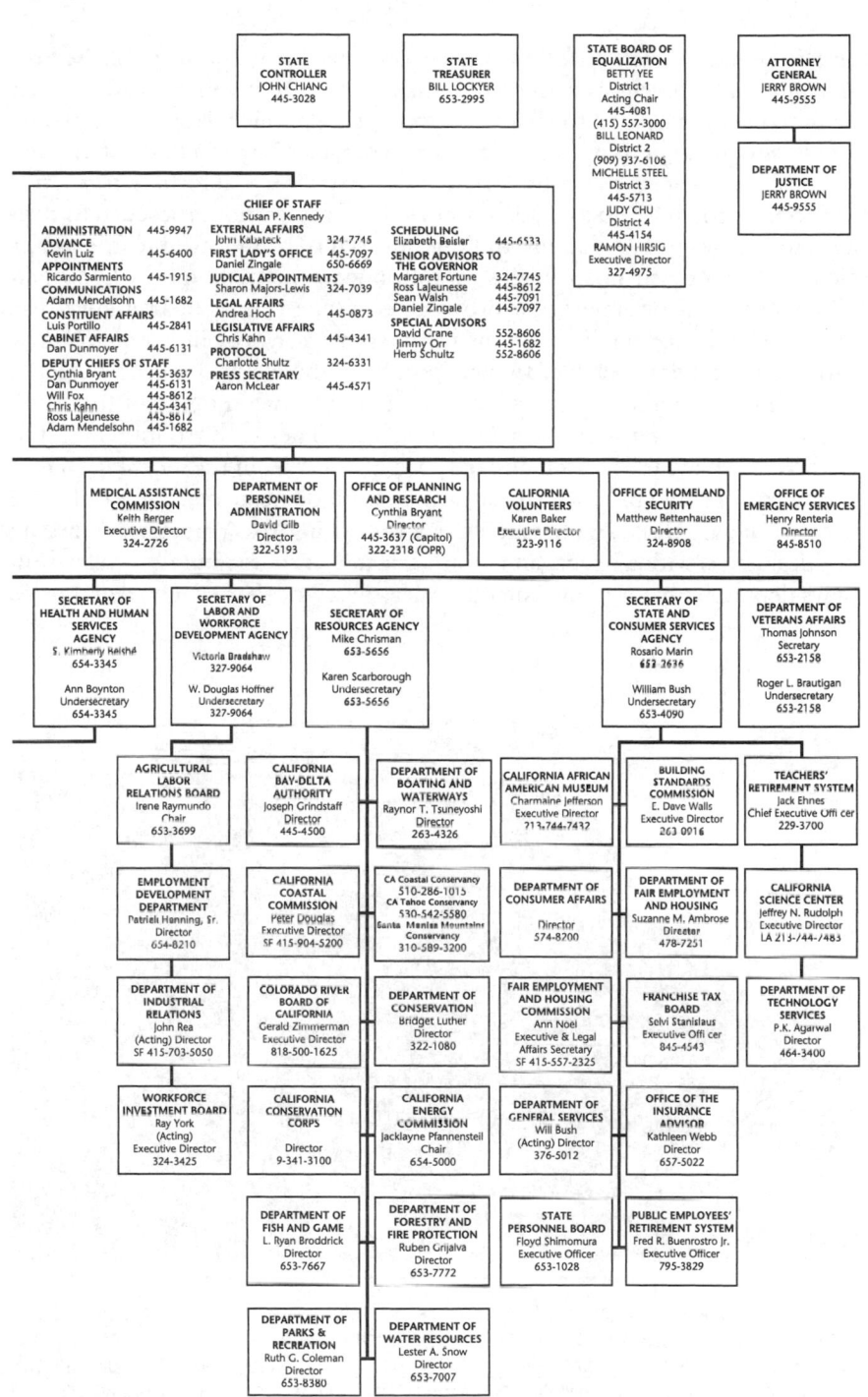

Figure 6-1 THE ORGANIZATION OF CALIFORNIA STATE GOVERNMENT'S EXECUTIVE BRANCH

SOURCE: California's Department of Technology Services, "Organizational Chart," www.cold.ca.gov/ Ca_State_Gov_Orgchart.pdf (accessed March 29, 2007).

and those most directly affected, namely organized labor in the public sector, strongly and actively campaigned against them. It became apparent that Schwarzenegger needed to change beyond using public relations and propaganda devices to prop up his image as an "outsider" fighting an entrenched political elite. A stage was constructed at Cal-Expo, the California fairgrounds in Sacramento, in February 2005 upon which the governor proceeded to turn a spigot, allowing fake red ink to flow out, symbolizing bureaucratic inefficiency. At a stop in Los Angeles to announce construction of a hydrogen filling station, Schwarzenegger drove a prototype hydrogen Hummer that had been built for public relations purposes to a hydrogen gas pump that turned out to be inoperable. In San Jose, he grabbed a broom and helped a road crew fill a pothole with asphalt to symbolize his commitment to repairing California's transportation infrastructure. The only trouble was, the pothole was new. It had been dug out by a crew earlier in the morning so that the governor could fix it. The most egregious bit of image making was the use of video news releases, fake video news clips using real reporters to discuss political issues with a propaganda spin attached and distributed to television news departments for use in their broadcasts free of charge. The video news

THE GOVERNOR PRETENDS TO FILL A HYDROGEN-POWERED HUMMER AT LOS ANGELES INTERNATIONAL AIRPORT IN 2004. WHAT THE CAMERA DOES NOT CAPTURE IS THAT THE HYDROGEN GAS PUMP AND THE ISLAND THAT IT SAT ON WERE FAKE: THEY WERE HOLLYWOOD PROPS BUILT STRICTLY TO PROVIDE A PHOTO-OP FOR THE GOVERNOR AND GENERAL MOTORS, THE MANUFACTURER OF HIS FAVORITE AUTOMOBILE.

releases distributed by the state focused on the "issue" of removing requirements for minimum lunch breaks for union employees.[10]

It mattered little that Schwarzenegger had failed to carry out his agenda. It
mattered less that the image he recycled was purely image. Rather, the act
wore thin and what was new and different in 2003 appeared old and banal by
early 2006. Society moved on to the next spectacle, and Schwarzenegger
could not hold his audience.

This was hardly a failed effort. For the power elite, the recall campaign
delivered exactly what was ordered. Here was a political event that had no significance beyond changing faces in Sacramento while solidifying two-party
absolute domination (the top two accounting for 80 percent of the vote) and
eliminating what had been marginally considered as solutions to debt. Tax
increases, which had stood little chance of implementation before, now stood
no chance. On top of that, Schwarzenegger chanted the pro-growth mantra
that has shaped the endless transformation of California's landscape for the
past 160 years, arguing that businesses had been fleeing the state because of
the rigid regulatory environment that had been created in the "out of control"
bureaucracy.[11] It is not surprising at all that the Schwarzenegger campaign's
largest contributors came from real estate, land development, and construction, with a prime individual supporter being the Stockton developer (and
owner of the San Diego Chargers football team) A. G. Spanos.[12] When the
governor switched chiefs of staff after the special election debacle, the new
chief, Susan Kennedy, was criticized for being a Democrat, but little attention
was given to her connection to a Los Angeles developer even though it did
get a mention in the *Los Angeles Times*.[13]

The narrative of a government hostile to business was affirmed without
actually dealing with the real problem of not enough revenues and too many
expenses in the state budget. Budgeting as a campaign issue was too complicated and messy; this story was more compelling. The political scientist
Murray Edelman concludes that the creation of political spectacles and stories
that accompany them is the substance of politics in much the same way that
Jean Baudrillard views social appearances substituting for reality itself.[14] There
is no reality to Schwarzenegger, but rather, he is an actor playing the role of
an actor in the role of a politician. Schwarzenegger's rise in California politics
needs to be viewed in this complicated interplay between fact and fiction,
substance and superficiality.

Schwarzenegger's apparently cynical view of government appealed to antitax and antigovernment advocates like Grover Norquist, who had gained a
national reputation in Washington through his close alliances with conservative members of Congress and the White House.[15] Schwarzenegger was
saying many of the same things that Norquist and other conservatives had
been saying. The defeat of Schwarzenegger's reform agenda in the special election coupled with his declining job performance ratings led to a complete
overhaul of the governor image in 2006. In January 2006, he announced a

commitment to rebuilding California's crumbling infrastructure and funding this reconstruction by borrowing enormous amounts of money through bond sales. With the state still facing large budget shortfalls and future debts from borrowing money to make payments on borrowed money, his budget proposals looked to be overly optimistic, and as many commented, reminiscent of the liberal Democrat Pat Brown in the 1960s. Schwarzenegger's proposals proved to be popular with California voters, as all five propositions, numbered Propositions 1A-1E, were approved by comfortable margins in the 2006 general election. An additional bond dealing with flood control and water quality (Proposition 84) also passed easily.

The governor found that he could have it both ways. He could appear to be a political liberal by supporting government programs and, simultaneously, he could be attractive to conservatives because the state would be paying for them with borrowed money instead of from tax revenues. It was a pro-growth, pro-development agenda either way, and the power elite did not have to worry about the costs of improving schools, repaving highways, and upgrading the levee system in the Sacramento Delta. In fact, those with sufficient investment capital could buy the bonds sold by the state and actually make more money with the interest that California would pay out when the bonds matured.

More remarkable was Schwarzenegger's political recovery in the 2006 gubernatorial election. With a 39 percent approval rating and 47 percent disapproval as late as April 2006, it seemed likely that a Democratic challenger would find it easy to knock off the incumbent (table 6-2). Instead, the controller, Steve Westly, and the treasurer, Phil Angelides, got tangled up in an acrimonious primary race in which both spent huge amounts of money to win the Democratic nomination. Westly, who had made a fortune in telecommunications and the Internet, spent $43 million, mostly out of his own pocket, and Angelides used up about $28.1 million for his campaign. Angelides prevailed by about 5 percent, but the real problem was the amount of money committed to the primary. Running against only nominal opposition in the Republican primary, Schwarzenegger was able to spend about $42 million on the general election, but Angelides had spent so much of his contributions to beat Westly that he could manage only a $10 million campaign against the governator. Schwarzenegger beat Angelides, 55.9 percent to 39.0 percent, a margin that seemed unbelievably large considering the incumbent's low approval numbers in the spring.[16] And this election again proved how democracy today takes a back seat to money.

In his 2003 recall campaign, Schwarzenegger repeatedly promised to get "special interests" out of Sacramento. Once in office, however, Schwarzenegger instead embraced interest groups, their lobbyists, and anyone willing to make contributions to his campaigns. In September 2006 he solicited campaign donations by holding off on signing bills into law until he could see how much money would come in either for or against the pending legislation. By 2007 he had set up the California Recovery Team, a tax-exempt

Table 6-2 Arnold Schwarzenegger's Job Performance as Governor, January 2004–March 2007 (percent)

	Approve	Disapprove	No opinion
March 2007	**60**	**29**	**11**
September 2006	48	37	15
July 2006	49	40	11
May 2006	41	46	13
April 2006	39	47	14
February 2006	40	49	11
October 2005	37	56	7
August 2005	36	52	12
June 2005	37	53	10
February 2005	55	35	10
September 2004	65	22	13
August 2004	65	22	13
May 2004	65	23	12
February 2004	56	26	18
January 2004	52	27	21
Party (March 2007)			
Democrats	58	33	9
Republicans	66	23	11
Nonpartisans/others	55	31	14

SOURCE: Adapted from the Field Poll, "Poll Archive," #2227, April 6, 2007, http://field.com/fieldpollonline/subscribers.
NOTE: Poll reflects performance among registered voters.

fund that could take in unlimited donations to support the governor's polit ical agenda. Among the donors to the Recovery Team was the insurance company State Farm, which was interested in limiting its liability in class action lawsuits as well as making sure that proposed changes to health care programs in California would not adversely affect the company. State Farm was not the only corporation making contributions, of course, but it is representative of a bigger problem in California and, indeed, American politics. At issue is the kind of direct "pay to play" system that Schwarzenegger endorsed. More money would buy closer, more intimate access, too. A donation of $25,000 would buy any contributor access to the Schwarzenegger home for a cocktail party, but bigger donations, between $100,000 and $250,000, meant an invitation back for dinner with Arnold and his wife, Maria Shriver.[17]

In the early part of the twentieth century, the political power brokers of California would meet with the economically powerful capitalist class in the proverbial back rooms of private clubs and restaurants, where cigar smoke filled the air and brandy and whiskey flowed freely. By the twenty-first century, Arnold Schwarzenegger had brought the California political system full circle. In addition to offering access for a price, he also reinvented the smoke-filled rooms of old by having a smoking tent erected in an inner court-yard at the state capitol building in Sacramento. Since smoking is prohibited in public buildings, it was a place where Schwarzenegger could legally smoke the cigars he enjoys, but it also became a place where various political leaders could meet with Schwarzenegger in a more casual setting, smoke a cigar with him, and maybe enjoy a schnapps with the governor. In a visit to Washington, D.C., Schwarzenegger caused a media stir by suggesting that President Bush needed a smoking tent to work out compromises with the Democrats.[18] What he ignored is the closed nature of this sort of political meeting. Only a select few can enter this inner sanctum of the power elite.

Schwarzenegger does not shy away from this image. He embraces it, as apparently do the voters of California. It's less important that the system drifts from democracy than that the governor appear to take charge. Wheeling-and-dealing with cigar in hand is more important than the substance of what is being decided upon. And perhaps it doesn't necessarily matter.

U.S. SENATOR DIANNE FEINSTEIN AND GOVERNOR ARNOLD SCHWARZENEGGER DISCUSS THE TENSE RELATIONSHIP BETWEEN STATE AND FEDERAL GOVERNMENTS, APRIL 2007. ALTHOUGH SCHWARZENEGGER PROMISED IN HIS 2003 CAMPAIGN TO DEMAND MORE FEDERAL FUNDING TO HELP CALIFORNIA PAY FOR SERVICES PROVIDED, THE BUSH ADMINISTRATION HAS LARGELY IGNORED THE STATE, PROBABLY BECAUSE CALIFORNIA'S PARTY POLITICS HAS LEANED HEAVILY DEMOCRATIC IN THE PAST DECADE.

Taking Stock

The governor has many very significant formal powers, but he has even more important informal powers. The governor acts as the symbolic leader of the state and can attract enough media attention to enable him to set the agenda for both his political party and all of California politics. California is a big state with plenty of mass media located in the large urban centers, which means that its governors also become important political players at the national level as well. Arnold Schwarzenegger's celebrity status elevates awareness of California politics to the international level too, because people around the world know that Arnold the actor has transformed himself into Arnold the governator. Although Schwarzenegger played many superhuman hero roles during his movie career, his powers as governor are checked by a plural executive system, in which voters elect a series of statewide officials. The system is intended to distribute executive branch power among many different offices instead of concentrating it in the governor. In the media-saturated society of the twenty-first century, however, the official duties of California's governor have scarcely seemed to matter, as Schwarzenegger has used his film images to present himself as a strong leader but one with a political agenda that quickly and thoroughly changed as his popularity ratings started to decline. He came to the governor's office claiming to be a reformer, but Schwarzenegger's real contribution to Sacramento has been to return politics to the smoke-filled, backroom deal making of the early twentieth century. As long as he looks strong, no one really seems to mind that the status quo seems stronger than ever. The power elite does not like change, and the governor has made sure that money will continue to play a vital role in the political process. Maintenance of the status quo is also the primary objective of the legal system, but in a system dominated by the rich and powerful, there can never be too many checks and balances. Real power cannot be put into the hands of the public.

QUESTIONS FOR DISCUSSION

1. How are the governor's appointment powers used to maintain an elite system of politics? Would it be possible for the governor to appoint people to government positions who are not well-connected politically or economically? Why doesn't it happen very often, if at all? What keeps the governor from acting differently?

2. The plural executive system is designed to make officials in statewide positions more accountable to the voters who elected them. Is it successful? What might keep it from being successful?

3. What do you think is meant by "the end of reality" and what part do mass media play in creating political figures like Arnold Schwarzenegger? Is political substance really a necessity for elected leaders, or is image all that matters?

NOTES

1. Marc Cooper, "Arnold Show: Canceled," *Nation,* November 28, 2005.
2. G. William Domhoff, *Who Rules America? Power, Politics, and Social Change,* 5th ed. (New York: McGraw-Hill, 2004).
3. Peter Nicholas, "Schwarzenegger's State Board Picks Raise Charges of Cronyism," *Los Angeles Times,* April 2, 2007; Aaron C. Davis, "Schwarzenegger Hands Former Staffers Plum Jobs," *North County Times,* November 17, 2006.
4. Carey McWilliams, *Southern California: An Island on the Land* (Salt Lake City: Gibbs-Smith, 1973 [1946]); Mike Davis, *City of Quartz: Excavating the Future in Los Angeles* (New York: Verso, 1990); Michael Blitz and Louise Krasniewicz, *Why Arnold Matters: The Rise of a Cultural Icon* (New York: Basic Books, 2004), xiii.
5. Carla Marinucci, "Governor Endorses Minutemen on Border," *San Francisco Chronicle,* April 29, 2005.
6. Jean Baudrillard, *The Perfect Crime* (New York: Verso, 1996), 2.
7. Gary Indiana, *Schwarzenegger Syndrome: Politics and Celebrity in the Age of Contempt* (New York: New Press, 2005); Blitz and Krasniewicz, *Why Arnold Matters,* 42–68.
8. Larry N. Gerston and Terry Christensen, *Recall! California's Political Earthquake* (Armonk, N.Y.: M. E. Sharpe, 2004).
9. Ibid., 16–25.
10. To view examples of these news releases, see a Center for Media and Democracy Web site: www.sourcewatch.org or www.prwatch.org. To see an example of a video news release produced by the insurance industry, see the Insurance Information Network of California, www.iinc.org (accessed May 15, 2007).
11. Gerston and Christensen, *Recall!,* 93–106.
12. Ibid., 105.
13. Robert Salladay, "Governor's Top Aide Was Paid by Developer," *Los Angeles Times,* February 10, 2006.
14. Murray Edelman, *Constructing the Political Spectacle* (Chicago: University of Chicago Press, 1988).
15. Peter Schrag, *California: America's High-Stakes Experiment* (Berkeley: University of California Press, 2006), 219–220.
16. Dan Morain, "Deep Pockets Carry the Day," *Los Angeles Times,* November 9, 2006; final results of all elections are available at the secretary of state Web site, www.ss.ca.gov.
17. Dan Morain, "With Bills in Play, Gov. Solicits Cash," *Los Angeles Times,* September 11, 2006; Peter Nicholas and Evan Halper, "State Farm Donates to Governor's Fund," *Los Angeles Times,* May 12, 2007; all of Schwarzenegger's connections to special interests are tracked by the Arnold Watch Web site, www.arnoldwatch.org (accessed May 14, 2007).
18. See George Skelton, "Word from the Tent: Governor Says He's Multi-tasker," *Los Angeles Times,* April 2, 2007; Erica Werner, "In Washington, Schwarzenegger Rebukes Feds, but Wants Favors," *San Francisco Chronicle,* February 27, 2006.

Chapter 7 The Dual System of Justice
From Dual Justice to No Justice?

A n unequal distribution of wealth, property, and privilege requires a legal system that will ensure that this distribution is not seriously disturbed or challenged. Crime is, first and foremost, a risk to those with property, and property rights within the context of law must be secured by a system that allows transfers and payments to occur on an orderly and legal basis. Nowhere is the gap between the wealthy and the rest more apparent than in the American legal system, and nowhere is the contrast between the haves and have-nots more vigorously concealed through institutional practices that are supposed to balance the scales of justice, yet never do. There are, as David Cole, a law professor, says, really two justice systems in this country: one for the haves, those with the financial means to adequately defend or protect their rights in a court of law, and another for those with limited financial resources and thus limited judicial protection.[1]

The American judicial system divides jurisdiction between the federal courts and state courts, but in theory both must adjudicate law consistent with the U.S. Constitution. The myth of American jurisprudence is that civil and human rights are protected by the Bill of Rights, creating a kind of cocoon around individuals to protect them from government intrusions and from other individuals who might try to impinge on those rights. The protection of the Bill of Rights is not, however, nearly as sacrosanct or secure as many are led to believe. The division of the court system maintains a system of dual federalism and the principle of dual citizenship as established by the early U.S. Supreme Court case *Barron v. Baltimore* (1833). The Court held that individuals are citizens of both the United States and the respective states in which they reside. The concept of dual citizenship has been altered through the years, particularly by the ratification of the Fourteenth Amendment in 1868, making citizens of all people born or naturalized in the United States and protecting those rights conferred by the federal government while reaffirming the dual nature of citizenship within state boundaries as well. It was also changed in the 1950s and 1960s when the Supreme Court under Chief Justice Earl Warren (1953–1969) came very close to suggesting that the Bill of Rights should be applied to all citizens, implying that federal law superseded state law. In *Brown v. Board of Education of Topeka* (1954), the majority opinion written by Chief Justice Earl Warren concluded that the equal protection clause was violated by the "separate but equal" education that had been validated by *Plessy v. Ferguson* in 1896. By 1961 the Court ruled in *Mapp v. Ohio* that procedural rights protecting people from unreasonable searches and seizures were also national standards applying to all citizens. As the Warren Court continued to extend Bill of Rights protections, some justices were concerned that the concept of dual citizenship might be changed. This came to a head in *Duncan v. Louisiana* (1968), in which the Supreme Court came very close to overturning *Barron* amid a strong dissent again from Justices John Harlan and Potter Stewart, who had been consistent critics of the Court's weakening of the dual citizenship principle.

In the years since *Duncan,* and especially after Earl Warren's retirement in 1969, the Supreme Court has gone in the opposite direction and *Barron,* and the principle of dual citizenship, still prevails. Although the Bill of Rights does apply, its application comes primarily through the state constitutions that protect those same rights and not via the federal government. This limits the reach of the federal justice system, but it also suggests that we may not be as protected as we think we are. Since the 1970s, the federal government has been fighting "wars" on crime, drugs, and now terror, consistently arguing that procedural rights protected under the Constitution (and reinforced by the Warren Court) handicap law enforcement in doing its job. As a result, both federal and state courts have loosened procedural requirements and have carved out a wide variety of exceptions in which, for instance, evidence seized under questionable circumstances can still be allowed to be introduced in trial.

More vitally, the notion of constitutional protection in the United States (and thus the states) is afforded only to citizens and not to noncitizens, be they in this country legally or otherwise. Although the Supreme Court has held that noncitizens are entitled to due process protection, those protections appear to have been weakened considerably since the passage of the USA Patriot Act in 2001. Under an extremely broad interpretation of wartime powers given to the executive branch, the president, and intelligence-gathering agencies, the government has held noncitizens designated as unlawful "enemy combatants" at Guantanamo Bay, Cuba; it has held noncitizens in the United States in custody without access to legal counsel or to a writ of habeas corpus (which would require the government to explain to a judge or magistrate why the individual is being held); and it has held citizens suspected of having connections to terrorism in custody, also without being charged and without right to habeas corpus. American citizen Jose Padilla remains in legal limbo years after being arrested in Chicago and without any clear sense of how or if the government will actually present a case against him.[2]

The erosion of constitutional protections is also to be found in the practice of what is called extraordinary rendition, in which people are grabbed by U.S. intelligence agents and sent to "black sites," where they are held and may be tortured.[3] The Patriot Act also authorizes the government to engage in "sneak and peak" searches, where material may be searched prior to obtaining a search warrant; until the act, the Fourth Amendment, which protects against unreasonable searches and seizures, had made it standard procedure for law officers to obtain such warrants before making searches. In the newest twist, it was found in 2006 that federal authorities had been wiretapping what they claim to be international communications of suspected terrorists without obtaining authorization from the secret Foreign Intelligence Surveillance Court (FISC, often called the FISA Court), as mandated by the Foreign Intelligence Surveillance Act (FISA) of 1978.

The weakness (and, in some cases, suspension) of constitutional protections is a particular concern for Californians, where immigrants make up a sizable proportion of the population and many are noncitizens. Most are legal, but some are illegal. Either way, the changes since 9/11 seem to suggest that noncitizens could be rounded up and deported without any due process protections and, in fact, could be detained without being informed why they are being held. Legal scholars are carefully watching the Jose Padilla case because it suggests that "enemy combatant" status could be applied to a U.S. citizen and would allow the government to strip the person of constitutional protections. As weak as past legal protections were, the changes implemented threaten to literally negate constitutional rights entirely by allowing the government to pick and choose who gets protected and who does not. These issues go well beyond California's judicial system: they are crucial for the entire American legal system.

The Warren Court (1953–1969) marked a watershed in the development of modern civil rights. During this time, the Court made new and expansive interpretations of the Fifth and Fourteenth Amendments' life, liberty, and property due process rights, shifting the Court's prior emphasis on the protection of economic liberty and property interests to the protection and promotion of other forms of liberty. More recently, and under the Bush administration's expansive interpretation of executive branch authority announced as part of its war on terror, the Court has been forced to reevaluate what constitutes due process in light of national security concerns. When the limits to governmental power are allowed to stretch whenever the government decides they must, protections of rights are jeopardized because neither citizens nor noncitizens can know the rules under those changing circumstances. For the power elite, this situation can create problems. When the elite is assured that power is firmly in its hands, the use of arbitrary power poses no threat. When, however, power is used so arbitrarily that property and privilege are themselves at risk, the "known unknown," to use a term coined by former defense secretary Donald Rumsfeld, can put political stability at risk, something economic interests most definitely do not like.

Criminal and Civil Law

The two most significant categories of law are criminal and civil law. In criminal law the government alleges that a crime has been committed that threatened public safety, morals, or health. Punishment is imposed: fines, incarceration, probation, parole, or combinations thereof. Civil cases are usually divided between contract law, which involves disputes over voluntary, agreed-upon actions (either written or oral agreements constitute contracts), and tort law, which is concerned with disputes arising from obligations in society involving some sort of negligence leading to property damage, injury, or both.

About 8 million to 9 million cases are filed in California annually. About 2 million cases are civil cases, slightly more than 2 million are criminal, and the rest are primarily traffic cases of varying degrees of seriousness.[4] California courts follow the pattern of most courts in the United States: about 90 percent of all criminal cases that make it to the court system end with a guilty plea or plea bargain, the defendant pleading guilty to lesser charges and receiving a reduced penalty. The image of the legal system is the one replayed in endless television dramas and films: the staid judge, the over-anxious prosecutor, and the committed defense attorney who is certain of her client's innocence. It is image and only image. Once a defendant is in the system, it is almost guaranteed that he or she will be found guilty, whether by plea or jury. The reason? Few of those accused have the resources to adequately defend themselves in the legal system. Although the famous *Gideon v. Wainwright* (1963) decision by the U.S. Supreme Court guaranteed the right to an attorney even if a defendant cannot afford one, the legal defense offered by court-appointed counsel is often meager in California at best. Public defenders are overworked and underpaid, attorneys assigned pro bono cases rarely put in more than a cursory effort, and defendants are often encouraged to take a plea bargain as the best and most economic solution.[5] From the prosecutor's vantage point, plea bargains move cases through a crowded docket, speed up a system that is supposed to offer a "speedy trial," and still provide the statistical benefit of a high conviction rate, which is important in a state where district attorneys and city attorneys are usually elected officials. A trial by a jury of peers is a California dream: less than 3 percent of criminal cases make it to a jury trial and less than 1 percent of civil cases are heard at trial. Out-of-court settlements in civil cases serve the same function that plea bargains do in criminal cases.[6]

The Three Tiers of California Courts

The **trial courts** in California are called superior courts. There are 460 trial courts with about fifteen hundred judges, and nearly all legal cases are first heard in these courts. They handle both criminal felonies and misdemeanors (including minor crimes and most traffic cases), small claims, family law (divorce and custody cases), and civil suits. Although the judge in trial courts must obviously follow the law and guidelines established by the court system, he or she has considerable judicial discretion in determining what evidence will be allowed, what witnesses may be called, and so forth. Judicial discretion makes it difficult to argue any case on appeal, and only the most egregious errors are subject to review. Even then, in only an extremely small number of cases is the error reversible.

The **Court of Appeal** is divided into six districts (San Francisco, Los Angeles-Ventura, Sacramento, San Diego-Riverside-Santa Ana, Fresno, and San Jose) and has 105 judges, who hear appeals from superior courts. Panels of three justices hear the cases, in which the two sides present oral arguments and file briefs. Courts of appeal may remand the case (that is, send it back to the trial court for reconsideration), order a new trial, or dismiss the charges. In most cases, they do nothing. Few cases make it to the Court of Appeal because of the high costs to the defendant of continuing a case to the next level and because of the wide latitude given to the lower court in conducting its proceedings.

The **California Supreme Court** has seven members (versus nine in the U.S. Supreme Court), presided over by the chief justice and six associates. It takes very few cases, mostly involving appeals based on interpreting the state or U.S. Constitution. An automatic right to appeal all death penalty cases to the supreme court is guaranteed.

Unlike federal judges, judges in California are elected. Trial judges frequently start as appointees as other judges move on, then are subject to reelection every six years. The governor appoints the justices on the courts of appeal and supreme court, subject to approval by the Commission on Judicial Nominees Evaluation (JNE) and the Commission on Judicial Appointments. Attorneys and public members sit on the JNE; the attorney general, chief justice of the state supreme court, and the senior presiding judge of the courts of appeal sit on the Commission on Judicial Appointments. If approved, the

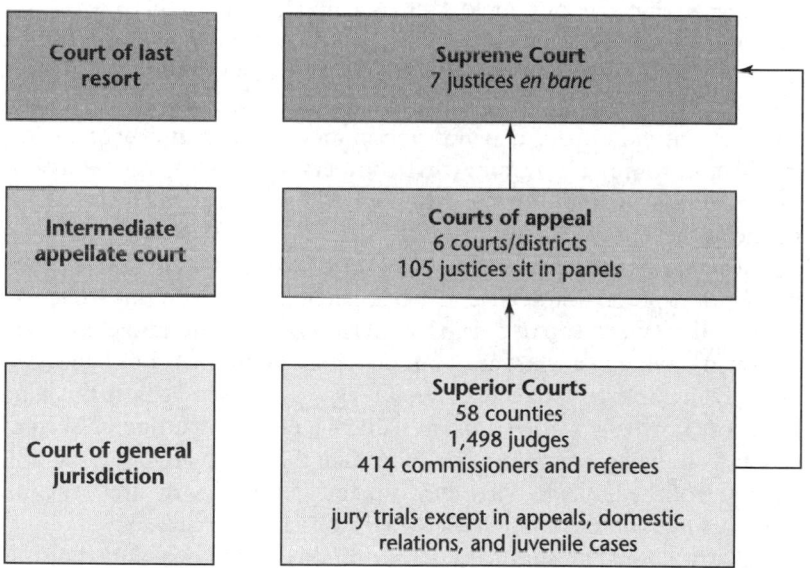

Figure 7-1 CALIFORNIA'S STATE COURT STRUCTURE

SOURCE: Adapted from the National Council on State Courts, www.ncsconline.org/D_Research/Ct_Struct/CA.htm (accessed March 30, 2007).

justices' names are put on the ballot for voter approval (through a plebiscite, meaning a "yes" or "no" vote) for a twelve-year term at the next gubernatorial election; if they are replacing a justice, they then serve out what remains of that justice's term before going on the ballot again for reelection.

Judges can be removed for misconduct or incompetence through the Commission on Judicial Performance, but this almost never happens. Most are issued an official warning or reprimand.

The election of judges is supposed to make judges more accountable as public servants to the people who elect them. In practice, few voters know anything about the judges they elect. If they are lucky, they may recognize a name from the last time they appeared on a ballot or caught a glimpse of them in action on *Court TV*, but this only occurs if a celebrity has been accused of some criminal act.

Problems and Controversies in California's Legal System

For the elite, the justice system works the way it is supposed to work for all. Questions of privacy, whether a search is reasonable or not, even how an arrestee is treated in custody can be challenged by those with the means to hire lawyers willing to file motions and to argue these points in court. For most people, that option is not available, and law enforcement knows it. Police are willing to cut some corners when it comes to detaining people, searching vehicles, and asking questions, because they know that most will not be able to challenge the legality of the procedures. For example, there is a high likelihood that a twenty-year-old black male will be stopped by police if found driving at night in what is recognized to be a white neighborhood. The black community and the police themselves refer to it as DWB, or Driving while Black. Critics refer to it as **racial profiling**.[7] Once stopped, it is not uncommon for that motorist to be put through "the routine," meaning that the person will not just be asked for license, registration, and proof of insurance (the standard when stopped for a traffic violation) but will be spread-eagled and searched. If the driver is lucky, he will be leaned onto the hood of the car; if he is unlucky, he will be sprawled down on the asphalt. The vehicle may be searched as well. In this scenario, the police may have no reason to detain this person beyond the suspicion raised by a black man driving in a white area, but police are aware that the chances of the person's being able to lodge a successful legal complaint against this kind of harassment is virtually zero. To their credit, the police departments keep these incidents from being even more common than they are by training the officers to be aware of the limits to what they can and cannot do. By itself, the justice system does not and cannot prevent illegal stops and searches.

The Patriot Act, the summary detention of noncitizens, and the still-to-be-determined scope of domestic spying in the post-9/11 era sent a chill throughout the American justice system that extends into the state courts as well. Challenges to the constitutionality of U.S. surveillance and spying may come from the state courts, but the justification put forth for nearly everything that the government has done (or that we are aware of) is that the president has increased power during war, thus making it legal.

California's legal system faces several other challenges beyond what is happening at the federal and international levels. In 1982, during the now-clichéd war on crime, voters approved a **Victims Bill of Rights** that created more mandatory sentencing, especially for crimes committed with guns. In 1994 the **Three Strikes law** mandated a minimum twenty-five-years-to-life sentence for a third felony conviction.

These laws changed the justice system in three important ways. First, they took away some of the legal discretion given to judges at the trial level by mandating sentencing guidelines that they could not change. This was in line with a national movement that similarly mandated fairly harsh minimum sentences for miscellaneous drug possession convictions. Judicial discretion was further limited by voters with a proposition that transferred from judges to district attorneys the decision of whether to try juveniles as minors or adults. The argument in all cases followed the same logic: judges were supposedly "soft on crime" and could not be left to decide on their own. Second, the laws encouraged the overcharging of accused criminals in order to gain more felony convictions quickly. By being charged with multiple felonies related to a single criminal act, for instance, the person could rack up three strikes faster, perhaps all at once. The Three Strikes law also mandates that if the first two felony convictions are categorized as "violent," "serious," or both, then the potential third strike case must be enhanced and tried as a felony even though it might not be under ordinary circumstances. Those in the legal system refer to these as "wobbler" offenses. Petty theft would usually be a misdemeanor, but if it is a third strike, it must be "tilted" over to be tried as a felony, and thus small criminal acts following serious ones might lead to a person's being locked up for a lifetime. Third, because more people were locked up for longer periods of time, a shortage of jail and prison space persists to this day.[8] The United States now leads the world in the number of prisoners in federal, state, and local systems (at more than 2.1 million) and ranks first globally for per capita incarceration (see table 7-1 for incarceration rates for U.S. states).[9] California's corrections system has more than 170,000 prisoners, most among the fifty states. To "store" so many prisoners, often referred to as **warehousing,** California has been hiring more prison guards and building more prisons, both of which are very costly, especially in a state where budget deficits have become routine. The corrections system, in turn, has been holding people for longer periods in the county jails instead of transferring them to state prisons and has used "catch and release" programs to allow some prisoners, mostly those convicted of drug possession, out of jail early. Anecdotally, a three-to-five year sentence means that the person will likely serve about nine months.

Aside from the total numbers in prison is the disproportionate number of minorities who are incarcerated, suggesting both that racism plays a

Table 7-1 Incarceration in the United States per 100,000 State Residents, by Race, 2002

State	White	Black	Hispanic	Ratio Black/White	Ratio Hispanic/White
Alabama	373	1,797	914	4.8	2.4
Alaska	306	1,606	549	5.2	1.8
Arizona	607	3,818	1,263	6.3	2.1
Arkansas	468	2,185	1,708	4.7	3.6
California	**487**	**3,141**	**820**	**6.4**	**1.7**
Colorado	429	4,023	1,131	9.4	2.6
Connecticut	199	2,991	1,669	15.0	8.4
Delaware	361	2,500	330	6.9	0.9
District of Columbia	46	768	260	16.5	5.6
Florida	502	2,877	684	5.7	1.4
Georgia	544	2,153	620	4.0	1.1
Hawaii	173	577	587	3.3	3.4
Idaho	502	2,236	1,103	4.5	2.2
Illinois	216	2,273	426	10.5	2.0
Indiana	373	2,575	602	6.9	1.6
Iowa	300	3,775	923	12.6	3.1
Kansas	397	3,686	753	9.3	1.9
Kentucky	466	3,375	2,059	7.2	4.4
Louisiana	421	2,475	1,736	5.9	4.1
Maine	207	1,731	759	8.4	3.7
Maryland	282	1,749	230	6.2	0.8
Massachusetts	204	1,807	1,435	8.9	7.0
Michigan	357	2,256	951	6.3	2.7
Minnesota	197	2,811	1,031	14.3	5.2
Mississippi	353	1,762	3,131	5.0	8.9
Missouri	402	2,306	730	5.7	1.8
Montana	358	3,120	1,178	8.7	3.3
Nebraska	226	2,251	824	9.9	3.6
Nevada	630	3,206	676	5.1	1.1
New Hampshire	242	2,501	1,425	10.3	5.9
New Jersey	175	2,509	843	14.3	4.8
New Mexico	311	3,151	818	10.1	2.6
New York	182	1,951	1,002	10.7	5.5
North Carolina	266	1,640	440	6.2	1.7
North Dakota	170	1,277	976	7.5	5.8
Ohio	333	2,651	865	8.0	2.6
Oklahoma	682	4,077	1,223	6.0	1.8
Oregon	488	3,895	777	8.0	1.6
Pennsylvania	281	3,108	2,242	11.1	8.0
Rhode Island	199	2,735	817	13.8	4.1
South Carolina	391	1,979	871	5.1	2.2
South Dakota	440	6,510	1,486	14.8	3.4
Tennessee	402	2,021	790	5.0	2.0
Texas	694	3,734	1,152	5.4	1.7
Utah	342	3,256	998	9.5	2.9
Vermont	183	2,024	799	11.1	4.4
Virginia	444	2,842	508	6.4	1.1
Washington	393	2,757	717	7.0	1.8
West Virginia	375	6,400	2,834	17.1	7.6
Wisconsin	341	3,953	863	11.6	2.5
Wyoming	740	6,529	1,320	8.8	1.8
National	**378**	**2,489**	**922**	**6.6**	**2.4**

SOURCE: Human Rights Watch, "Race and Incarceration in the United States: Human Rights Watch Press Backgrounder," February 22, 2002, www.hrw.org/backgrounder/usa/race/pdf/table1.pdf (accessed April 2, 2007).
NOTE: Highlighted entries represent the top ten states for each category. Since Pennsylvania and Vermont are tied at 11.1 for the ratio of black to white prisoners, eleven states are highlighted in that column.

significant part in how those accused are treated in the system and that minorities are overrepresented at the poorest rungs of the socioeconomic ladder and thus most likely to land in jail. As of 2002, California had incarcerated 3,141 blacks per 100,000 in population, compared with 820 Latinos and 487 whites. This distribution is consistent with the national averages, which stood at 2,489, 922, and 378, respectively, for the same year.[10]

Advances in DNA testing have raised new concerns about the number of people wrongly convicted of crimes and now held in prison. The Innocence Project, which started at the Cardozo School of Law in New York and has now spun off to other organizations throughout the country, has been reexamining evidence to try to reopen cases in which DNA exonerates the person convicted of the crime. The project is limited to death penalty cases in which the convicted may be wrongly executed and for which DNA is available (meaning blood evidence, rape kits, hair and skin samples, and the like). Even with this narrow focus, there is a strong indication that many people are in prison for crimes they did not commit (although the Innocence Project is reluctant to draw such broad conclusions).[11] Use of the death penalty raises questions not only about those who may be wrongly accused but also about its use violating international law. Fearing that the death penalty might be used against political opposition in non-democratic countries, human rights organizations have long pressured the United Nations to stop the use of capital punishment around the world and find support for this idea in the Universal Declaration of Human Rights, passed by the UN in 1948, and the International Covenant on Political and Civil Rights, which came into effect in 1976. According to Amnesty International, 129 countries have either abolished the death penalty completely or have stopped its practice while still keeping it legal for extraordinary circumstances. Sixty-eight other countries retain capital punishment, but only a handful of countries actually still use it.[12] The United States finds itself in the company of China, Iran, and Saudi Arabia in continuing to use the death penalty, all countries with poor human rights records, to say the least.

As of May 2007 a moratorium remains in effect on the use of the death penalty in California. In early 2006 a federal judge placed a hold on the use of lethal injections in the state because the practice might constitute cruel and unusual punishment. California has been trying to change its lethal injection procedures to satisfy the judge in this case, but so far the ban remains in place.[13]

The direction criminal law has taken is that of locking up the bad guys. In civil law the power elite has been working to protect private business interests from being responsible for what they produce in the context of a nationwide movement for tort reform. The argument for tort reform usually starts with a set of images: greedy trial lawyers out for a buck look for corporations to sue, hoping that the corporation will settle such "nuisance lawsuits," leading to a lucrative payout for client and unscrupulous attorney. That imagery has led to tort reforms in California. In 1975 the **Malpractice Injury and Compensation Reform Act** was passed, limiting damages for pain and suffering to

$250,000 and placing limits on lawyers' fees. One of the objectives of organizations like the American Tort Reform Foundation (linked to other ultra-conservative groups and foundations) is to place additional limits on product liability as well. A 1960s ruling by the California Supreme Court established the principle of strict liability, which is now followed nearly universally in the American legal system. Strict liability means that companies can be held strictly liable for the design, manufacturing, and marketing of defective products regardless of how carefully they were made and irrespective of any negligence involved in that production process. Tort reform groups seek to place caps on the amount of money that can be awarded in these liability cases, a direct benefit to producers by taking away the threat of large liability judgments that should serve as an incentive toward making better and safer products. Knowing what the maximum loss might be in such instances, the cost of the risk to consumers can more easily be covered in the price of a product.

Voters in California passed **Proposition 64** in 2004, which removed the possibility of class action suits being brought against companies engaged in unfair business practices. The plaintiff now must show direct injury or harm in order to sue for an unfair business practice, and only the state attorney general or local government prosecutors may enforce laws against unfair business practices. In effect, small businesses cannot file civil suits against big businesses that may be gaining advantages on the cost of goods, labor, and so forth. Their only option is to ask the government to help them. The proposition was backed by a host of business interests and passed by a 59 to 41 percent margin. Did people understand what they were voting for? They did understand the images, and terms like trial lawyers, nuisance lawsuits, and deep pockets, not recognizing that the deep pockets were the ones supporting this change. Score another victory for the elite, with more to come.

Taking Stock

Although most Americans believe that we are all equal under the law, there are really two systems of justice in the United States: one for the wealthy and another for the rest of us. As with the other institutions of California government, an enormous earthquake fault divides society into two separate and unequal pieces. The justice system exposes other fault lines as well. In the wake of the terrorist attacks of 9/11, the federal government has effectively removed most constitutional protections from those who are not U.S. citizens and reside in this country either legally or illegally, making it possible for the government to imprison, deport, or even torture individuals who have no right to due process or habeas corpus. Citizens, in theory, are more protected, but if the federal court system upholds the right of the U.S. government to detain Jose Padilla as an enemy combatant, it will grant government the power to take away constitutional protections from American citizens too. The California court system demonstrates how limited resources leave most people vulnerable to the dual system of justice. More than nine out of ten people charged with crimes will either plead guilty or accept a plea bargain that brings a lesser charge or that promises less punishment, mostly because they lack the financial means to fight the case brought against them. The vast majority of civil cases are settled before they go to trial for the same reason: it costs money to fight them. California's appeals courts and the state supreme court hear cases on appeal, but again, very few cases make it that far. The political perception that the courts system has not been sufficiently tough on crime and on criminals has led to changes in California sentencing laws, most notably passage of the Three Strikes law in 1994. The state's prison population has mushroomed to more than 170,000 inmates, and Three Strikes has meant that prisoners must be warehoused for longer periods of time. Here the fault lines of racial and ethnic differences are reinforced by those of social class, as minorities with limited economic resources end up overrepresented in the state's prison population. At the local level, police have to make instantaneous judgments as to whether a possible crime has been committed. It is at this level that people can see and experience the immediate effects of the political process, and it is a key part of understanding how California government works.

QUESTIONS FOR DISCUSSION

1. How does expanded governmental authority to detain individuals, to search property without initial warrant, and to collect information about what a person is doing affect the rights of everyone in American society? What if you have done nothing wrong and have nothing to hide? Should these changes in the law concern you?

2. Why are so few cases heard on appeal? Does this prove that the original trial court got the decision right?

3. Is the large number of black and Latino prisoners in California's corrections system really a product of inadequate legal representation, or might it be that minorities simply commit more crimes? How might this also be connected to questions of socioeconomic status and class?

NOTES

1. David Cole, "Two Systems of Criminal Justice," in *The Politics of Law: A Progressive Critique,* ed. David Kairys, 3rd ed. (New York: Basic Books, 1998), 410–433.
2. Nat Hentoff, *The War on the Bill of Rights—and the Gathering Resistance* (New York: Seven Stories, 2004); Barbara Olshansky, *Democracy Detained: Secret Unconstitutional Practices in the U.S. War on Terror* (New York: Seven Stories, 2007); several human rights organizations have extensive discussions and documentation on this topic as well: see Amnesty International, www.amnestyusa.org, and Human Rights Watch, www.hrw.org.

3. Stephen Grey, *Ghost Plane: The True Story of the CIA Torture Program* (New York: St. Martin's, 2006).

4. For the latest statistics and an overview of how California courts are organized, see "California Courts," www.courtinfo.ca.gov.

5. See George Fisher, *Plea Bargaining's Triumph: A History of Plea Bargaining in America* (Stanford: Stanford University Press, 2004); see also Dirk Olin, "Plea Bargain," *New York Times Magazine,* September 29, 2002.

6. See the California Courts Web site, "A Visitor's Guide to the California Superior Courts"; "Exploring the Work of California Trial Courts: A 20-Year Retrospective," www.courtinfo.ca.gov/reference/4_12courtsupct.htm.

7. David A. Harris, "Driving while Black: Racial Profiling on Our Nation's Highways," www.aclu.org/racialjustice/racialprofiling/15912pub19990607.html; see also Joe Feagin, *Systemic Racism: A Theory of Oppression* (New York: Routledge, 2006).

8. Kevin Starr, *Coast of Dreams: California on the Edge, 1990–2003* (New York: Knopf, 2004), 97–105.

9. See the Sentencing Project, "Incarceration," www.sentencingproject.org/IssueAreaHome.aspx?IssueID=2; Marc Mauer, *Race to Incarcerate* (New York: New Press, 2006); Christian Parenti, *Lockdown America: Police and Prisons in the Age of Crisis* (New York: Verso, 2000).

10. Human Rights Watch, "Race and Incarceration Backgrounder," www.hrw.org/backgrounder/usa/race/, February 27, 2002 (accessed May 22, 2007).

11. For information related to the Innocence Project, see www.innocenceproject.org.

12. Amnesty International, "Facts and Figures on the Death Penalty," http://web.amnesty.org/pages/deathpenalty-facts-eng (accessed May 22, 2007).

13. Bob Egelko, "State Proposes Changes in Lethal Injections to Satisfy Judges," *San Francisco Chronicle,* May 15, 2007.

Chapter 8 **Local Governments and Obsessive Development**

Growth machines and the cities, bureaucratic institutions, and corporations that power them, have to exist in real, geographic space. Land must be put to use and it must be commodified along with the labor that creates that use; from this, profit flows. The logic of growth is supported at both the state and the national level, but it is locally that development of land translates directly to growth, and so local government at the county and city levels make it happen. The need to invent and reinvent land use means that the visible landscape is constantly changing and being rebuilt, so that everything that was there ten, twenty, or thirty years ago now becomes a dreamscape. Books are filled with nostalgic pictures of things that are not there any more, and the transformation of landscape accelerates with the incessant need to grow even more and at a faster pace.[1] A visit to a city council meeting, in person or on the local cable access channel, quickly gives a glimpse into what it's all about: approval for changes to the city plan, changes to zoning, and questions of issuing variances to residences and businesses that have not conformed to the rules. It is a system guided by rules, and yet when rules are enacted to control or to limit the rate at which growth is to occur, those rules serve primarily symbolic functions rather than actually placing restrictions on development itself, as the urban geographers Kee Warner and Harvey Molotch suggest.[2] The image of the political process separated from the economic imperatives of increasing profit is thus neatly maintained.

How Local Governments Are Organized

California has fifty-eight counties. County governments provide services, including police, fire, and road maintenance, to mostly rural areas that are not incorporated as cities. There are two types of counties in the state:

- **General law counties.** The state constitution provides for **general law counties,** which are organized under laws enacted by the state legislature. Of the fifty-eight counties, forty-six are general law counties. "Each of the forty-six counties has an elected five-member board of supervisors serving four-year terms, plus other elected county officials, such as the sheriff, district attorney, tax collector, coroner, and county clerk. Progressivism made each of these positions nonpartisan, so party affiliation cannot be listed on the ballot.

- **Charter counties.** Allowed to organize under their own rules, **charter counties** have, in principle, more flexibility and control over how they govern. For trivia fans, Los Angeles was the first charter county in 1912 (after the state constitution was amended to provide for it), and it has been followed by ten more, mostly in urban areas. San Francisco is a chartered city-county, meaning that it is a hybrid; it has a county board of supervisors and a mayor but no city council.

There are 477 incorporated cities in California. Incorporation provides an economic advantage in that the city is entitled to sales taxes and motor vehicle fees collected there that would otherwise be disbursed among the entire county. Cities are able to set their own city plans and zoning ordinances rather than rely on the county board of supervisors to do this task, There are two types of city organizations too:

- **General law cities.** The vast majority of cities are **general law cities,** which are organized under state law, usually following a council-manager form with an elected city council and an appointed city manager who manages the day-to-day operations of city government.
- **Charter cities.** Again, the charter option gives greater flexibility and a semblance of home rule not afforded under general law. **Charter cities** may provide a greater array of services than a county would. Currently 107 of the 477 cities are chartered.

Cities are incorporated through the county's **Local Agency Formation Commission (LAFCO),** which includes two county supervisors, two representatives from incorporated cities in the county, and a public representative chosen by the other four. If LAFCO decides that a city is politically and economically viable, the board of supervisors holds a hearing to approve the plan and it then goes to the voters for approval. If areas want to secede from an existing city, the process is the same, but voters from both the area seeking secession and those in the city that it is seceding from must approve the change. In 2002, voters in the San Fernando Valley portion of Los Angeles narrowly approved secession, but voters in LA overall voted against it; in Hollywood, both locals and the city at large voted it down.

In addition to city and county governments, there are 983 school districts in California with elected school boards, and there are more than 4,700 special districts covering many different services: transportation (such as Bay Area Rapid Transit—BART), cemeteries, sanitation, vector control, air quality (South Coast Air Quality Management District—SCAQMD), and water (Metropolitan Water District—MWD). Most of these districts have a direct impact on residents' day-to-day lives, but almost no public attention is given to them and unless something extraordinary happens, the mass media ignore them.[3]

There are also currently 386 **redevelopment agencies** with considerable power over making planning decisions in urban areas and subject to almost no direct oversight. Redevelopment agencies have become a powerful engine for growth machines because they have little accountability. In most cases, members of the city council convene as the head of the redevelopment agency. Accountability comes in the form of being a council member, subject to election, not directly as part of the agency.[4]

Redevelopment agencies have considerable power within a defined boundary. An area designated for redevelopment will be identified as being "blighted" in some way, and the agency (having effectively given itself the authority to do so) encourages new businesses to move in through gentrification of old buildings and facilities or by promoting new construction. Redevelopment can be encouraged in several ways. The agency can use public funds to secure low-interest loans to stimulate business interest; it can condemn abandoned properties and claim control over them through eminent domain (in which an owner must turn over private property for public use in return for just compensation); or it may offer a variety of deals to developers to coax them into building in the redevelopment zone. Agencies may lease or sell properties held by them to the developers at below-market rates, cover some of the construction costs, waive property taxes for a designated number of years, waive sewer hook-up fees and upgrades, and so on. The primary goal is to get the developers in and to make redevelopment happen (figure 8-1). The results can be rapid and startling. In downtown Long Beach, for example, redevelopment zones in the old central business district and along Shoreline Drive (home to the Long Beach Grand Prix auto race) are now filled with trendy restaurants, nightclubs, and movie theaters. There is little to remind people of the homeless and the poor who dominated the street scene twenty years ago. The homeless never disappear, of course, but are simply pushed along to some other part of town or to the skid row areas of other cities. But for redevelopment purposes, out of sight, out of mind, and the machine keeps churning out dollars for those corporations with the means and connections to participate.

The Fiscalization of Land Use and the Legacy of Proposition 13

No single initiative has had a greater impact on California politics than **Proposition 13,** passed by a comfortable margin of voters in 1978. It is so famous, in fact, that its number has been retired.

The story of how and why Proposition 13 came to be so important goes back to the economic recession of the 1970s. The system that pegged the value of the U.S. dollar and other currencies to deposits of gold had collapsed, in large part because of global competition that led to an overvaluation of the dollar. At the same time the Organization of Petroleum Exporting Countries (OPEC) cut production in order to decrease supplies and drive up the price of oil, leading to gasoline rationing. These events caused inflation to spiral in the 1970s, exceeding 10 percent from 1973 to 1978 and fueling near-panic buying of real estate by those who saw it as a hedge against inflation and by

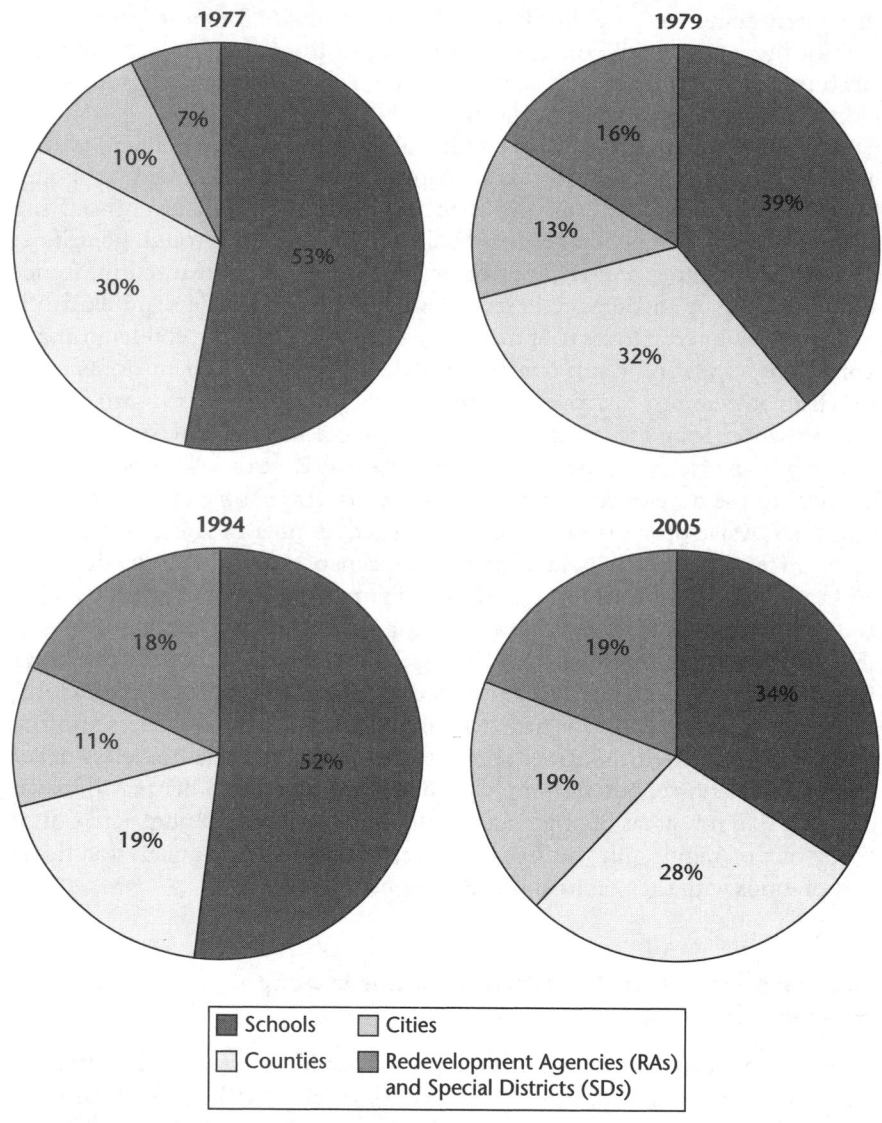

Figure 8-1 CALIFORNIA'S SHIFTING TAX DISTRIBUTION: INCREASING SHARE FOR REDEVELOPMENT

SOURCE: Legislative Analyst's Office, "Cal Facts 2006: California's Economy and Budget in Perspective," www.lao.ca.gov/2006/cal_facts/2006_calfacts_state_local.htm.
NOTE: 1977—Before 1978, local agencies determined the property tax rate and its distribution of revenues. 1979—Proposition 13 (1978) set a maximum tax rate of 1 percent and shifted control over the distribution of property taxes to the state.
1994—Facing fiscal pressure in the early 1990s, the state modified the distribution of property taxes to give a greater share to schools (thereby reducing state school spending).
2005—The state shifted a greater share of property taxes to cities and counties to offset their losses due to the (1) reduction in the vehicle license fee rate and (2) use of local sales taxes to pay the state's deficit.

those simply trying to lock in interest rates before they increased further. Assessments at that time ran somewhere between 3 and 3.5 percent of market value, but with the values going up so rapidly, taxes in some places were increased three or four times a year.

Proposition 13 fixed the property tax at 1 percent of the assessed value retroactive to 1975, limited increases in the tax to 2 percent per year, and limited new assessments to when the property was bought or sold, or when new construction went up on the parcel. It also required that any tax increases be approved by two-thirds of the legislature in each house and that any and all local taxes be similarly subject to two-thirds voter approval. Although some of the provisions have been modified since (to be discussed in the next chapter) most of Proposition 13 remains in effect.

Led by the antitax crusader Howard Jarvis and his ally Paul Gann, the campaign for Proposition 13 (known at the time as the Jarvis-Gann Initiative) appealed primarily to homeowners who were facing huge tax bills, even though all property owners stood to gain from these tax cuts. It was thought by many that this initiative would lead to financial armageddon, but much of the immediate impact was absorbed by a tidy budget surplus that had accumulated under the watch of Governor Jerry Brown. The effects of the proposition, however, persist and shape the nature of growth and land development.

Property taxes that used to be revenue streams for local governments became the purview of state government, which then redistributed taxes back to the place where they came from. The two-thirds voter approval requirement made it difficult for local governments to raise taxes, and an antitax climate made it impossible. So a dependency was created. Local governments, which were left with almost no means to raise additional funds themselves, had to rely on the state to send back money that was collected locally. Through the 1980s, counties and cities did what they could to cut budgets and cover costs. Park facilities were allowed to deteriorate, libraries cut back on book purchases and operating hours, museums began to charge entrance fees. Many services, especially those offered by special districts, now required separate fees and service charges. Some localities sought to increase the flow of money by increasing taxes on hotel rooms; this hidden tax hits up tourists, who are usually made aware of it only when they see their bill on the morning they check out; some municipalities legalized gambling and card clubs to bring in more money; and a handful of places struck sponsorship deals to connect brand to city. Huntington Beach was the first to do this in 1999, signing a deal with Coca-Cola to feature its products on city properties as an official "Coke city." The economic solution, naturally enough, is to deepen the corporate connection and to have commercialism impinge even further on the public sphere.[5]

The logic of growth is fixed into place by the logic of taxation. Local governments need to see the sale of property or new construction in order to have the property value reassessed at current market values. They also need to have sales taxes generated within their city or county, because under state formula they are entitled to 1.75 percent of the state's 7.25 percent sales tax collected in their community (it used to be 2 percent until Governor Schwarzenegger's plan to borrow money to pay for loans due—Proposition 57—cut that by a quarter of a percent). Thus, because it is difficult to increase taxes any other way, local governments have to encourage growth so that new assessments raise the tax base. Just as important, if the new development happens to be a commercial property, it can reap the harvest of the sales taxes generated by that business as well. This is referred to as the fiscalization of land use. Changes in land use and transfers of property create revenue for local government, and the incentive is in place for public officials to push for growth to pay for fire and police departments, street sweeping, and trash pickup.

Development in the form of infilling, a process in which underutilized properties are purchased by developers (often encouraged or subsidized by redevelopment agencies) and filled in either with intensified residential development or with retail uses, or redevelopment of existing properties is usually offered as a win-win proposition. Noting that there is a demand for housing, real estate developers are quick to point out that infilling is simply a response to a growing urban economy and that land use must change to accommodate these evolving needs. In the case of redevelopment, growth means profit for the businesses involved, especially if the redevelopment agency is willing to absorb a good deal of the costs associated with opening new stores or in helping to pay for infrastructural improvements to accommodate more intensive land uses, such as widening streets or adding new sewer connections. The redevelopment agency, in turn, responds directly to the operation of the growth machine and is able to claim that new property and sales tax revenues will allow local government to pay for more cops on the beat, more fire stations, and help improve schools. These arguments are made virtually every week in some city council chamber or redevelopment agency hearing somewhere in this state, and they put those who question the logic of growth at a definite rhetorical disadvantage. Who could possibly be against more cops, more fire stations, and more computers in the classroom? Growth advocates also point out that development creates new jobs, both in construction and in the new businesses that eventually move into the revitalized community.

But the arguments are circular. More government resources are needed precisely because growth is occurring. When the population increases, for instance, more schools need to be built or more portable classrooms (now mainstays of almost any California public school) need to be brought onto the playground to accommodate the growing number of families. Any potential benefit to existing school facilities is nullified. And big-box retailers may tout the creation of jobs in the city but fail to mention that most of these jobs pay something close to minimum wage while providing little or no additional benefits such as health care coverage for their employees. The logic of growth insists that these changes are a natural part of a market economy, and so there is nothing that can be done to stop them. As the economics professor Michael Perelman suggests, the naturalness of this is the essence of constructing the myth of the free market and makes it virtually impossible to argue for seeing economic behavior in any other way. They may not be great jobs, one might hear, but people are better off working than not having any jobs at all.[6]

Fiscalization continues to push suburbanization to more distant areas of urban centers. Areas previously "undeveloped" can be made valuable by building homes or businesses on them, thus jacking up the value of the property. The concept of edge cities, where commuting patterns link people not to jobs in the central business district but to surrounding suburbs where there are ample employment and shopping opportunities, is used to justify enormous developments at what seem to be extreme distances from the traditional downtown. In Southern California, huge developments in the Newhall Pass and Lake Castaic area have converted primarily grasslands and some farmland into areas filled with housing. An even larger development, called the Centennial Project, plans to house 70,000 people in the Fort Tejon area, hoping to create a suburb for both Los Angeles and the Bakersfield area.[7] New homes equal new property taxes. Within already urbanized communities, local governments encourage infilling. In Orange, Riverside, and San Diego Counties, infilling has swallowed up the last remnants of agriculture, as the last strawberry fields and orange groves have been infilled with tract housing. Redevelopment agencies push fiscalization further still by anchoring redevelopment with big box retailers, which generate a large amount of sales taxes. Big boxes like Wal-Mart, Costco, Home Depot, and Target depend on cities to dangle carrots of subsidized construction, tax breaks, and the like before deciding where to locate new stores. Retail businesses, which generate new construction and new sales taxes, are, for local government, the proverbial cash cow.

Although the fiscalization of land use is sometimes discussed as a problem, its pivotal role in the growth machine makes it unlikely that this function will change anytime soon. Property values have increased so dramatically since 2001 that the political benefits of land development have become greater than ever. As new homes and businesses have been built, their assessed value has come in at inflated market rates; because property tax bills are pegged at that rate, local revenues look very healthy. At the state level, the ongoing operating budget shortfall, projected to be about $3 billion for fiscal year 2007–2008, could be worse were it not for healthy increases in nonwage earnings, that is, investment income, which tends to be concentrated among the wealthiest 10 percent of Californians.[8] Those nonwage incomes have been augmented by the increase in real property prices and stock prices, making the rich richer; in addition, the higher property prices can be used to borrow and buy even more property, enhancing the effect yet again.

However, the rapid increase in housing prices has led to a variety of new "loan instruments" (as the loan industry likes to refer to them) to help home buyers who entered the market to take advantage of record-low interest rates

Table 8-1 Home Purchases Financed by Interest-Only Loans, 2002 and 2005 (percent)

County or metropolitan area	2002	2005
San Francisco	18	70
Marin	18	70
San Mateo	18	70
San Jose	9	61
Vallejo	6	78

SOURCE: Data from Kelly Zito, "High Interest in Interest-Only Home Loans," *San Francisco Chronicle,* May 20, 2005.

(especially between 2001 and 2005) but did not necessarily have enough cash available to make down payments normally required for a traditional, usually fixed-rate, mortgage. A deregulated, integrated industry known collectively as Finance-Insurance-Real Estate (or FIRE) quickly made new varieties of loans available. These include interest-only loans, which allow purchases with no money down and typically involve adjustable rate mortgages that do not require payment on principal (the actual price of the home) until three, five, or seven years down the road (table 8-1). More controversially, FIRE expanded the practice of subprime lending, which enables those with poor or nonexistent credit to qualify for a mortgage. Because subprime customers are considered a greater risk, the overall interest rates on these loans are generally higher, but they offer greater flexibility to buyers who don't have cash on hand by allowing them to forgo down payments. There is risk to the borrower too, because these subprime loans tend to have adjustable mortgages that could mean larger payments in the future. The most extreme example of a subprime loan involves what are called Alt-A (alternative documentation) loans for which the borrower does not need to provide the lender information on income at all; the loan is granted based on credit score alone (figure 8-2). For both home buyer and FIRE, mortgages have become a game of chance.

The advantage of these features to homebuyers is that they can get into a house despite currently inflated prices. The disadvantage is that interest rates have already started to move upward (and given their record lows, up was virtually the only option) and house payments will shoot up substantially once the interest-only loan period ends. Economists suspect that many buyers are borrowing money against the (inflated) value of their homes, meaning that debts are accumulating on an unprecedented level and that the entire system can come crashing down.[9] This is not just a California problem but one tied to rising national debt, trade deficits, and the effects that both of these have on the value of the U.S. dollar.

The consequences of the interconnections between land use, government revenues, growth, and the global economy have not yet been fully realized. The interconnectedness suggests, however, that the system is an extremely fragile one. A continued increase in interest rates by the Federal Reserve Board

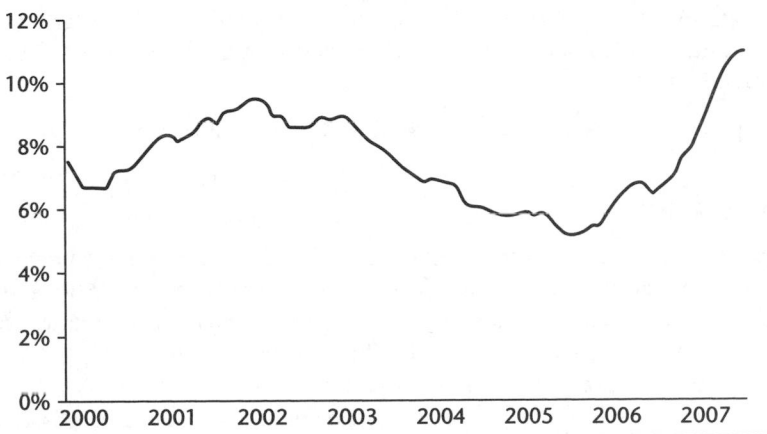

Figure 8-2 SERIOUSLY DELINQUENT SUBPRIME MORTGAGES

SOURCE: Adapted from Joseph A. Giannone and Christian Plumb, "Fremont Shares Soar on Stake, Loan Unit Sales," Reuters News Service, May 22, 2007, www.reuters.com/globalcoverage/subprime?src=052207_1641_doublefeature_.
NOTE: Defined as two or more monthly payments late, based on dollar value of outstanding residential mortgages.

to cool inflation will also cool the housing market. Those with any kind of adjustable rate mortgage will immediately face larger mortgage payments. In 2005 almost 48 percent of all home loans issued in California were interest-only loans. By 2006 about 36 percent of all loans were adjustable rate mortgages, about 9 percent in the highest risk subprime category.[10] Where will the extra money come from? As a *San Francisco Chronicle* article suggests, even small changes can cause disaster for those living on the economic edge. As gas prices surge upward and people take on more credit card debt, which increased by 6.5 percent in 2006, interest rates are a concern for all borrowers and not just those with subprime loans. The number of real estate foreclosures would, however, likely increase first with those holding subprime loans, and there are indications that the so-called real estate bubble started to burst in 2007. Late payments on subprime loans increased to over 10 percent and the overall foreclosure rate in California increased by 36 percent in early 2007 compared with the national average of just 7 percent.[11]

For state and local government, growth machines have provided a temporary revenue fix without the need for those governments having to deal with the longer-range problems of continued budget deficits and bonds that must at some point be paid back. The risk that all this encompasses is captured by Kevin Starr, who notes:

Once Americans had come to California to get away from it all. Now the peoples of the world were arriving, as Arnold Schwarzenegger had, to take their chances with life on the edge. For many, the edge was dropping off into nowhere. For others, it offered a toehold, at least a road sign, and sometimes even a lottery ticket, in the direction of a better way of life.[12]

If we put our hopes on a lottery ticket, we are in a lot of trouble.

Taking Stock

The obsession with economic growth and the continuous need to invent and then reinvent land use drives the local political process. It is in the local sphere that the growth machines operate at full power, helped along by the work of redevelopment agencies that funnel public money into redevelopment zones in order to encourage private developers to turn blighted areas into newly refurbished growth nodes where profits can again be made. There is an insistence in our culture that the economy must be about letting the free market run free, but nothing could be further from the truth. Without appropriate incentives offered up by government, redevelopment would not occur, and so these redevelopment agencies have to find ways to coax businesses into doing what they supposedly should do of their own accord and yet do not. Fear of taxes has become a common feature of American politics, and its roots go back to the successful passage of Proposition 13 by voters in 1978. Proposition 13 certainly did lessen the tax load for property owners in California, but that tax savings has come at long-term economic costs. Local governments must encourage even more development in order to increase revenue streams coming into counties and cities. Property tax reassessments depend on a turnover of property, and a portion of sales taxes comes back to the place where they were collected, meaning that more business means more money back to local governments that they can then use to promote, of course, still more growth. And so it goes. As the so-called real estate bubble has expanded in California, housing prices have skyrocketed, and FIRE has stepped in to offer a variety of loan options that allow more people to take advantage of low interest rates while placing themselves in more debt and at greater economic risk than ever before. The bubble will eventually burst, and there are some indicators that it is already starting to deflate. But what will the consequences be for a state that has found itself in a chronic budget crisis? That crisis, of course, has its roots in Proposition 13.

QUESTIONS FOR DISCUSSION

1. If redevelopment agencies did not exist, would economically depressed or blighted areas ever develop on their own? Why or why not?

2. Proposition 13 guarantees that a reassessment on property value will not occur until the property changes hands. How might this create tax inequities between, say, neighbors living next door to each other? It also

sets the property tax at 1 percent of the initial assessed value (with small increases allowed per year). How might the property tax itself affect the ability of homeowners to make their mortgage payments?

3. Why do you think that FIRE is willing to take on more risky kinds of loans? Why are individuals and families willing to gamble on various interest-only and subprime loans? Why is government willing to allow this kind of gambling to take place?

NOTES

1. There are many books that deal with nostalgia for places and things that no longer exist. See for example, Charles Phoenix, *Southern California in the '50s* (Santa Monica, Calif.: Angel City Press, 2001).

2. Kee Warner and Harvey Molotch, *Building Rules: How Local Controls Shape Community Environments and Resources* (Boulder, Colo.: Westview Press, 2000), 59–77.

3. For a pro-redevelopment perspective, see the California Redevelopment Association Web site, www.calredevelop.org; an extensive collection of information on local government can be found at the California Local Government Information Web site, www.igs.berkeley.edu/library/localweb.html.

4. By law, additional oversight of redevelopment is provided by the California Department of Housing and Community Development and by the State Controller's Office. In practice, however, little regulatory oversight is applied as long as the redevelopment agencies file required reports and documents. See the Housing and Community Development Web site, www.hcd.ca.gov/rda.

5. See Commercial Alert, "City for Sale," www.commercialalert.org/issues/government/city-for-sale.

6. Michael Perelman, *Railroading Economics: The Creation of the Free Market Mythology* (New York: Monthly Review Press, 2006).

7. David Kelley, "Small-Town Feel Planned for Big Centennial Project," *Los Angeles Times,* April 25, 2005.

8. Legislative Analyst's Office, "Analysis of the 2006–2007 Budget Bill," and "Overview of the Governor's Budget: 2007–2008," both available at www.lao.ca.gov.

9. See Michael Hudson, "The New Road to Serfdom," *Harper's,* May 2006, 39–46.

10. David Streitfeld, "They're In—but Not Home Free," *Los Angeles Times,* April 3, 2005; Gina Martin, "Mortgage Delinquencies Low, but Trouble Lurking," Wachovia Economics Group, September 18, 2006, http://mediaserver.fxstreet.com/Reports/df0150b8-eddf-4233-8d92-3c0995725393/4aa167ab-6aaa-4d72-a334-6ddd55ae9638.pdf.

11. Bob Tedeschi, "Mortgages Too Much for Many," *San Francisco Chronicle,* May 20, 2007; Michael Rappaport, "California Foreclosures Nearly Twice U.S. Rate," *San Bernardino Sun,* April 19, 2007.

12. Kevin Starr, *Coast of Dreams: California on the Edge, 1990–2003* (New York: Knopf, 2004), 630.

Chapter 9 "The Chronic"
California's Permanent Budget Crisis

The Addiction Redefined

Beginning with the recall election of 2003, Arnold Schwarzenegger's stump speech has included a line about legislators being "addicted to spending."[1] There is a chronic problem in California's budget, but it is not spending that has caused it. Rather, governors and legislators have chronically been addicted to the neoconservative tenet of taxation being the original sin of government. The image of a huge, wasteful, and irresponsible state bureaucracy that conservatives like to conjure up continues to justify the antitax climate that was established with the passage of Proposition 13 in 1978 and the other laws that place serious constraints on creating new revenues through taxation and limit the legislature from being able to shift money around to pay for the most-needed programs. This system is the system of the power elite, for it keeps as much wealth in private hands as possible and the hope remains that tax burdens can be reduced even further should the government go bankrupt and have to reorganize entirely.[2] In the meantime, chronic tax phobia entails not an addiction to spending but a chronic budget crisis in which borrowed money is used to make up differences between revenues and spending.

The Budget Process, Revenues, and Spending

In theory, California's budget must be balanced. In practice, this is more fiction than reality, although the state did amass substantial budget surpluses beginning in the late 1990s, flush from the stock market bubble and profitable (at least for a time) investment in the dot-com companies. As the stock market fell along with the value of these dot-coms, revenues for the state fell; unemployment increased, cutting personal income tax revenues; and a series of political changes placed added financial burdens on state governments to take over and fund programs previously managed by the federal government. State surpluses turned into enormous deficits in excess of $30 billion in 2002 and 2003 (and revenues declined by more than $21 billion), ushering in the gubernatorial recall in 2003.

The governor submits the budget proposal in January. That proposal then goes to the **Legislative Analyst's Office** for review and the LAO flags parts of the budget for further review by the legislature as they work toward approving the budget by the end of June and the start of the next fiscal year (July 1).

Table 9-1 California's Budget Anxieties: The Rise and Fall of Revenues and Unemployment

Year	Total state revenues ($)	Total unemployed (no.)	Unemployment rate (%)
1998	144,985,000,000	963,000	6.00
2000	172,481,000,000	836,000	4.90
2002	151,245,000,000	1,163,000	6.70
2004	229,289,000,000	1,080,000	6.20
2006	—	958,000	4.90

SOURCE: U.S. Census Bureau, *Statistical Abstracts*.
NOTE: — = not available.

Once sent to the legislature, the budget goes to the assembly's Ways and Means Committee and the senate's Budget and Fiscal Review Committee. The budget is then split into different bills and assigned to different committees for hearings, amendments, and the usual legislative proceedings. By mid-April, the multiple budget bills should go to the assembly and senate for votes, and differences in the approved bills get hashed out in the Conference Committee. A critical step along the way is the **May Revise,** in which the governor's office issues an update based on the latest numbers of how much money is coming in and how much is going out. The Revise may require parts of the budget to be reworked. As was true even in politically friendlier times, many disagreements and hang-ups slow down the budget process, and a lot of logrolling is needed in order to secure the needed two-thirds majority for approval (as an appropriation). In the final negotiations, California relies on the Big Five to do most of the heavy lifting: the governor, assembly Speaker, assembly minority leader, president pro tem of the senate, and the senate minority leader. Personality can figure heavily in this process, especially in an era of term limits, when the influence of leaders over party members has been reduced. Schwarzenegger has done much of his personal wheeling and dealing in the smoking tent erected outside the Capitol, where he smokes cigars and helps work out compromises between the party leaders.[3] Historically, compromises are not always easily reached and, since the 1980s, budgets have frequently been late. During George Deukmejian's term as governor the state had to issue IOUs to some state employees because the budget was so late that California ran out of money.

The budget for fiscal year 2005–2006 left California with a reserve of about $10.1 billion, the result of the 2004 special election organized by Schwarzenegger in which voters approved bond sales to pay off existing debts, effectively borrowing money to pay off borrowed money; they also approved a second proposition that created a so-called budgetary reserve fund. In principle, the reserve fund was to be used as a "rainy day fund" should the budget again spiral into huge deficits. That rainy day, however, has already come, and the reserve has been used in the budgets for 2006–2007 and 2007–2008.

In effect, it allows the governor's budget to conceal budget shortfalls by simply allowing that reserve fund to cover the difference between actual expected revenues and overall state spending. In 2006–2007, revenues for the state were about $95 billion but expenditures totaled about $102.1 billion, a deficit of about $7.1 billion; that difference was covered by the reserve fund, which was then reduced to $2.9 billion. In 2007–2008, the pattern was more or less repeated, with revenues scheduled to total about $102 billion and expenditures exceeding $103 billion (see table 9-2). The good news is that the reserve fund will probably not be entirely drained in the short term, but the bad news is that annual deficits are projected for the budgets running through 2009, so the gap between money coming in and more money going out will become something of a permanent fixture in the state budget process. Moreover, if there is any sudden change in the amounts of revenue coming in or amounts going out, there will not be much of a reserve or cushion to count on, and thus the state will be left in a kind of permanent budget crisis. Such is life living on a fault line.[4]

California ranks the tenth highest among the fifty states as regards the per capita tax burden. It has the fifth highest personal income tax, nineteenth highest sales tax, and thirty-fifth highest property tax, the legacy of Proposition 13. When calculating state and local taxes as a percentage of personal income (which is a better indicator of burden relative to how much money one earns), California ranks twentieth in the country.[5]

The 2007–2008 budget proposal estimates that about 44.8 percent of revenues will come from the personal income tax, about 27.3 percent from the sales tax, 8.4 percent from the corporate tax, 4.3 percent from motor vehicle fees, 2.8 percent from highway user fees, and the rest from a variety of taxes on insurance, tobacco, liquor, and so on (see table 9-3 for total amounts of these and other revenue sources for the last nine budget years).[6] Consistent with a system that benefits elite interests, the corporate tax burden has decreased in California while the personal income tax and sales tax have increased over time. But even though the upper income brackets pay more income tax, their share of the wealth continues to increase as nonwage income (mostly on investments) continues to widen the gap between the haves and the rest of California.[7]

As to spending, the 2006–2007 budget includes a proposed 40 percent for K–12 public education, about 29 percent for health and human services, 10.7 percent for higher education, and 9.7 percent for corrections and rehabilitation. Compared with previous post-recall budgets, the 2007–2008 edition includes a few interesting wrinkles. First, passage of a series of bonds to improve and renovate California's transportation infrastructure as well as money dedicated to water resources has allowed cuts in the budgets in these two areas. Rather than spend money from the general fund (essentially the treasury for the state), California will borrow the money instead. The largest cuts in spending are to be found in the categories of business, transportation, and housing (a reduction of 47.5 percent from the 2006–2007 budget) and

Table 9-2 General Fund Revenues for Fiscal Years 1999–2000 through 2007–2008 (dollars in thousands)

Category	Code	Source	1999–2000	2000–2001	2001–2002	2002–2003	2003–2004	2004–2005	2005–2006	2006–2007	2007–2008
Major revenue	1	Alcoholic beverages taxes and fees	282,165	288,451	292,627	290,564	312,826	314,252	318,276	320,800	324,500
	2	Corporation tax	6,638,762	6,899,302	5,333,025	6,803,559	7,019,216	8,670,065	10,316,467	10,311,000	10,816,000
	3	Cigarette tax	132,200	126,664	121,612	114,894	117,137	119,055	118,022	121,000	122,000
	4	Horse racing (pari-mutuel license fees)	5,955	4,382	3,296	2,037	2,429	2,655	2,422	2,335	2,335
	5	Estate, inheritance, and gift tax	928,148	934,708	915,627	647,372	397,848	213,036	3,786	0	0
	6	Insurance gross premium tax	1,299,777	1,496,556	1,595,846	1,879,784	2,114,980	2,232,955	2,202,327	2,220,000	2,354,000
	7	Trailer coach license (in-lieu) fees	28,422	26,337	15,372	15,592	18,678	21,586	24,892	25,357	25,844
	8	Motor vehicle license (in-lieu) fees	0	0	0	0	0	0	0	0	0
	9	Motor vehicle fuel tax (gasoline)	0	0	0	0	0	0	0	0	0
	10	Motor vehicle fuel tax (diesel)	0	0	0	0	0	0	0	0	0
	11	Motor vehicle registration	0	0	0	0	0	0	0	0	0
	12	Personal income tax	39,574,649	44,514,297	33,046,665	32,709,761	35,398,983	42,738,007	49,876,823	52,042,000	55,598,000
	13	Retail sales and use tax (realignment)	0	0	0	0	0	0	0	0	0
	14	Retail sales and use tax	21,137,297	21,276,843	21,355,315	22,415,138	23,847,329	25,758,635	27,580,979	27,775,000	29,347,000
	15	Telecommunications tax				0	0				
	16	Retail sales and use tax (fiscal recovery)							0	0	0	0
Major revenue total			70,027,375	75,667,540	62,679,385	64,878,701	70,229,426	80,070,246	90,443,994	92,817,492	98,589,679
Minor revenue	20	Trial court revenues	0	444	0	0	0	0	0	0	0
	21	Emergency telephone users surcharge	0	0	0	0	0	0	0	0	0
	22	California State University fees	0	0	0	0	0	0	0	0	0
	23	Income from pooled money investments	471,952	821,243	354,988	189,577	123,312	232,012	447,193	579,000	571,000
	24	Income from surplus money investments	4,948	4,494	4,131	37,075	5,919	4,791	4,021	4,910	4,910
	25	State lands royalties	11,912	13,438	15,131	78,470	113,763	174,919	295,573	242,523	270,723
	26	Abandoned property	197,744	133,785	287,848	257,533	669,319	657,759	334,206	369,657	329,983
	27	Settlements and judgments	515,051	392,611	75,771	5	4,011	5,068	87,969	22,322	15,001
	28	All other minor revenue	321,139	574,177	1,190,883	12,337,092	5,008,601	829,660	1,820,820	1,124,279	1,881,673
Minor revenue total			1,522,746	1,940,192	1,928,752	12,899,752	5,924,925	1,904,209	2,989,782	2,342,691	3,073,290
SCO adjustments	30	Adjustments to reconcile to controller	1,405	802	1,242	0	0	6,544	0	0	0
SCO adjustments total			1,405	802	1,242	0	0	6,544	0	0	0
Transfers and loans	29	Transfers and loans	379,032	−6,180,836	7,653,229	2,785,113	713,029	228,490	−6,630	−641,605	−385,509
Transfers and loans total			379,032	−6,180,836	7,653,229	2,785,113	713,029	228,490	−6,630	−641,605	−385,509
Grand total			71,930,558	71,427,698	72,262,608	80,563,566	76,867,380	82,209,489	93,427,146	94,518,578	101,277,460

SOURCE: California Legislative Analyst's Office, "General and Special Funds Revenues, 2007–08 Budget as Proposed (January 2007)," www.lao.ca.gov/sections/econ_fiscal/ Historical_Revenues.xls (accessed April 1, 2007).

NOTE: Revenues for 2007–2008 as proposed in January 2007. Note that this table shows general fund revenue, which unlike total revenue (see table 9-1) does not include several large revenue sources. Most research focuses on general revenue for comparative purposes.

Table 9-3 California Taxes: Where They Come From, What They Are, and Where They Go

State taxes	Current rate	Comments/description
Personal income	Marginal rates of 1% to 9.3%. Additional 1% surcharge on high incomes (7% AMT)	Married couples with gross incomes of $27,426 or less need not file. The top rate applies to married couples' taxable income in excess of $86,934. The surcharge is placed on taxable incomes of $1 million or more.
Sales and use	6.25%ª	Applies to final purchase price of tangible items, except for food and certain other items.
Corporation		
General corporations	8.84%ᵇ (6.65% AMT)	Applies to net income earned by corporations doing business in California.
Financial corporations	10.84% (6.65% AMT plus adjustment)	For financial corporations, a portion of the tax is in lieu of certain other taxes.
Alcohol and cigarette		Tax is collected from manufacturers or distributors. Equivalent taxes are collected on sale of other tobacco products.
Wine and beer	$0.20/gallon	
Sparkling wine	$0.30/gallon	
Spirits	$3.30/gallon	
Cigarettes	$0.87/pack	
Horse racing license fees	0.4% to 2%	Fees/taxes are levied on amounts wagered. Rate is dependent on type of racing and bet, and where the wager is placed.
Insurance	2.35%	Insurers are subject to the gross premiums tax in lieu of all other taxes except property taxes and vehicle license fees.
Property	1% (plus any rate necessary to cover voter-approved debt)	Tax is levied on assessed value (usually based on purchase price plus the value of improvements and a minimum annual inflation factor of 2%) of most real estate and various personal and business property.
Local sales and use	1% to 2.5%ᶜ	Collected with state sales and use tax. Revenues go to cities, counties, and special districts.
Vehicle license fee	0.65%ᵈ	Tax is applied to depreciated purchase price. It is collected by the state and distributed to cities and counties.
Other local	Varies by jurisdiction	Types of taxes and rates vary by jurisdiction. Includes utility users tax, business license tax, and transient occupancy tax.

SOURCE: Legislative Analyst's Office, "Cal Facts 2006: California's Economy and Budget in Perspective," www.lao.ca.gov/2006/cal_facts/2006_calfacts_state_local.htm (accessed March 22, 2007).
NOTE: AMT = alternative minimum tax.
a. Includes rates levied for state-local program realignment and local public safety, and repayment of deficit-financing bonds.
b. A 1.5 percent rate is levied on net income of Subchapter S corporations (a type of corporation which, because it has relatively few shareholders, is taxed as a partnership).
c. A portion of sales and use tax revenues formerly received by local governments (0.25 percent) is used for debt service on the state's deficit-financing bonds. Local governments are compensated through additional property taxes.
d. The state shifted additional property tax revenues to cities and counties beginning in 2004–2005 to compensate for the vehicle license fee rate reduction from 2 percent.

in resources/environmental protection (cut by 30.8 percent). Second, it includes a large increase—slightly over 33 percent—for the general operation of the government itself. Schwarzenegger campaigned on making government leaner in both 2003 and again in 2006, but his own budgets have contradicted these promises. Third, the governor has suggested selling off the California lottery system to a private company, thus giving California a quick injection of cash that it could use for other purposes. In the world of financial and budgetary addiction, this kind of a quick money fix is identical to what happens to third-world countries faced with having to make a loan payment but lacking the hard currency to do so. Under structural adjustment programs implemented by the International Monetary Fund, the country is encouraged to sell off state-run enterprises to raise the cash they need to service their debts. California's budgeting, in effect, is beginning to resemble that of countries in Latin America and all along the Pacific Rim.[8]

Budgetary Constraints: Micromanagement as an Antitax Strategy

Proposition 13 triggered a series of measures that has handcuffed both the governor's office and the legislature. Most of these changes were implemented through the initiative process and were financially supported by groups wanting to create a system that limited the taxing and spending responsibilities of government as much as possible. The propaganda and public relations techniques of campaigning have successfully convinced voters of California that "the people" need to micromanage the budget because "out of control" public officials are incapable of doing so and are unwilling to rein in their own behavior. Discretionary spending is no longer an option for California's legislature; these changes have eliminated discretion almost entirely.

The more important constraints placed on the budget process include:

- **Proposition 13 (1978).** The primary effect of Proposition 13 was on local governments, as discussed in Chapter 8.
- **Proposition 4 (1979).** Known as the Gann Initiative (from Paul Gann, of Jarvis-Gann fame), this proposition mandated that budget increases be proportional to rises in the Consumer Price Index (CPI). This mandate was modified in 1990 with Proposition 111, which relaxed the requirement with the acknowledgment that the cost of living in California was higher than the national average, so the California CPI was to be used instead.
- **Proposition 6 (1982).** Proposition 6 more or less eliminated the state inheritance tax, even though only the very wealthiest families were actually subject to its effects.
- **Proposition 98 (1988).** Proposition 98 required that 40 percent of the state's budget taken from the general fund be allocated to K-12 education plus the community college system. A provision allowed for temporary suspension of this measure in the event of an emergency. Such an

emergency was declared by Schwarzenegger in 2004–2005. Faced with a huge budget deficit, Schwarzenegger suspended the 40 percent allocation for a year with the promise that it would be restored in the next budget. It was not, leading to a showdown between the governor and the powerful teacher's union, the California Teachers Association.

- **Proposition 218 (1996).** This proposition requires voter approval for all local tax increases.

Other propositions in recent years have introduced the mechanism of earmarking funds for specific purposes, thus not allowing the government to shift spending around. Proposition 98 was the most dramatic earmark and made sure that the government would not shortchange schools. Others have included approval of the state lottery (1984) with funding going to education; a guarantee that 0.5 percent of the state sales tax revenue would go to local fire, police, and emergency services (1993); the earmarking of the sales tax from gasoline sales for transportation (2002); and an allocation of general fund money to before- and after-school programs (2002). This program has been suspended because of the continued budget crisis but is scheduled to be fully funded with an allocation of more than $550 million in 2007. Three other "ballot box budgeting" measures were approved in 2004, but a fourth, which would have raised a telephone tax to pay for an emergency care system, was defeated, largely under the weight of an opposition campaign funded by the phone companies.[9]

Although the intentions behind initiatives like Proposition 98 may be noble, their effects on assembling a budget have been nothing short of terrible. The good intentions have been used by special interests to mask what these initiatives are really about: limiting the ability of government to provide services to the people who elect them. It appears that even the power elite must place adequate checks on political power to make sure that the system does not malfunction and do more than it is supposed to do.

Gray Davis got most of the blame for the budget crisis of 2002 and 2003, but he was much more conservative with state finances than he was given credit for. He used the veto power frequently to keep spending down against the wishes of legislators from his own party, and although he was blamed for not telling the public about how dire the circumstances really were, both Davis and the legislative analyst Elizabeth Hill did sound repeated warnings that apparently no one wanted to hear. The broader context, however, suggests that although Davis should carry some of the blame, the political agenda of recent years, which has emphasized education reform and a war on crime, has created a need for expenditures when there is little to spend and few options available to change the formula.

In the 1960s California had been ranked one of the highest states in the nation for funding for education, but after that, education funding had steadily declined, in large measure because the composition of the school system changed from primarily baby boom white suburban children to mostly black and Latino urban ones. Control over school funding through property taxes was turned over to the state after the California Supreme Court's ruling in *Serrano v. Priest* (1971) that the differences in spending between rich school districts and poor violated the equal protection clause of the constitution. The impact on California schools was mixed, for although it helped lessen the funding disadvantages that students in poor areas had to deal with, it also moved the funding question to the state level, where the education budget had to compete for dollars against other state programs. Additionally, the financial advantages that schools in relatively well-to-do areas have over poorer neighborhoods remain a part of California's education system. Wealthier areas find ways of making sure that money gets funneled to their schools.

With educational funding in state hands, real cuts had to be made after passage of Proposition 13. Beginning in the 1980s with Proposition 98, some effort was made (with the strong support of teachers and its powerful union voice, CTA) to make sure that further cuts would be averted. But the real impetus for education reform came from a 1983 federal government report published on education that warned, "Our nation is at risk."[10] In a national setting, it set off a reform movement devoted almost exclusively to returning schools to the three Rs (reading, writing, and arithmetic) and to establishing an extensive system of standardized testing to make students, teachers, and parents more "accountable." In the 1990s both Pete Wilson and Gray Davis took up the charge and dedicated more resources to education reform, which became one of the main political issues of that decade. The huge investments in public education (including textbook purchases, reduced K–3 class sizes, and lots of standardized testing), however, could not be sustained, because the revenues were just not there. It could be done when there were surpluses to play with in 1999–2000, but that money went away and there was nowhere to go to get new flows of money. On the assumption that standardized tests have any significance, scores have improved somewhat since 2000, but reading scores rank among the lowest in the fifty states and math scores hover around the national average. As of 2002–2003, California ranked thirtieth in per capita spending at $7,244 per student (though it ranked eleventh in per capita income) and fiftieth in student-teacher ratio.[11] It does rank number one in teacher salaries, an increase in which was seen as a way to keep good teachers in the profession.

Schwarzenegger irritated teachers and the potent CTA by negotiating a temporary stop to Proposition 98 funding, then refusing to reinstate the funding in 2005–2006. When Schwarzenegger tried his special election attack on the tenure system and on unions, the teachers fought back with a vengeance. It may be all for naught. Latinos account for about 44 percent of the student population and Asian students another 9 percent; reading score improvements in a system in which more than half the students are either non–native speakers themselves or from non-native-speaking families will thus be incremental without more funding help. Special education programs are also extremely costly (because of the very low student-teacher ratio) and play an increasing role as more children are diagnosed with autism, a disorder that is taking on near-epidemic proportions in this country.[12]

Continuing funding problems for public education have been responsible for increases of fees and tuitions across the board for 3 million community college students, 400,000 California State University students, and 200,000 University of California students. The state system that once subsidized higher education has now moved much closer to a pay-as-you-go system, for which students (and presumably parents) have to foot the bill. In addition, cuts in funding for federal and state student loans and hence their availability add to the costs of a college degree.

The war on crime and the parallel war on drugs led to more mandatory sentences, including the "Three Strikes law" and the subsequent warehousing of prisoners. Although proponents extol the virtues of this new tough-on-crime attitude, it is costly to keep people locked up. Between 1982 and 2003, the prison population in California increased from 32,000 to 161,000,[13] and there are more prison guards working in the system now than there were prisoners back in 1982. There are other costs in fighting these wars as well, including those incurred by the increase in the police force, more equipment for it (what would Los Angeles be without the ubiquitous LAPD helicopter?), and more cases to prosecute.

The Disintegrating Federal System and Effects on the States

California's financial difficulties are part of a larger national pattern. The federal government is facing its own debt problem, fueled by deep tax cuts for the wealthy, massive military spending for the war in Iraq, and an absolute refusal to consider how the government will ultimately pay for everything. Instead, Congress has made cuts to social programs, has contemplated more cuts, and looks for other ways to make permanent the tax cuts that benefit the wealthiest segments of society. During the Clinton administration, economic advisers, Wall Street executives, and the Federal Reserve Board pushed the administration to cut the federal deficit and to pay down at least part of the national debt. With strong support from Republicans, funding for a series of social programs was reduced and the duties of administering these programs devolved back to the states. The change in "welfare" turned Aid to Families with Dependent Children (AFDC) into its current form of Temporary Assistance to Needy Families (TANF). Unlike AFDC, TANF limited the time that a family could stay on welfare and included welfare-to-work provisions intended to move people out of TANF and into the workforce. For state governments, the most important changes came in the administration and funding of TANF. States and not the federal government ran the program, and the funding was capped so that even if more people in

California might qualify for TANF, the total amount of money for the program would not change. Changes at the federal level effectively put the squeeze on state and local governments, as they had to take on the rising costs of administration and the potential costs of having more people in the welfare ranks. Responsibility shifts downward, or devolves, in government, and TANF placed more responsibility on individuals and families to deal with their own socioeconomic plight. This trend has deepened during the Bush administration, and there has been little interest in Washington in maintaining let alone creating new kinds of social programs to help people with few means to help themselves. As the cultural theorist Henry Giroux has observed, the unwillingness of the federal government to act as quickly as it should have after the devastation of Hurricane Katrina in Louisiana in 2005 may mark a new era of what he calls the "politics of disposability," in which people's lives no longer really matter.[14]

The devolution of power back to the states carries with it a large financial burden. Funding from the federal government typically gets reduced (as it did with TANF), and if the state wants to continue the program it must come up with a good portion of its own money. Unwilling to make deeper cuts in social programs, California maintained much of the funding when the federal money was cut, making its shortfalls of 2002–2003 even worse. Included in these programs was the expensive Medi-Cal program, designed to supplement the pitifully weak Medicare; Supplemental Security Income (SSI), meant to reinforce the limited scope of Social Security; First Five, which provides preschool intervention and health service referrals; and the current Healthy Families program, which offers low-cost medical and dental insurance for children and teenagers.[15]

The *Los Angeles Times*, on October 29, 2002, concluded that the "State Spent Its Way into Budget Crisis."[16] The spending for education, for fighting crime, and for providing a social safety net at a time when the federal government's commitment to provide the same diminished, was spent for all the right things. The problem is how to pay for it. In this state and in this country, the elite seem fairly determined to hang on to every cent they have and allow governmental responsibilities to be pulled back to a bare minimum. In the twentieth century, the promise of the welfare state was to give something back to society. The gap between owners and workers, haves and have-nots might not disappear, but at least the state offered some semblance of security and well-being that would keep society reasonably content and legitimize the authority of the state system providing these benefits. By the twenty-first century, this kind of system appeared to be in ruins. Ronald Reagan in the United States and Margaret Thatcher in Great Britain introduced the global system to the neoconservative (and often libertarian) notion that private economic interests are by definition superior to public interests served by governments. This, they maintained, was the natural order of things. Thatcher summed it up best: get used to it because, as she so coldly put it, "there is no alternative."

This worldview has prevailed. Governments step to the side and it is simply accepted that private interests, entrepreneurs, and corporations will do the job best. But can this kind of a system be maintained? If so, how? What will it mean for California, what will it mean for the United States, and what will it mean for the world? Those are the questions we turn to next.

Taking Stock

Governor Schwarzenegger had it wrong. Politicians are not "addicted to spending"; rather, the power elite is chronically addicted to its own wealth. Over the past three decades, since the passage of Proposition 13, any attempts to substantively raise taxes in order to provide, maintain, or enhance state services have been met with stiff political opposition and warnings of economic apocalypse. We all know the story because so many politicians tell it: the rich need their money because they will reinvest and we will all benefit from its trickle-down effects; the poor need to be more self-reliant and if government helps them, there will be no incentive to take matters into their own hands; middle-class families have a hard enough time making ends meet, so why burden them unfairly with more taxes? And yet, when it has come to the real needs of society, there appear to be some things that merit attention: improving the school system, repairing the famed freeway systems, doing something about crime, and providing at least some social services for those who have had their funding reduced dramatically by a federal government even more intent on spending money without worrying about who will pay for it all. But one can't have it both ways, and until there is a realization that one cannot have a government without spending some revenues, the crisis will continue. The governor, legislature, and voters of California thought they came up with a solution by borrowing money to pay off old debts and to help pay for needed upgrades to schools and roads and for new prisons to house an ever-growing prison population. But where will the money come from in the future if this same spend-but-don't-pay system remains in place? The mountain of debt begins with credit card debt, rises with the risks inherent in subprime lending, then grows to dizzying heights with state and local bond sales, and eventually, $9 trillion of debt compiled by the federal government. Something has to give.

QUESTIONS FOR DISCUSSION

1. Could the need for government services in California increase in the future? If so, how? When? How might government respond? Do you think it will respond?

2. Proposition 98 and its requirement that 40 percent of the budget go to K–12 plus community college education has placed constraints on how

the state must spend its money. But isn't there an up-side too? What are the benefits of Proposition 98 and do they outweigh the difficulties that it has created?

3. Critics of modern capitalism have pointed out that social programs provided by government can effectively buy off the most militant elements of society. As long as the government provides an array of essential services that most people can share and benefit from, there will be less willingness to rebel against that system. What happens when government starts cutting back on the kinds of services it provides? What happens when essential programs are eliminated completely? Will there be revolution, or will anybody even notice?

NOTES

1. Todd Wallack, "Governor's Workforce Is Growing Again—Despite His Talk of Curbing Spending, State Set to Add 11,000 Jobs over Two Years," *San Francisco Chronicle,* June 30, 2005.

2. Peter Schrag, *California: America's High-Stakes Experiment.* (Berkeley: University of California Press, 2006), 206–230.

3. Peter Nicholas, "The Private Side of His Governance," *Los Angeles Times,* April 3, 2006.

4. For all details pertaining to the budget, see the Legislative Analyst's Office Web site, www.lao.ca.gov. In particular, see "2007–2008: Overview of the Governor's Budget"; "Overview of the 2007–2008 May Revise"; "2006–2007: Overview of the Governor's Budget."

5. Public Policy Institute of California, "Just the Facts: California's Tax Burden," www.ppic.org/content/pubs/jtf/JTF_TaxBurdenJTF.pdf, January 2007 (accessed May 30, 2007); California Budget Project, Policy Points, "Who Pays Taxes in California?" www.cbp.org/pdfs/2006/0604_pp_whopaytaxes.pdf (accessed May 30, 2007).

6. Governor's Budget 2007–2008, "Proposed Budget Summary," www.ebudget .ca.gov/BudgetSummary/BSS/BSS.html. These figures should be compared with those of the Legislative Analyst's Office, above. Note, for instance, that these apply to the total revenues and not strictly to those coming from the general fund (accessed May 30, 2007).

7. According to the California Budget Program, more than 50 percent of general fund revenues come from personal income tax compared with 35.4 percent in 1980–1981. Corporate taxes, by contrast, have decreased from 14.6 percent of revenues in the general fund to 10.9 percent in the same year. See California Budget Project, Policy Points, "Who Pays Taxes in California?" www.cbp.org/pdfs/2006/0604_pp_whopaytaxes.pdf (accessed May 30, 2007).

8. Legislative Analyst's Office, "Overview of the 2007–2008 May Revise," www.lao.ca.gov/2007/may_revise/may_revise_051507.aspx (accessed May 30, 2007).

9. Schrag, *California: America's High-Stakes Experiment,* 136.

10. Peter Sacks, *Standardized Minds: The High Price of America's Testing Culture and What We Can Do to Change It* (Cambridge, Mass.: Perseus, 1999), 65–93.

11. See EdSource Online, "School Rankings 2003–2004," www.edsource.org/sch_rankings.cfm (accessed May 29, 2007).

12. While autism rates increase, there is considerable disagreement as to what is causing it and whether this constitutes an "epidemic" in classical medical terms. For one perspective, see Robert F. Kennedy Jr., "Deadly Immunity," *Rolling Stone*, www.rollingstone.com/politics/story/7395411/deadly_immunity, posted June 20, 2005 (accessed May 29, 2007).

13. Legislative Analyst's Office, "Cal Facts 2006," www.lao.ca.gov/2006/cal_facts/2006_calfacts_trends.htm#crimjust (accessed May 29, 2007).

14. Henry A. Giroux, *Stormy Weather: Katrina and the Politics of Disposability* (Boulder, Colo.: Paradigm Publishers, 2006).

15. Schrag, *California: America's High-Stakes Experiment*, 118–122; for a sense of what kinds of programs California funds, see also the Healthy Families Web site, www.healthyfamilies.ca.gov.

16. Jeffrey L. Rabin, "State Spent Its Way into Budget Crisis," *Los Angeles Times*, October 29, 2002.

Chapter 10 Conclusions
The Limits to Democracy and the Limits to Government

The Autopia attraction at Disneyland serves as the perfect metaphor for what democracy in California is all about. Visitors can steer their own vehicles, they can push on the gas pedal to make them go and take their foot off to make them stop, but their control over the miniature cars is limited by the center rail that keeps everybody on track and by the length of the ride. You can't go too fast because there is a regulator on the speed and you can't go too slowly or cars behind you will force you to keep stepping on the gas. And you always end up back at the station.

The power elite have managed to dominate California politics the same way. Elections are held; voters can choose candidates, with the emphasis always placed on the differences between the parties being represented; and a handful of issues frame the agenda of what is at stake—education, crime, taxes, immigration reform. But Californians always end up back at the station. It is a ride that the elite have built, after all, with guarantees that the spirit of Progressivism made it more democratic than ever, but it is a ride in which the rail of growth and development keeps everybody moving in exactly the same direction.

That is not to say that nothing has changed, because different elites do have differing views of what needs to be done, what services need to be provided, and what facilities need to be built. From the 1940s to the 1960s, for instance, California's infrastructure, including schools, freeways, and an ambitious aqueduct system (to supplement two others that Southern California had already outgrown) did provide tangible changes to the way that future Californians would lead their lives. Republican or Democrat, professional legislature or not, the logic of growth was the same. Never did anyone question the sanity of allowing the population to grow at such a fast pace, and no one really questioned how the landscape was being transformed. But the power elite at that time recognized that all of this came at a price: someone would have to pay for it. To that end, the costs of government and of building California were absorbed by the public. They were costs that even the elite was forced to share, because they, too, had to pay taxes, and their bills were inevitably going to be bigger.

The economic recession that hit America in the 1970s began to change the way this scenario worked. By the 1980s, government and the spending of money for "public good" became anathema. Growth and development, however, did not stop, nor did it even slow down. Growth machines invented new methods to reshape the land, now by directly funneling profits into the pockets of corporate retailers, land developers, and the construction industry. Development and redevelopment by private interests served the public good, for there was an insatiable demand for housing and for more big-box stores, where people could spend their money (credit or ATM?) on appliances assembled in Malaysia, clothes stitched in China, or shoes manufactured in a free-trade zone in Honduras. Taxes, we began to be told, are a waste. Keep money in the hands of consumers and the wheels of commerce can turn ever faster.

In October 2003, brush fires swept through large portions of San Diego County and the mountain resort areas of the San Bernardino Mountains. Although conservative talk-radio hosts were quick to blame Gray Davis and "the liberals" for inadequate responses to the fires, something else was revealed: in the haste to build and to grow, large areas of northern San Diego County had been developed in the last twenty years with minimal fire and emergency services. Fire departments could not respond because fire stations did not exist; San Diegans had to wait because the response had to come from elsewhere.[1] The federal government slowed the response down further as President Bush refused to declare a state of emergency, foreshadowing the kind of delayed response that was to be repeated on a much larger scale in New Orleans in 2005.[2]

This is the future, today. One can only try to imagine what would happen in the event of a greater catastrophe. California ranks dead last in per capita Homeland Security funding, despite two plots uncovered in which Los Angeles was known to be the target. Wyoming, Vermont, and North Dakota top the list.[3] We have seen some major earthquakes in the past decades, but the state, now home to more than 36 million people, has yet to experience a magnitude 8 earthquake. San Francisco 100 years ago was a much different place from what it is today. It is sad to think that a devastating quake would, in the end, only rev up the growth machine to a scale not yet imagined.

California in a Global Context

California's economic present and future are tied inextricably to a global economy. The San Pedro/Long Beach port complex, the Alameda Corridor rail and truck system that supports it, and Los Angeles International Airport serve as the major gateway for trade with the Pacific Rim.[4] This trade, however, relies on an extremely fragile relationship between American consumers, who purchase huge amounts of goods produced in China, with much of the money that China earns being circulated back to the United States by way of treasury bond and security purchases. With no sense of exaggeration, China gives the United States back money so that it can buy more. All the while, outsourcing becomes more prevalent in this country as jobs are moved overseas, where labor costs are substantially lower. Manufacturing was the first to go; call centers offering customer service moved to the American Midwest and are now relocating to India; engineering, various research and development jobs, and biomedicine are next. Not every job can be outsourced, of course. There will always be a need for truck drivers or nurses or teachers in the classroom, but the extent to which even supposedly safe jobs can be outsourced is surprising. Even as the bulk of imported goods from the Pacific Rim flow through the enormous container facility in the dual ports of Los Angeles and Long Beach, some of that cargo has been recently diverted to Mexico where it is loaded off (at lower cost) and the goods then transported to the American Midwest via rail and truck, with plans under way to expand use of this transportation corridor in the future.[5]

Other employment opportunities leave the state but not the country, as growth machines in other states offer better deals to get companies to move to their communities. Each time this occurs, some jobs may be gained but little attention is paid to the quality of jobs and what kinds of wages will be earned. Moreover, in seeking to attract business, these same growth machines may be undercutting their own tax base, making it harder to pay for essential state and local services. Tourism is often looked at as a "growth industry" and has its advantages in that it is seen as a relatively clean way of developing land use to cater to visitors who will visit local attractions, stay in hotels, dine in restaurants, and, naturally, buy lots of useless souvenirs. As the historian Hal Rothman points out, however, even tourism involves a kind of "devil's bargain" as the local community is changed by the presence of visitors, and economic concessions to a tourist trade now dominated by large transnational corporations are inevitable.[6]

But the people keep coming to California, hoping to get that toehold, as Kevin Starr puts it. Rather than finding a dream or expecting to build a utopia, California today is a place for survival. The likelihood of survival among the elites is assuredly higher than for the rest of us, so we are satisfied with just being given a chance. California is divided as the world is divided; a fault line separates "them" from "us."

The philosophers Gilles Deleuze and Félix Guattari describe a society split by the economic system that makes us who we are. Capitalism, they argue, decodes flows and creates a **deterritorialization** of the social being.[7] Using Freudian terminology, they argue that it creates a "schizophrenic accumulation of energy or charge" that runs through the entirety of the capitalist system. This can be seen in California as it can throughout the global system today. On the one hand, capital and capitalism is free to roam the earth. Financial flows, investment, and currency itself flows instantaneously through a global information network.[8] The products of capitalism, the things we wear, the things we eat and drink, the stuff we put in the gas tank, similarly move with relative ease through this deterritorialized space. Indeed, jobs can move, as we have seen. But a contradiction enters here, for although capitalism can be (and must be) mobile, the people—the workers, human capital—cannot be mobile. The dream of wealth is attainable only through the goods that this market system produces (goods that may not ever be attained by most people on this planet), but the ability to move in this system is restricted by a system of governments. Try to cross a border and guards will soon appear with snarling German shepherds and weapons drawn. Therein lies schizophrenia: a desire to move, to have, to be; but that desire inevitably will go unfulfilled.

Late in 2003 a Pentagon document was leaked to the press revealing that the military was preparing for an international crisis brought about by global warming and dramatic climate change. The document made front-page headlines in Europe but was ignored by the mainstream American media. Even as the Bush administration continued to insist that the scientific community was still not sure that global warming was even happening, the Pentagon was describing a world in which rising sea levels, extreme weather phenomena, and shifts in heating and cooling patterns will create chaos. The goal, they concluded, was to build a security system around the United States to keep those on the outside from coming in and taking a share of the increasingly scarce resources that the United States would have to offer.[9]

The controversy over changes in immigration law in 2006 needs to be seen in this light. This is the first serious step in constructing a "Fortress America," just as for years, a "Fortress Europe" has aimed to keep the outsiders out and the insiders in. It is not clear, however, that this American fortress is capable of withstanding the changes to come. Tens of millions of people in the urban areas of Southern California, Arizona, and Nevada depend on fresh water that comes from remote sources, namely, the Rocky Mountains and the Sierra Nevadas. A prolonged drought has already limited the water supplied by the Colorado River, and what happens if climate change limits the supply permanently? There are technological fixes such as desalination to consider, but these kinds of infrastructural changes do not appear overnight. Similarly, it is possible to imagine changes that would rapidly reduce the amount of carbon emissions actually going into the atmosphere, but no one seriously wants to deal with them. As a typical member of the elite power structure, Arnold Schwarzenegger epitomizes a noncommitment to making much of a change at all. While voicing support for limiting greenhouse gas emissions, he is careful to note, "We don't want to go after business and make business leave the state."[10] The environment will permanently be changed, but God forbid that growth be inconvenienced.

In a recent book, James Kunstler argues that the world is headed toward a **long emergency** brought on by the convergence of three catastrophic changes: the end of an oil-based economy, the collapse of nature brought on by global warming, and a total disintegration of the global economic system.[11] There is a lot to think about here, for we may already be in the long emergency. What is both shocking and troubling is that so few are willing to acknowledge the problems we now confront. The power elite remains, as always, concerned with where money can be made and how the economy can continue to grow, while the rest of society remains unaware, obsessing again over who will be the next "American Idol" or which young actress is the latest to check into rehab.

A Final Note of Optimism

The textbook ending, naturally, is to exhort students to get involved in politics, to find out more about their legislators, to take action by letting them know what needs to be done, yadda, yadda, yadda. These are but useless and burned out clichés. In order to capture the attention of those in power, people must experiment with different approaches and develop new tactics. Firing off an angry letter to one's elected assemblyperson has not had any discernible impact on California politics for the last 150 years, and that is not likely to change any time soon. The history of California as recorded by Carey McWilliams or Mike Davis and experienced by the Wobblies or the students on the Berkeley campus leads to the same conclusion: direct, participatory action is the only way to break the status quo.

Analyzing the power elite fifty years ago, C. Wright Mills ends with the observation that elitism breeds immorality.[12] Those in power do not see the immorality in which they are immersed. Mills's assessment then could not be any truer today. But it should also be noted that elite power breeds arrogance. Those in power are so arrogant that they don't see it for what it is. They self-confidently refuse to believe that it could be any other way, creating a blind spot when it comes to defining their place in the political and economic order of things. The 1960s are a recent example of how the elite may not recognize how quickly and unexpectedly that power may come to be challenged. The image of the American middle-class dream—life in the suburbs, shiny car in the driveway, new appliances in the kitchen—concealed a growing discontent in American society. Although the United States was at the pinnacle of economic and political power in the world system, something was not right, and the people recognized it well before those in power did. They can't see it because they judge the strength of the system by how well they, that is, the elite, are doing. They ignore who is not benefiting and who is being pushed aside: that is their blind spot. And it creates an opening, a possibility for democracy to work.

It is that blind spot that must give hope.

Taking Stock

It has always been about looking ahead, believing that economic growth and development is a necessary part of California's future. But are there not limits to this growth? How long can this expansion continue, and do we want to live in a state where the population may be twice the size that it is today? We may never get the opportunity to answer these questions. Climate change may alter the picture completely, not only in regard to coastal living in an era when sea levels are expected to rise, but most certainly in regard to reducing snow packs that Californians must rely on for freshwater supplies. This may be a completely different world that we are entering, and what scientists expect will happen according to reports issued by the United Nations Intergovernmental Panel on Climate Change (available at www.ipcc.ch) is frightening. As suggested here, the power elite are in large measure responsible for getting us to this situation, and one can only hope that the rest of society recognizes what is at stake and pushes hard for changes that need to occur, politically, economically, and even culturally. The world as defined by its people has to change because the natural world is already changing.

QUESTIONS FOR DISCUSSION

1. Gasoline prices in California have been above $3 per gallon fairly consistently since 2005. How high do gas prices have to go before people start driving less? What would happen to California if crude oil really does run out in the next 20–25 years, as some models predict?

2. How "schizophrenic" do you feel in the current capitalist system? Consider this: are there material things that you want to have but also know that you probably cannot have them because they are too expensive? How does this make you feel?

3. Political activism in the 1960s helped support the civil rights movement, created resistance to the Vietnam War, and led many to question the values embedded in a consumer-oriented capitalist society. San Francisco, Oakland, and Berkeley were centers of activity at that time. Can the 1960s be repeated today? Where?

NOTES

1. Mike Davis, "California Burning," *Nation*, November 24, 2003.
2. Jim Miller, "Afterword: Out of the Ashes of the Old?" in *Under the Perfect Sun: The San Diego Tourists Never See*, by Mike Davis, Kelly Mayhew, and Jim Miller (New York: New Press, 2003), 361–373.
3. See Department of Homeland Security, FY 2006 HSGP Allocations, www.dhs. gov/xlibrary/assets/grants_st-local_fy06.pdf (accessed May 30, 2007). Although the total figures of resources allocated to California are impressive, the per capita allocation gives decided advantages to less populous states.
4. Stephen P. Erie, *Globalizing L.A.: Trade, Infrastructure, and Regional Development* (Stanford: Stanford University Press, 2004).
5. Outsourcing may involve so-called "creative" jobs too. See Richard Florida, *The Flight of the Creative Class: The New Global Competition for Talent* (repr., New York: Collins, 2007); on the outsourcing of transportation see Richard D, Vogel, "The NAFTA Corridors: Offshoring U.S. Transportation Jobs to Mexico," *Monthly Review* 57 (February 2006): 9.

6. Hal Rothman, *Devil's Bargains: Tourism in the Twentieth-Century American West* (Lawrence: University Press of Kansas, 1998).
7. Gilles Deleuze and Félix Guattari, *Anti-Oedipus: Capitalism and Schizophrenia* (Minneapolis: University of Minnesota Press, 1983), 34.
8. Ankie Hoogvelt, *Globalization and the Postcolonial World: The New Political Economy of Development* (Baltimore: Johns Hopkins University Press, 2001).
9. Mark Townsend and Paul Harris, "Now the Pentagon Tells Bush: Climate Change will Destroy Us," *Observer/UK*, February 22, 2004, available at CommonDreams.org, www.commondreams.org (accessed May 30, 2007).
10. Marc Lifsher, "Gov. Calls for Curbs on Emissions," *Los Angeles Times*, April 12, 2006.
11. James Howard Kunstler, *The Long Emergency: Surviving the End of Oil, Climate Change, and Other Converging Catastrophes* (New York: Grove Press, 2005).
12. C. Wright Mills, *The Power Elite* (New York: Oxford University Press, 1956), 343–361.

For Further Research

Books and Articles

CALIFORNIA POLITICS AND SOCIAL HISTORY

Arax, Mark, and Rick Wartzman. *The King of California*. New York: Public Affairs, 2003.

Baldassare, Mark. *California in the New Millennium*. Berkeley. University of California Press, 2000.

Banham, Reyner. *Los Angeles: The Architecture of Four Ecologies*. New York: Harper and Row, 1971.

Blitz, Michael, and Louise Krasniewicz. *Why Arnold Matters: The Rise of a Cultural Icon*. New York: Basic Books, 2004.

Brechin, Gray. *Imperial San Francisco*. Berkeley: University of California Press, 2001.

Chacón, Justin Akers, and Mike Davis. *No One Is Illegal*. Chicago: Haymarket Books, 2006.

Chan, Sucheng, and Spencer Olin. *Major Problems in California History*. New York: Houghton Mifflin, 1997.

Davis, Mike. *City of Quartz*. New York: Verso, 1991.

———. *Dead Cities*. New York: New Press, 2002.

———. *Ecology of Fear*. New York: Vintage, 1998.

Davis, Mike, Kelly Mayhew, and Jim Miller. *Under the Perfect Sun*. New York: New Press, 2003.

Deverell, William, and Tom Sitton, eds. *California Progressivism Revisited*. Berkeley: University of California Press, 1994.

Didion, Joan. *Where I Was From*. New York: Knopf, 2003.

Gerston, Larry N., and Terry Christensen. *Recall! California's Political Earthquake*. Armonk, N.Y.: M. E. Sharpe, 2004.

Henderson, George. *California and the Fictions of Capital*. Philadelphia: Temple University Press, 1998.

Hundley, Norris, Jr. *The Great Thirst*. Berkeley: University of California Press, 1992.

Indiana, Gary. *Schwarzenegger Syndrome: Politics and Celebrity in the Age of Contempt*. New York: New Press, 2005.

Isenberg, Andrew C. *Mining California*. New York: Hill and Wang, 2001.

Kahrl, William. *Water and Power*. Berkeley: University of California Press, 1982.

May, Kirse Granat. *Golden State, Golden Youth*. Chapel Hill: University of North Carolina Press, 2002.

McWilliams, Carey. *California: The Great Exception*. Berkeley: University of California Press, 1999. First published 1949.

Mitchell, Don. *The Lie of the Land*. Minneapolis: University of Minnesota Press, 1996.

Mowry, George E. *The California Progressives*. New York: Quadrangle, 1976. First published 1951.

Orsi, Richard. *Sunset Limited*. Berkeley: University of California Press, 2005.

Parson, Don. *Making a Better World*. Minneapolis: University of Minneapolis Press, 2005.

Pincetl, Stephanie S. *Transforming California*. Baltimore: Johns Hopkins University Press, 1999.

Rawls, James J., and Walton Bean. *California: An Interpretive History*. New York: McGraw-Hill, 2002.

Schrag, Peter. *California: America's High-Stakes Experiment*. Berkeley: University of California Press, 2006.

Starr, Kevin. *Americans and the California Dream*. New York: Oxford University Press, 1973.

———. *California: A History*. New York: Modern Library, 2005.

———. *Coast of Dreams*. New York: Knopf, 2004.

———. *The Dream Endures*. New York: Oxford University Press, 1997.

———. *Embattled Dreams*. New York: Oxford University Press, 2002.

———. *Endangered Dreams*. New York, Oxford University Press, 1996.

———. *Inventing the Dream*. New York: Oxford University Press, 1985.

———. *Material Dreams*. New York: Oxford University Press, 1990.

Stewart, Dean, and Jeannine Gendar, eds. *Fool's Paradise: A Carey McWilliams Reader*. Berkeley: Santa Clara University/Heyday Books, 2001.

Walker, Richard A. *The Conquest of Bread*. New York: New Press, 2004.

AMERICAN POLITICS AND SOCIAL HISTORY

Boggs, Carl. *The End of Politics*. New York: Guilford, 2000.

Bonner, William, and Addison Wiggin. *Empire of Debt*. Hoboken, N.J.: Wiley, 2006.

Chomsky, Noam. *Profit over People*. New York: Seven Stories Press, 1999.

Collins, Chuck, with Felice Yeskel. *Economic Apartheid in America*. Rev. ed. New York: New Press, 2005.

Domhoff, G. William. *Who Rules America?* 5th ed. New York: McGraw-Hill, 2005.

Duncan, Richard. *The Dollar Crisis*. Singapore: Wiley, 2005.

Ehrenreich, Barbara. *Nickel and Dimed: On (Not) Getting By in America*. New York: Holt, 2002.

Kivel, Paul. *You Call This a Democracy?* New York: Apex, 2004.

Limerick, Patricia Nelson. *The Legacy of Conquest.* New York: Norton, 1987.

McChesney, Robert. *The Problem of the Media: U.S. Communication Politics in the Twenty-First Century.* New York: Monthly Review Press, 2004.

McGerr, Michael. *A Fierce Discontent.* New York: Oxford University Press, 2003.

Mills, C. Wright. *The Power Elite.* New York: Oxford University Press, 1956.

Parenti, Michael. *Democracy for the Few.* 7th ed. New York: Wadsworth, 2001.

Perelman, Michael. *Railroading Economics.* New York: Monthly Review Press, 2006.

Phillips, Kevin. *Wealth and Democracy.* New York: Broadway Books, 2002.

Pollin, Robert. *Contours of Descent.* New York: Verso, 2005.

Reisner, Marc. *Cadillac Desert.* New York: Penguin, 1987.

Schumpeter, Joseph A. *Capitalism, Socialism and Democracy.* New York: Harper Perennial, 1976.

Slotkin, Richard. *Gunfighter Nation.* New York: Atheneum, 1992.

Turner, Frederick Jackson. *The Frontier in American History.* New York: Holt, 1926. First published 1921.

White, Richard. *"It's Your Misfortune and None of My Own": A New History of the American West.* Norman: University of Oklahoma Press, 1991.

Wolff, Edward N. *Top Heavy.* Updated ed. New York: New Press, 2002.

Worster, Donald. *Rivers of Empire.* New York: Oxford University Press, 1985.

SOCIAL CRITICISM AND THEORY

Baudrillard, Jean. *The Perfect Crime.* New York: Verso, 1996.

Davis, Mike. *Planet of Slums.* New York: Verso, 2006.

Deleuze, Gilles, and Felix Guattari. *Anti-Oedipus.* Minneapolis: University of Minnesota, 1983.

Easton, David. *A Framework for Political Analysis.* Chicago: University of Chicago Press, 1979. First published 1965.

Foucault, Michel. *Power/Knowledge.* New York: Pantheon, 1980.

Giroux, Henry A. *Stormy Weather.* Boulder: Paradigm, 2006.

Hoogvelt, Ankie. *Globalization and the Postcolonial World.* Baltimore: Johns Hopkins University Press, 2001.

Kunstler, James Howard. *The Long Emergency: Surviving the End of Oil, Climate Change, and Other Converging Catastrophes.* New York: Grove Press, 2005.

Lasswell, Harold. *Who Gets What, When, How.* New York: P. Smith, 1950. First published 1936.

Logan, John, and Harvey Molotch. *Urban Fortunes.* Berkeley: University of California Press, 1987.

Marcuse, Herbert. *One-Dimensional Man.* Boston: Beacon Press, 1964.

Online Resources

FOR CALIFORNIA GOVERNMENT

California Budget Project: www.cbp.org. An independent organization focusing on economic and policy analysis and targeting the well-being of low- and middle-income Californians.

California Courts: www.courtinfo.ca.gov. The Web site for the judicial branch of California with data and other information related to the judiciary.

Department of Finance: www.dof.ca.gov. Web site for the chief fiscal policy adviser to the governor.

Fair Political Practices Commission: www.fppc.ca.gov. The Web site for the commission, a bipartisan, independent group that administers and enforces California's campaign finance and lobbying rules.

Legislative Analyst's Office: www.lao.ca.gov. The home page of the nonpartisan agency that advises and oversees fiscal and other policy for the state. The LAO is meant to be the "eyes and ears" of the legislature, and the Web site contains historical and current data on the budget.

Legislative Counsel's Official California Legislative Information: www.leginfo.ca.gov. The official Web site for information on California's legislature, including information about current bills, members, and a roster of daily events.

Public Policy Institute of California: www.ppic.org. Extensive collection of original research related to all aspects of California politics and economy.

Secretary of State: www.ss.ca.gov. Provides information on elections past, present, and future, including filing data pertaining to campaign contributions in state elections.

The State of California Web site: www.ca.gov. The gateway to online resources dealing with all three branches of government.

POLITICAL COMMENTARY, ISSUE ADVOCACY, AND OPINION

Arnold Watch: www.arnoldwatch.org. The site's own description sums it up best: "Watching the hidden hand of special interests in the Schwarzenegger Administration." Some of it is pretty funny, too.

California Political Daily: www.calpday.com. Daily summary of important California news and commentary.

California Redevelopment Association: www.calredevelop.org. The Web site for a professional organization representing redevelopment agencies in California. Redevelopment from the viewpoint of those who do it.

Calitics: www.calitics.com. Daily blog with a decidedly progressive, left-wing perspective with excellent links to other useful California-related media sites.

CQPolitics: www.cqpolitics.com/california. Postings of political news, focused primarily on California representatives in Congress. CQPolitics has postings for other states, too.

Grist: Environmental News and Commentary: http://gristmill.grist.org. A nonprofit resource for environmental journalism that is self-described as "gloom and doom with a sense of humor."

Rough and Tumble: www.rtumble.com. Daily summary of news articles and commentary related to California politics.

They Rule: www.theyrule.net. An Internet site with searchable data showing how corporations are actually interlocked through their boards of directors. The names are not always entirely updated, but the picture of interlocks remains clear just the same: this *is* the power elite.

DATA RESOURCES

Center for Responsive Politics: www.opensecrets.org. Tracks money in politics at both federal and state levels, including data broken down by industries and interest groups; also provides an accounting of money in PACs and 527s.

Data Place: www.dataplace.org/. A data repository sponsored by the Fannie Mae Foundation with good state and local data and excellent maps and graphs.

National Conference of State Legislatures: www.ncsl.org. A clearinghouse for data and information on state legislatures.

National Institute on Money in State Politics: www.followthemoney.org. A variety of searchable databases investigating the role of money in state politics.

UC Data: http://ucdata.berkeley.edu:7101/. University of California at Berkeley's principal archive of computerized social science and health statistics information, including a wealth of data on California (Field Poll Press releases and other demographic data).

U.S. Census Bureau: www.census.gov. Census data and information from the U.S. decennial and other censuses. See especially the Statistical Abstracts for state-related information.

Glossary

astroturf lobby groups. Lobbying groups that appear to be real grassroots community political movements but in fact are organized and funded by larger, often corporate interest groups. (Chapter 5.)

author system. A system by which a bill in the legislature is cared for by its author, who shepherds it through the process. This is one of the procedural differences between how the California legislature and the U.S. Congress works. (Chapter 5.)

bracero system. A program created during World War II by the federal government that brought contracted temporary farmworkers from Mexico to work California fields. The system ended in 1962. (Chapter 3.)

California Land Act (1851). An act that required proof of ownership of the rancho properties. Used as a means of taking control of property away from the californios once California became a state. (Chapter 3.)

californio. A member of the landed class that rose to prominence while California was still under Mexican rule prior to statehood. Although californios themselves were often of mixed ethnic or racial background, they claimed a Europeanized ethnic superiority to the indigenous native populations around them. (Chapter 3.)

central place theory. A theory in the field of geography that argues for a logical distribution of market centers based on size and market opportunities. (Chapter 1.)

charter cities. A type of governmental organization for cities that gives them greater flexibility and a semblance of home rule not afforded under general law. (Chapter 8.)

charter counties. Counties that are allowed to organize under their own rules and thus have, in principle, more flexibility and control over how they govern. (Chapter 8.)

citizen politicians. Politicians who try to finance their own way into political office by spending enormous amounts of personal wealth to bypass the traditional route of working their way up the party organizational ladder and moving from "lower" elected positions to more prominent statewide positions. (Chapter 4.)

contract lobbying. Lobbying done on a temporary, contractual basis, to argue any position that the client needs. Contract lobbying firms, in effect, offer "hired guns" to lobby. (Chapter 5.)

Court of Appeal. The Court of Appeal is divided into six districts and hears appeals from superior courts. Panels of three justices hear cases in which the two sides present oral arguments and file briefs. Courts of appeal may remand the case, order a new trial, or dismiss the charges. (Chapter 7.)

deterritorialization. A term coined by the philosophers Gilles Deleuze and Félix Guattari, since used by others as well. Using Freudian terminology, they argue that capitalism creates a "schizophrenic accumulation of energy or charge" that runs through the entirety of the socioeconomic system, because capital and the goods that it produces may flow freely across geographical space but people—workers in the system—are still territorially bound and their movements limited by a political system of states, borders, passports, and work permits. Capitalism is deterritorialized but people are not. (Chapter 10.)

edge cities. Developments that have taken place in areas seemingly too far from traditional central business districts but that have been made possible by new commuting patterns. Edge cities provide all the amenities of the central business district so that people may not have to commute to the central city. Rather, they stay in the edge city or commute within the suburban edge. (Chapter 3.)

elite politics. Rule by the wealthy and influential, regardless of how "democratic" a system may seem to be; a plutocracy: rule by and for the rich. (Introduction.)

fiscalization of land use. The process by which economic growth is promoted by encouraging the (often subsidized) transfer of land to private interests in order to get tax revenues that increased due to reassessments of property based on changes in ownership and land use. (Chapter 3.)

general law cities. A type of city that is organized under state law, usually following a council-manager form with an elected city council and an appointed city manager who manages the day-to-day operations of city government. (Chapter 8.)

general law counties. A type of county that consists of an elected (but nonpartisan) five-member board of supervisors serving four-year terms, plus a series of other elected county officials, including the sheriff, district attorney, tax collector, coroner, county clerk, and others. (Chapter 8.)

gerrymandering. Districts clearly drawn with the intent of pressing partisan advantage at the expense of other considerations. Usually a pejorative term used to describe reapportionment or redistricting. (Chapter 4.)

great exception. As Carey McWilliams notes, California became the great exception, because everything that capitalism required had to come in from outside sources, bypassing settlement of the rest of the West and making California ready immediately for statehood. (Chapter 1.)

growth coalitions. Those in the community who support the idea of development as put forth by the growth machines. (Chapter 1.)

growth machines. Made up of those who control the land and its resources (often corporations or wealthy entrepreneurs), supported by local governments and a host of bureaucracies that bring together both private and public interests at local, state, and national levels and push for the constant development and redevelopment of land as a means of promoting economic growth. Growth machines follow a logic of growth that says that all economic expansion is, by definition, good and therefore must be supported. (Introduction.)

hard money contributions. Money directly contributed by individuals and organizations that is regulated primarily under the Federal Election Campaign Act (FECA) of 1971. (Chapter 4.)

initiative. Measures to be approved or rejected by voters, such as new laws or constitutional amendments, placed on the ballot by citizens who have collected a sufficient number of signatures. In California, the legislature may later amend the initiative, but amendments are also subject to voter approval unless designated otherwise. The initiative is pure direct democracy, for it allows voters to make law when elected officials are

unwilling or unable to take action. (Chapter 4.)

interlocks. A political and economic system wherein the same people sit on many different boards of directors at the same time such that everybody in the power elite works together to make sure that the same corporate logic can be maintained across the privatized system. (Chapter 2.)

internment camps. Camps to which Japanese Americans were sent by executive order during World War II. (Chapter 3.)

labor movement. The struggle for workers' rights, which were fought for by unions without significant political support. Those in the labor movement relied on public protest and street demonstration because they lacked other venues to be heard. The power elite relied on police action and use of force to suppress the labor movement in California, especially during the 1910s through the 1930s. (Chapter 3.)

Legislative Analyst's Office (LAO). A nonpartisan bureau within California's government that has the task (among other budgetary responsibilities) of reviewing the governor's budget and flagging portions for further review by the legislature. (Chapter 9.)

Local Agency Formation Commission (LAFCO). A commission formed to oversee the incorporation of cities. (Chapter 9.)

long emergency. The hypothesis that the world is headed toward a time of crisis brought on by the end of an oil-based economy, environmental collapse brought on by global warming, and a total disintegration of the global economic system. (Chapter 10.)

Malpractice Injury and Compensation Reform Act (MICRA). Passed in 1975, limits pain and suffering damages

to $250,000 and places limits on lawyers' fees. (Chapter 7.)

May Revise. Part of the budget review process in which the governor's office issues the latest numbers of how much money is coming in and how much is going out; this update may require parts of the budget to be reworked. (Chapter 9.)

military-industrial complex. An economic relationship describing the close connection between industries dedicated to the making of armaments (and other military hardware) and the political decision making process that supports these industries. President Dwight Eisenhower warned of the growing power of the military-industrial complex in 1961, but its power has largely expanded since, despite Eisenhower's apprehension. (Chapter 3.)

nonpartisan independent bureaus. Politically independent bureaus that support the work of the legislature. (Chapter 5.)

party affiliation. Citizens' identification with a particular political party. (Chapter 4.)

plural executive system. A system whereby statewide executive officeholders are elected separately by the voters rather than being appointed by the governor. The system is intended to increase the accountability of officials and dilute executive power. (Chapter 6.)

Political Reform Act. Passed in 1974, an attempt to regulate campaign financing. The act established rules for public disclosure of all donors and campaign expenditures. (Chapter 4.)

power elite. C. Wright Mills's conceptualization of the American political system dominated by an economic ruling class but supported by political and cultural leaders who reinforce a system in which power is concentrated in the hands of the few; *see* elite politics.

private government. The decision-making process within the corporate world that stands outside public accountability. (Chapter 2.)

professional legislature. The California legislature was professionalized in 1966, when legislating was made a full-time job that carried a full-time salary. (Chapter 5.)

Progressive movement. A political movement begun during the Progressive era that ran from about 1910 to 1930, directed primarily toward breaking the power of the railroad trusts by calling for political reforms, including the introduction of primary elections, nonpartisan offices, and avenues for direct democracy. (Chapter 3.)

Proposition 4 (1979). Mandated that budget increases be proportional to rises in the consumer price index (CPI). In 1990 Proposition 111 relaxed the requirement, acknowledging that the cost of living in California was higher than the national average, so the California CPI was to be used instead. (Chapter 9.)

Proposition 6 (1982). More or less eliminated the state inheritance tax, even though only the very wealthiest families were actually subject to its effects. (Chapter 9.)

Proposition 13 (1978). An initiative passed by California voters in 1978, fixing the property tax at 1 percent of the assessed value and limiting increases in the property tax to no more than 2 percent per year. Properties are not reassessed until the property is developed or changes hands. Proposition 13 took property tax collection away from local governments and put it under state authority. Although limited to property tax assessments, the antitax message delivered by Proposition 13 has had a lasting effect on all aspects of California's budget process. (Chapter 8.)

Proposition 34 (2000). Establishes hard limits on contributions to individual campaigns as well as to political action committees (PACs) in California. (Chapter 4.)

Proposition 64 (2004). Initiative that did away with the possibility of class action suits brought against companies engaged in unfair business practices. (Chapter 7.)

Proposition 98 (1988). Required that 40 percent of the state's budget taken from the general fund be allocated to K–12 education plus the community college system. The 2004–2005 budget, however, took advantage of a provision in the proposition that allowed for temporary suspension of this measure in the event of emergency. (Chapter 9.)

Proposition 218 (1996). A measure that requires voter approval for all local tax increases. (Chapter 9.)

racial profiling. A type of policing that is based upon typification (racial type, or "profile") rather than on the actual behavior of an individual; one's race or ethnicity becomes a determinant in raising suspicion. (Chapter 7.)

rancho system. Large land grants given to a handful of settlers who then dominated California's early economic and political development. (Chapter 3.)

reapportionment. The drawing of new boundaries for congressional and state legislative districts, usually following a decennial census; also referred to as redistricting or, in a more negative sense, gerrymandering. (Chapter 4.)

recall. A mechanism of direct democracy that allows citizens to collect signatures sufficient to allow a vote on the ouster of an incumbent politician prior to the next regularly scheduled election. (Chapter 4.)

redevelopment agencies. Local government agencies with considerable power over making planning decisions in urban areas and subject to almost no direct oversight. (Chapter 8.)

referendum. A form of direct democracy that allows the electorate to either accept or reject a law passed by the legislature. There are two types of referenda. A compulsory referendum is placed on the ballot when the legislature approves constitutional amendments or the issuance of most bonds. A petition referendum can be thought of as a recall of a law already passed by the legislature. (Chapter 4.)

soft money. Campaign contributions that are not regulated and may be made in unlimited amounts. Until changes to federal law placed some new restrictions on soft money contributions, the national parties benefited most from such contributions. Today, soft money is donated primarily to political action committees and 527s, which are only partially regulated. (Chapter 4.)

superior courts. *See* trial courts.

Supreme Court. California's highest court, consisting of seven members, presided over by the chief justice and six associates. (Chapter 7.)

term limits. The limitation of the length of time an elected official may serve. State senators are limited to two four-year terms, assembly members to three two-year terms. (Chapter 5.)

Three Strikes law. A law passed in 1994 that mandated a minimum sentence of twenty-five years to life for a third felony conviction. (Chapter 7.)

trial courts. In California, the superior courts where nearly all legal cases are first heard. These courts handle both criminal felonies and misdemeanors (including minor crimes and most traffic cases), small claims, family law (divorce and custody cases), and civil suits. (Chapter 7.)

Victims Bill of Rights. A bill passed in 1982 that created more mandatory sentencing, especially for crimes committed with guns. (Chapter 7.)

warehousing of prisoners. A corrections system dedicated to locking up prisoners for extended periods of time instead of attempting to rehabilitate them. This has led to overcrowding of the prison system, despite construction and expansion of prisons in California. (Chapter 7.)

weak party system. One of the characteristics of California's legislature going back to the Progressive era that means that committee chairs are not necessarily assigned through seniority (which goes to the ranking majority member) and that some committees may be chaired by minority members. (Chapter 5.)

Index